Victor Hugo
and the
Visionary Novel

His name surrounding ruins.
Son nom entourant des ruines.

Victor Hugo

and the

Visionary Novel

VICTOR BROMBERT

Harvard University Press
Cambridge, Massachusetts
and London, England

Copyright © 1984 by the President and Fellows of Harvard College
All rights reserved
Printed in the United States of America
10 9 8 7 6 5 4 3 2

Library of Congress Cataloging in Publication Data

Brombert, Victor H.
Victor Hugo and the visionary novel.
Bibliography: p.
Includes index.
1. Hugo, Victor, 1802–1885—Fictional works.
2. Myth in literature. I. Title.
PQ2304.M88B76   1984   843'.7   83-26584
ISBN 0-674-93550-0 (cloth)
ISBN 0-674-93551-9 (paper)

To Beth

To Sheila and Jean Gaudon

Acknowledgments

I owe a special debt to a number of Hugo scholars: Pierre Albouy, Jean-Bertrand Barrère, André Brochu, Jean Gaudon, Claude Gély, Richard B. Grant, Guy Rosa, Jacques Seebacher, Anne Ubersfeld. Many of them contributed to Jean Massin's splendid chronological edition, which has become an indispensable working tool.

Conversations over the years with the late Pierre Albouy, and with my friends Sheila and Jean Gaudon, have been very enriching.

I also wish to express my gratitude to all those who have read Hugo with me at Princeton, as well as in seminars I offered at the Johns Hopkins University and the University of California at Berkeley.

Special thanks are due to Joseph Frank, whose friendship, intellectual presence, and penetrating comments on several of the chapters have been particularly inspiring.

A Senior Fellowship of the National Endowment for the Humanities enabled me to begin work on this book. Repeated assistance from the Princeton University Committee on Research in the Humanities and Social Sciences contributed to its completion.

Some sections of this book appeared in an earlier and quite different form in *Nineteenth-Century French Studies* 5 (Fall–Winter 1976–77); *New Literary History* 9 (Spring 1978); *The Romanic Review* 70 (March 1979); and *Stanford French Review* 3 (Fall 1979). For permission to reprint in a revised form I wish to thank the respective editors.

I am especially grateful to Maria Ascher, who has given the manuscript expert care; it is difficult to imagine a more highly qualified and attentive editor.

I am also indebted to Simone Balayé, Roger Pierrot, and Charles A. Porter for generously helping me obtain reproductions of Hugo's drawings, and to Ewa Lewis, Suzanne Sinton, and Carol Szymanski, who in various ways have provided much-valued assistance.

Finally, my loving thanks go to B.A.B., who may not suspect how much I owe her, but who knows, better than anyone else, why I had to write this book.

V.B.

Contents

Illustrations

The quality and variety of the more than two thousand drawings by Victor Hugo which are reproduced and catalogued in volumes 17 and 18 of Jean Massin's edition of the complete works (and it is far from a complete listing) would suffice to establish Hugo's reputation as a visionary artist. Many of these drawings can be seen at the Maison Victor Hugo, on the Place des Vosges in Paris. Others illustrate manuscripts held by the Bibliothèque Nationale. Still others are dispersed in various collections. Hugo's graphic work was for him an important form of self-expression. It often parallels his written work, at times precedes and inspires it. It often displays an obsession with his own name or initials. Hugo was in the habit of offering drawings to friends and family members. But he also liked to surround himself with his own favorite drawings.

The graphic works that illustrate this book have been selected because of their thematic relevance to the different chapters, as well as to the visionary nature of Hugo's imagination.

Titles in quotation marks are Hugo's own.

Following page 48:

1. Octopus. *Pieuvre.*
2. Conscience in front of an evil deed.
   "La conscience devant une mauvaise action."
3. The judge. *"Judex."*
4. The executioner. *"Le bourreau."*
5. The Vianden ruin seen through a spider web.
   La ruine de Vianden à travers une toile d'araignée.

Victor Hugo
and the
Visionary Novel

1

Approaches

Le roman c'est le drame hors cadre.

The novels of Victor Hugo are as much of an anomaly as the legend of the man. To judge *Les Travailleurs de la mer* or *Les Misérables* by the standards of the French realist novel from Balzac to Zola is to miss the surprisingly modern nature of his fiction making, which undermines and decenters the subject, using character and plot to achieve the effects of visionary prose narrative. Hugo is as far removed from Stendhal's self-conscious and ironic lyricism as he is from Flaubert's obsessive concern for tight constructions and technical mastery. The dramatic and psychological power of Hugo's novels depends in large part on the creation of archetypal figures. Their poetic and thematic unity derives from his ability to conceive the linguistic analogue for larger forces at work. The sweep of his texts and the moving, even haunting visions they project are a function of the widest range of rhetorical virtuosity.

Hugo was perfectly aware of the magnitude of his undertaking. At the age of twenty-one, reviewing a novel by Walter Scott, he called for a new type of fiction that would give epic scope to the moral and social consciousness of his period. Years later, as he approached the writing of *Les Misérables*, he wanted more than ever to achieve a fusion of epic and dramatic elements. Such a fusion, he felt, was the proper business of the novel—that new and unique literary phenomenon ("merveilleuse nouveauté littéraire") which also was a powerful social force. At the end of his career, surveying his own works, he was more than ever convinced that the novel—his kind of novel—was a drama too big to be performed on any stage. By his own definition, every one of his novels was a "drame hors des proportions ordinaires"—a drama of more than ordinary dimensions.[1]

During his lifetime, Hugo's reputation as poet and novelist was almost as enormous as his ambition. Though he had detractors, unrestrained praise from the most diverse quarters generally greeted his productions. When *Notre-Dame de Paris* appeared in 1831, Lamartine did not hesitate to refer to its author as the Shakespeare of the novel. Nor was the praise, echoing throughout the nineteenth century, limited to France. Swinburne, who felt that Hugo was one of the greatest elegiac and lyric poets, stood in awe of the sustained power and "terrible beauty" of his novels, hailing him as the greatest prose writer of his generation—in fact, "the greatest writer whom the world has seen since Shakespeare." Walter Pater, a somewhat more sober admirer, considered the energy, the "strangeness," the grim humor, and the compassion of Hugo's work characteristic expressions of the very best in Romanticism. Dostoevsky, who early in life had compared Hugo to Homer, not only insisted that *Les Misérables* was superior to *Crime and Punishment*, but continued to revere Hugo as a prophetic voice, as a modern spokesman for the idea of spiritual regeneration. In a similar vein, Tolstoy saw Hugo—especially Hugo the novelist—towering over his century as a model of the highest type of artistic and moral consciousness.[2]

Even masters of irony ceased being ironic when writing about him. Flaubert proclaimed that Hugo, more than anyone, had made his heart throb, that he simply adored the "immense vieux"—the grand old man. Compared to him, Flaubert felt, all other contemporary writers, himself included, looked pale: "Hugo . . . enfoncera tout le monde." He admired the "power" and the "genius" of *Notre-Dame de Paris* and was dazzled by the "colossal" poetry of *La Légende des siècles*—"lines such as have never before been written." Likewise, Baudelaire asserted in a dithyrambic essay that modern French poetry would be poor indeed had this rare and providential poet not appeared. Baudelaire extolled Hugo's extraordinary verbal resources, his ability to decipher the great dictionary of nature, to dig into the inexhaustible treasure of the "universal analogy." And it is worth recalling that Rimbaud, who read Hugo's fiction the way one reads and relishes poetry (*"Les Misérables* sont un vrai poème") granted him privileged status in his celebrated literary credo known as "La Lettre du voyant."[3]

Does Hugo still speak to us? Or must his fame be attributed to a romantic taste for grandiose visions and myth making? The complex reactions of a figure such as Jean-Paul Sartre cast light on our own ambivalences. Sartre was unavoidably suspicious of Hugo's idealistic humanism. Having set out to denounce all literary *cléricatures*, as well as the implicit ideal of a communion in the absolute of art, Sartre could hardly be expected to endorse the vatic poet entranced by his self-appointed role as the spokesman for transcendence. (Sartre refers ironically to Hugo as the "favorite interviewer of God.") Yet Sartre recognized, with admiration and envy, that Hugo was the only French writer who had been able to reach the masses and who was still read by the working classes. It is only half ironically that, in *L'Idiot de la famille*, he speaks of Hugo as the supreme lord of his epoch, the "incontestable souverain du siècle." Sartre's own language grows surprisingly hyperbolic when he speaks of Hugo. He is not merely impressed by Hugo's prodigious vitality, by his sense of his own life as a project and destiny, and by his prestige in political exile, but refers to him as "cet homme étonnant"—a man endowed with almost superhuman power: "il possède je ne sais quelle puissance surhumaine."[4]

If Sartre consistently treats Hugo as exceptional in every sense of the word, despite Hugo's self-glorification as high priest of Literature and Word incarnate, it is doubtless because he recognized in him the supreme nineteenth-century exemplar of the committed, *engagé* writer. Sartre's views on the writer's function and responsibilities are explicitly set forth in *Qu'est-ce que la littérature?* and in the short manifesto introducing the first issue of *Les Temps Modernes*: the writer must not miss out on his time; he must espouse his period; he must avoid indifference and understand that silence can be shameful. More fundamentally, the writer must give society an uneasy conscience (*conscience malheureuse*) and will thereby necessarily clash with all conservative forces. Ultimately, the notion of *engagement* is philosophical: the acute awareness that evil is not simply a product or by-product; that it cannot be conveniently denied, reduced, or assimilated by the rhetoric of idealistic humanism; that it remains a hard reality and that literature has therefore an obligation to deal with "extreme situations." By Hugo's own definition there can be no innocent bystander, either in daily life or in the face of history. "Qui assiste au crime assiste le crime"—any bystander is necessarily an accomplice. Hugo's aphorism has, by anticipation, a Sartrian ring.[5]

To say, as did André Gide, that Hugo is the most powerful assembler of images and master of syntax in the French tradition is true enough, but is almost as wide of the mark as Gide's much-quoted "Victor Hugo, hélas!" Jean Cocteau's famous quip comes closer to the truth: "Victor Hugo was a madman who thought he was Victor Hugo."[6] For Hugo's supreme talent was essentially of a mythopoetic nature. He was able to convert personal experiences into a destiny, and then relate this destiny to the disturbing configurations of contemporary history. Facts and phantasms of a family drama (hostility between father and mother, rivalry between brother and brother) overlap and blend from the outset with the drama of external events (the Napoleonic adventure, Waterloo, the Restoration), thus creating a powerful bond among private obsessions, political evolution, and a strikingly personal reading of history. Hugo's literary consciousness, early in life, becomes the stage for a historical psychodrama whose symbolic actors are the Father, Napoleon, the King, and the guillotine. The true monsters, however, are within. It is by drawing them out into the open that

Hugo constructs himself; the man becomes a text. Hence the importance of literary documents such as *Promontorium somnii* and *William Shakespeare* which deal with the vertiginous poetry of dreams and the abyss of genius.

Perspectives change. Hugo no longer appears as the prodigious pyrotechnist posing as God's special interlocutor. The past two decades have brought into sharper focus—largely because of contemporary concerns—the relationship between poetic vision and ideology, as well as Hugo's love-hate relationship with history. Recurrent images in his work—the statue, the Tower of Babel, the spider, the human monster, the sea changes, the grimacing buffoon—can all be traced to a fundamental design. The well-known antitheses and oxymorons, the seditious tropes, far from proposing irreconcilable opposites, function as harmonizing elements. The prophetic voice can be related to Hugo's graphic art and to a morally inspired hallucination that makes him a brother to Goya. Yet the visionary thrust of his work is always controlled by a will to lucidity, by a longing for order. *Chaos vaincu,* the title of the allegorical play in the novel *L'Homme qui rit,* points to Hugo's need to overcome his own inner anarchy, as well as to the political tensions of the public figure trying to reconcile commitment to progress with allegiance to the past.

There is no denying that Hugo's name and vast body of writing fell into disfavor during the first half of the twentieth century. The reasons for this are complex. There was the obvious reaction against his glorification—indeed apotheosis—culminating in the magnificent funeral of a national hero. Yet despite the idolatry, or *hugolâtrie,* which extended beyond his death in 1885, Hugo remained misunderstood. He was emasculated by the pieties of the Third Republic, which fixed him in the statuesque pose of *père bénisseur* of democratic virtues; repressed by new generations of writers, who were uncomfortably aware of his crushing superiority; and betrayed by anthologies, which consistently included only his flashier or more sentimental pieces. Yet no writer's work is less suited to being immobilized in the display case of an anthology. Hugo set his sights not on the poem but on poetry, not on the novel but on fiction making, not on the well-wrought artifact (though he is a splendid craftsman and lord of language) but on poetic process and becoming.

There has been, in recent years, a growing pattern of critical reassessment that has nothing to do with hagiography. Earlier work by J.-B. Barrère and Pierre Albouy set the tone and the high standards. In the 1960s the chronological edition of Hugo's complete works, under the editorship of Jean Massin, became the rallying point for a distinguished group of young scholars of unusual critical sensitivity—among them Jean Gaudon, Jacques Seebacher, Guy Rosa, Claude Gély, Henri Meschonnic, and Anne Ubersfeld, whose study of Hugo's theater (*Le Roi et le Bouffon*, 1974) has far-reaching implications. But whereas the poetry and the theater acquired a renewed luster in this modern perspective, the novels, in part because of their size and complexity, continued to pose a serious challenge to Hugo critics.

Yet modern theoretical concern with narrative and metaphor, ideology and tropes, myth and historiography—not to mention thematic and deconstructive readings that tend to question the centrality of the subject and the authority of the auctorial voice— should have been sufficient reason to explore the unusually fertile terrain of Hugo's prose fiction. It is, for instance, hard to imagine a fictional world that more strikingly anticipates Mikhail Bakhtin's theory of the novel as a problematic genre which, through parodic subversion of the canonic genres, not only undermines the hieratic world of the epic but defies all the hierarchies of established tradition, thus participating in a dynamic and essentially revolutionary process of renewal and becoming. According to Bakhtin, this transformational and future-oriented potential of the novel— by definition a noncanonical genre-in-the-making—finds its source in the tradition of Menippean satire, and its vivifying inspiration in the liberating forces of popular laughter.[7]

Nothing illustrates the dynamic tensions in Hugo's work better than the dialectics of laughter, which he repeatedly endows with revolutionary significance. Hugo in fact defines *revolution* as the hour of laughter; hence the importance of the king's buffoon: the threatening grimace of the oppressed challenges the cruel laughter of the oppressor. The misshapen faun who faces the laughing gods on Olympus in Hugo's poem "Le Satyre," and who finally overpowers them with his cosmic song, is the mythical embodiment of a victory from below, of which there are many variations in his novels. But laughter is also the prerogative of the oneiric artist. In *Promontorium somnii* he refers to the hilarity of dreams; in the poem "Les Mages" he sees the creative genius as the high priest of laughter. The poet-novelist's visionary and political themes thus merge.

Hugo's prose narratives obviously cannot be approached as conventional novels. Paradoxically, this writer who aimed at, and succeeded in, reaching the largest possible public also made new and difficult demands on the reader. Closer to romance and myth than to the realist tradition, projecting linguistic and metaphoric structures that achieve what has been called the *roman poème*, the novels of Hugo, always steeped in a sociohistorical context, tend toward the elaboration of a new epic which no longer sings the heroic exploit but the moral adventure of man. Hugo converts politics into myth, much as he translates private obsessions into collective symbols. This transformational thrust is made possible by an exceptional stylistic and formal range. On the occasion of Balzac's funeral, Hugo let it be understood that for him the novel was a protean genre that takes on "all forms and all styles."[8]

The insistence on a multiplicity of tones and structural centers may indeed cast light on the originality of Hugo's fiction, for his novels tend to be centrifugal. As Jean Gaudon shrewdly observed in discussing the aesthetics of digression, Hugo deliberately undermines the monocentric conception of the novel, as part of a larger attempt to break with "pseudo-Aristotelian concepts."[9] Viewed in this perspective, Hugo appears at the origin of the modern "polycentric" novel—as the creator of a liberating but always problematic countercode.

Further complicating the problematic nature of Hugo's novels is their political and historical resonance. This resonance is far from homophonic. When Hugo published *Littérature et philosophie mêlées* in 1834, he inveighed against the notion of a naïvely activist art. Such an *art enrôlé*, he felt, was blunt, childish, and degrading.[10] All through his life, even in his moments of greatest dedication to the "usefulness" of art, he questioned the utilitarian assumptions of militant literary discourse, decrying all attempts to reduce art to the level of propaganda. This hardly meant that he was eager to withdraw; rather, his notion of involvement was more demanding. It meant a commitment to painful transition and change, to moral issues that could not be resolved by the glib answers and trivial victories of the day.

Hugo's first important novel, *Le Dernier Jour d'un condamné*, a stern denunciation of capital punishment and the inequities of the law, is polemically charged. Its powerful images and drama do not, however, function as a simple appeal for legal or penal reforms. The poetic and psychological intensity of the text corresponds to a more fundamental project: Hugo's need to create in the reader (but first in himself) a maximal unease—the equivalent of a *conscience malheureuse*. It is a book whose ominous presence pervades Hugo's subsequent writings.

Hugo's capacity for social and political indignation remained very much alive. So did his sense of history as tragedy. We need hardly speculate about whether or not he would have remained silent on the subject of concentration camps and genocide. Certainly he would not have waited to denounce such things as the Stalinist purges, the Holocaust, and the Gulag archipelago. Evil was for him not just a metaphysical shadow, an idea to be dissolved or dismissed by abstractions, but an immanent and irrecusable reality that stirred his salvational instincts.

No nineteenth-century writer had a keener sense of his own time. If Hugo liked to think of himself as having been born with the century ("Ce siècle avait deux ans . . ."; "je suis fils de ce siècle"),[11] this was not merely self-dramatization but an expression of solidarity with the events and the destiny of his own post-revolutionary period. The nineteenth century, according to him, was without precedent. It was the offspring of an idea. And that idea—the Revolution—was, in his terms, the grand climacteric of humanity, the turning point in a providential scheme. History remains the overwhelming presence. In a deep sense, all of Hugo's novels are historical—though they also challenge the assumptions of the historical novel. This ambiguity is revealing. Revolution became for Hugo the life-giving force of modern history. But the monstrosity of revolutionary violence, which truly obsessed him, also explains the dream of transcending revolution, of seeking a higher harmony through an exit from history, through the negation of the destructive principle which he associated with any linear historical concept.

Hugo's political evolution from the ultraroyalism of his adolescence to his democratic and even prorevolutionary convictions accounts in part for the ideological and thematic tensions in his works. The articulations of religious faith and political beliefs, the transitions of history, the legitimacy of violence, the trauma of regicide and parricide, the incompatibilities of linear and cyclical concepts of time—these are some of the haunting motifs of his novels. Political conversion resulted in conflicting commitments to the past and to the future. In his later years, recognizing the eternal gap between generations, Hugo wrote that hope would come when old people learned to be forward looking and the younger generation learned to feel allegiance with the past. But already much earlier, he saw the need to reconcile divergent temporal pulls. When he asserted, in an article significantly entitled "Guerre aux Démolisseurs," that the past is almost as sacred as the future, he merely expressed the bidirectional historical tension inherent in the revolutionary consciousness.[12]

The entire nineteenth century, especially as it experienced the ideology of revolution, was condemned to think ahead with a sense of history's weight; for the French Revolution itself, though it remained to be fulfilled, was already an event and model of the past. The paradox was glaring: the to-be-achieved revolution was, unavoidably, to be spoken of in the past. And the present—the entire nineteenth century—was a time of gaps and discontinuities, a time of rehearsal in every sense of the word.[13] In such a context, the individual and the collective consciousness were likely to come into conflict with themselves and with each other. The young Hugo welcomed the clash and was to find it a fruitful subject. Why not, he asked, confront the "revolutions of an individual" with the "revolutions of society"? The modern term "psychohistory" would hardly have surprised him. Early in his career, he indicated a desire to write, in the near future, a major work that would be "at once psychological and historical."[14]

Polyvalence, ironic parallelisms, discordant time schemes—these have a modern ring. Hugo's "modernity" exists, of course, on several levels. In terms of literary history, Hugo anticipated the Symbolist creed. He viewed the book as a spiritual instrument, and the world as a text whose signs had to be deciphered. His true modernity, however, is to be found elsewhere—in the fascination with inscriptions, traces, effacements, mirror effects, and dissolving processes, and in the belief that not only history but reality itself is a "text."

Hugo's unwillingness to establish fixed boundaries between genres and to see art as simply reflecting a stable reality helps blur the line of demarcation between his poetry and prose, between his novels and his other works. Any serious discussion of Hugo's novels must necessarily look beyond them, and in particular seek illustrations and intertextual commentary in the body of his poetry. Hugo's expressive powers and range of vision seem to be corollaries of his versatility. He is the only major French nineteenth-century writer to have felt equally at home in lyric and epic poetry, in the novel, and in the theater—and to have made a powerful impact in all these genres. No similar claim, whatever their genius, can be made for Stendhal, Balzac, Flaubert, Zola, Dickens, Dostoevsky, or Tolstoy.

Such versatility affects not only the poetic but the visionary quality of Hugo's fiction. Hybrid forms, fusions, and amalgams create surprising links between the world of fantasy and moral concerns; for the visionary power of the novels is not simply a matter of stunning visual imagery, of hints of insight in blindness, but of an underlying moral and spiritual turbulence. The eye itself becomes a metaphorical abyss. This *oeil gouffre* suggests visionary occultation and boundlessness, as well as an exploratory descent into imaginary nether regions, where "looking at" is replaced by "seeing" (Hugo explicitly distinguishes between *regarder* and *voir*) and where forms tend to vanish, as they already do in the early poem "La Pente de la rêverie," making room for an inverted but revelatory vision *from below*. The orphic Satyr, in Hugo's famous allegory of the visionary poet, thus sees the tree from the point of view of the roots; he glimpses the dark underside of creation.[15]

But if Hugo's visual references often point to the iconographic world of a Dürer or a Piranesi, his deeper visionary tendencies are determined by grim social and historical realities, by utopian dreams and fears, and by the need to relate private phantasms to the thrust of external events. His moral and poetic vision thus situates the dark underside, the *revers ténébreux*, in a social context: in the world of poverty, dereliction, and crime—the world of the oppressed. And if spiritual salvation, for Hugo, does come from below, this is not merely because of a poetic and symbolic descent to the nether regions but because moral and political salvation is to come out of the horror and violence of the social underworld.

The interplay of visionary and ideological elements, which will be a central concern of the chapters that follow, is also a measure of Hugo's highest ambitions. In notes for a preface to *La Légende des siècles*, he clearly stated his desire to situate his work at the relatively unexplored and difficult outposts where epic and dramatic modes converge, at those points of junction from which he would be able to cast light on the "shadows" that darken human life.[16]

The determination to make an impact through a literary career was in itself not unusual at the time. The recent example of Chateaubriand provided the specific model of literature as presence-in-the-world. Like others in the post-Napoleonic era, Hugo believed that the pen should replace the sword. (That his own father had been a general under Napoleon invested the opposition of warrior and poet with added significance.) Hugo's was not an ordinary literary ambition, however. More intensely and more consistently than others, he believed that writers had a mission, that they were to be the educators and leaders of the recently awakened *peuple*, that they were to regenerate society, prepare the future, and write, as it were, on paper and in life, the immanent epic of humanity's progress.[17] Above all, he came to see literature as a spiritual power, and the poet as *sacerdos magnus*.

Hugo rarely allowed the pressures of history and politics to take precedence over the deeper commitments of art. He repeatedly asserted, in particular in *William Shakespeare*, that revolution was to serve art and, beyond art, the spiritual needs of man. The very texts that establish the closest bond between art and revolution are the ones that also link symbolization to a yearning for the *sacred*. The vatic voice, in *William Shakespeare*, proclaims the chief tenets of Symbolism, all of which transcend politics: the poet's intuition of the occult sense of existence; the heroic quality of poetic vision; the gospel of correspondences; the belief that the world is a text that speaks to us but needs to be deciphered—that there are semiotic links between the realms of the visible and the invisible, binding infinite manifestations to a single principle.

The fruitful tensions among ideological, poetic, and spiritual needs make up the drama of Hugo's texts and are, to a large extent, the subject of this book. They remained unresolved to the end, and were present from the beginning. Hugo took pride in his political evolution. In "Ecrit en 1846," he claimed that it was not reason alone but a vision of history ("L'histoire m'apparut") that undermined his royalist beliefs and converted him to the cause of revolution: "Me voici jacobin." But he also knew that history was not all, that its claims could in turn become despotic. In the same poem, he also professes his allegiance to himself: nothing in his heart has changed ("Non, rien n'a varié").[18] Perhaps the most remarkable thing about Hugo's life is that his evolution—political, metaphysical, aesthetic—illustrates not so much change as continuity. All the great themes, all the major preoccupations, were there from the start.

This sense of identity, of selfhood and sameness, characterizes what he himself defined as *Ego Hugo*. It explains his determination to be foremost in all genres, to cover the widest possible range in style and tone, to reflect and elaborate the chief concerns of his time. It is possible, of course, to speak of an inordinate sense of pride, of a boundless dilation of the ego; but this devotion to his own eminence and singularity can also be seen as a supreme form of literary integrity that places his voice in the service of values greater than himself. Hugo's most lasting ambition was to be at once unique and representative. Perhaps that is why he felt that his life could be summed up by two words: *solitaire, solidaire*.[19]

My relationship with Hugo began when, as an adolescent during the Occupation of France, I read *Les Contemplations* and *L'Année terrible* with love and awe. During that dark period, when all of Europe seemed condemned to exile or worse, the tragic dignity of Hugo's voice struck a responsive chord. I have not been able to forget the bitter joy with which I recited to myself his sonorous and acrid lines. I had, of course, read other poems of his in school; and I had admired, though hardly opened, the heavy volumes of his complete works on my father's shelves. But that Hugo seemed patriarchal and distant. What made the difference when I discovered those two collections of verse in 1940–41 was that I could suddenly relate a voice, a style, and a rhetoric to the drama of history—to our collective drama.

This newly discovered Hugo became so much a part of my personal and historical experience that when, after the war, I began seriously to study literature, it did not at first occur to me that his works could be subjected to the ordinary scrutinies and subtleties of literary criticism. In time, I learned that criticism could also be an act of love, that it was in fact always in danger of becoming merely a sophisticated and sterile exercise when there was not a close and loving contact with the language of a text, as well as a communion with its spirit.

Early exposure to Hugo's poetry prepared me to read his novels as poetic constructs. Years of teaching and writing about the works of some of the other great nineteenth-century novelists prepared me to appreciate the extraordinary interest and originality of his fiction. My aim in this study is to account for these qualities by closely analyzing forms, themes, and techniques, and also by relating individual works to a larger vision. Attention to the rhetoric of fiction and to problems of narrative will help bring into focus the artistic achievement, the poetic and conceptual density, of each of the novels. Looking at recurrent motifs, themes, and problems—taking care, meanwhile, to respect the unity and integrity of these novels as works of art—will enable us to locate and analyze, at different levels, the larger issues involved. Violence-in-history, the battleground of the human conscience, the themes of revolution, the dynamics of destruction and change, the ambiguities of laughter and of the grotesque, the inequities of human laws, the epic of regeneration, the elaboration of a personal theology—these are only a few of the richly interwoven subjects. They in turn help cast light on some of the underlying preoccupations of the nineteenth-century novel. Hugo is not the only writer to concern himself with the struggle between the individual and society, the intellectual's glorification and latent fear of the masses, the guilt and hope associated with the memory of regicide and all challenges to authority, the awareness of historical discontinuities; but in his work the symptomatic themes take on a particularly haunting and even mythical form.

The artistic and thematic complexity of Hugo's novels cannot, obviously, be accounted for by a simple study of plot and characters. To deal successfully with Hugo's narrative, it is necessary not only to draw on the combined resources of formal, thematic, and even "deconstructive" criticism but to situate the textual configurations in an ideological context, against the broader background of the history of ideas. My approach relies a great deal on close textual criticism, on reconnoitering the text's linguistic and figural patterns. To be truly meaningful, however, a study such as this must test the capabilities of criticism in dealing with the intricate network of aesthetic, social, political, psychological, and ethical preoccupations.

The analysis of novels, because of their length, creates a special difficulty and a special challenge. Is it ever possible to treat a novel with the care, subtlety, and total awareness of craft with which good criticism approaches masterpieces of poetry? Yet should this not be the desired ideal? Love and respect for the texture and inner coherence of great narratives, the ability to relate every detail to a whole, could also be the aims of the critic of fiction. Though it is unlikely that we can ever come to know a large novel the way Quasimodo knows the cathedral, which he inhabits and of which he has become a part, we can perhaps hope to attain a degree of intimacy that will make it possible to move inside the vast construct with precision and freedom. Such precision and freedom are not meant, however, to display the critic's prowess. They are to serve the better understanding of great works.

Neither one of Hugo's early novels can qualify as great. *Han d'Islande* (1823), begun when Hugo was nineteen, and *Bug-Jargal*, published a few years later but begun when he was sixteen, may reveal the young man's talent and allow retrospective glimpses into his psyche and formative processes; but in neither of these books has the novelist found his distinctive voice. That voice would come into its own a few years later, in 1829, with the publication of *Le Dernier Jour d'un condamné*. But though my study properly begins with a close reading of this novel, it would be a mistake to dismiss the two juvenile texts as irrelevant to Hugo's later development and preoccupations. The two early attempts at fiction present features and motifs which, in a variety of ways, will recur as central, even obsessive themes in later contexts.

When *Han d'Islande* appeared, Stendhal wrote a cutting review for the *New Monthly Magazine*. He made fun of the catalogue of atrocities, yet recognized the "enormous talent" of the author and quite rightly suspected that this story about a human monster, blood baths, dark plots, and the horror of the scaffold might have been written tongue-in-cheek, partly as a spoof.[20] Hugo's own three prefaces to successive editions of the novel are ironic and parodic, pointing out the mannerisms of his own text and the outlandishness of the names and of the epigraphs. The novel itself is filled with self-mocking authorial intrusions, facetious remarks, bookish drolleries. The epigraph to the concluding chapter could serve as a warning to the naïve reader: "What I have said as a joke, you have taken seriously." A certain black humor will continue to color even Hugo's more idealistic texts.

The plot of *Han d'Islande* is not only grim but melodramatic to the point of defying sober paraphrase. A blood-curdling Icelandic brigand-monster terrorizing entire regions of Norway, mutinous miners misled by evil conspirators, a viceroy's anonymous son in love with a damsel who has been imprisoned along with her persecuted father, the adventures of a knight-errant who tries to save the father and win the daughter, a sadistic executioner taking pleasure in hanging his own brother, vast numbers of fighting men crushed or burned alive—these are only some of the features of this orgiastic literary exercise.

Han d'Islande is a study in horror. It begins in a morgue, with pale white light falling on disfigured and decomposing bodies. It reads from the outset like a caricature of a Gothic novel, a *roman noir*. Han mutilates his victims to the accompaniment of maniacal laughter. It is hard to tell who is more horrible: the executioner, a master of the art of torture who derives exquisite satisfaction from inflicting pain; or Han, who, in front of the woman he once raped, displays their son's skull—now a cup from which he drinks human blood.

This parody of a Gothic novel—the blending of elements drawn from fantastic tales, gory tragedies, humorous narratives, and historical fiction in the manner of Walter Scott—produces a hybrid text that plays with recognizable fictional modes as though to test and challenge their capabilities. The principle of hybridity, soon to become part of a more conceptualized experiment in *Notre-Dame de Paris*, will prove to be a constant structural and thematic feature in Hugo's mature work.

When Hugo in 1833 wrote the third preface, he looked with some condescension on the excesses of this "naïve work" (by now *Notre-Dame de Paris* had been published). But he also asked that his early work be read with his future work in mind. Referring to the talent of the nineteen-year-old author of *Han d'Islande,* Hugo uses three times the verb *deviner* (to guess or divine), suggesting intuitive as well as anticipatory qualities.[21] From the start, Hugo chose to view his work as a life project, an evolution to be grasped in its totality by a retrospective glance. It is, of course, precisely such retrospection that today allows us to see, behind the elements of parody and mystification, behind the juvenile inebriation with language, a text filled with immediate concerns and lasting obsessions. The conventionally improbable love story reflects the difficulties, material obstacles, parental opposition, and secret betrothal that preceded Hugo's marriage to Adèle Foucher. But more significant by far than these autobiographical elements are the combined thematic presences of the moral monster, of social rebellion, of the figure of the executioner, and of a spiritual quest. Still loosely threaded, these elements prepare for the mighty canvases of the great novels.

Hindsight indeed allows one to read into this early confrontation of monster and hero (they later tend to merge) a very special moral and mythical dimension. Behind the superficial thrills of horror provided by the human beast looms a vocation of pure evil which, in its mystery and gratuitousness, has an almost theological cast: "My nature is to hate man." Forever wandering ("il erre toujours"), Han is at one point explicitly compared to the Antichrist.[22] But if the monster wanders, so does Ordener, the hero. The quest motif signals more than an ordinary adventure of high romance in which the fearless knight-errant saves the captive lady and her father. The hero's eagerness to fight the monster leads him to the primordial cave. Through an entrance that Hugo compares to one of the *bouches de l'enfer,* Ordener descends into an abyss, to the underground city of the mutinous miners—a clear prefiguration of the lower depths and the social hell of the *misérables,* a world that Hugo was to describe at great length in his later novels.

Elements of horror—whether monster or mob—sustain the visionary power of the text. The landscape is animated and mythologized. Bizarre roving clouds rush by a red moon; ancient forests grow on the banks of a lake as does hair on a human head; shrubs climb over fallen walls and let their flexible arms hang over the edge of a precipice. But it is the perspective on this weird landscape that is most revealing of Hugo's latent visionary tendencies. As the hero stands by the lake, the narrator speaks of a singular "optical illusion" that allows him, as though through an abyss piercing the globe, to see the sky "through the earth."[23]

Such an optical illusion implies not only dizzying verticality but total inversion. Its correlative is the subterranean meeting place where an armed mob has gathered for rebellion. In this metaphorical underworld, filled with threatening figures and improvised weapons, visionary and ideological elements converge. It is also a point of intersection at which some of Hugo's later ideological tensions are foreshadowed. Even at this early stage, in the apparently nonpolitical context of *Han d'Islande*, notions of revolt and popular unrest produce unease and ambivalence. To be sure, oppressive laws and arbitrary taxation seem to justify some vague cries for justice; there is talk of old women dying of cold and hunger. Hugo makes it clear, however, that Ordener joins the rebels not out of sympathy for their anger or for a definable cause but for a private reason, in order to save an *individual*. The son of the viceroy finds himself associated with an angry mob of "blind partisans" and "revolting bandits" for reasons at once "powerful" and "secret" which the narrator, in a revealing aside, says he prefers not to analyze.

The mixture of fascination and revulsion caused by the idea of social revolt is the more striking as revolt is not the overt subject of the novel. In fact, negative signals about rebellion abound. It is a "conspiracy," an "insurrection"; the rebels are a "gang" thriving on chaos, filling the air with savage sound and fury. The wild mob, which in a number of ways prefigures the truants and criminals of the Cour des Miracles in *Notre-Dame de Paris*, is associated with murder, rape, sacrilege, and arson. That mob is, moreover, identified with the monster. The conspirators pretend to put Han at the head of the insurgents. Revolt itself thus takes the shape of a monster. It is as though Hugo were intuitively afraid of those impulses which were later to draw him to the cause of revolution and which tended to justify the horrors of civil disorder and of fratricidal wars. In *Han d'Islande* the issue is not yet faced directly. A happy ending blurs the problem and dissipates the unease. After the monster has conveniently destroyed himself, news is brought to the now pacified miners that the king has of his own free will remitted the burdensome tax.

These latent ideological tensions are confirmed by the threatening presence of the executioner—the *bourreau*. This ominous figure is early evidence of Hugo's life-long concern with capital punishment, and of his struggle against what he continued to define as legal murder. The pervasive presence of the executioner in *Han d'Islande* goes far beyond the requirements of a horror story. Repeated allusions and references to Joseph de Maistre, the arch-conservative political theorist who had glorified the executioner as the foundation of social order, clearly suggest a polemical orientation. Certain passages in the novel that describe the "master of high justice" as a pariah-like high priest of "sinister ceremonies" come straight out of de Maistre's *Soirées de Saint-Pétersbourg*. The implicit denunciation of de Maistre will be more focused and conceptualized in *Le Dernier Jour d'un condamné*. But certain pages that deal with the pomp of judicial murder, and that depict the cruelty of the crowd come to observe at close quarters the features of the *misérable* about to die, read like first versions of some of the later novel's most haunting scenes.

The executioner is also the most concrete embodiment, in the early novel, of the theme of fratricide: the last person he puts to death is his own brother. The irony is symbolic of the deeper complicity, later explored by Hugo, especially in *Les Misérables*, between the worlds of crime and punishment. And beyond that disturbing relationship, the irony also points to what will remain for Hugo a permanent obsession associated with the figures of Cain and Abel: original violence and the existence of evil.

Han dies, but the "power of evil" to which Hugo refers cannot so easily be exorcized. Deep moral concerns are the dramatic undercurrents of this adolescent text. They create tensions among a number of themes: the idealistic quest of the individual, the violence of the group, the monster in man and in nature. Vague utopian yearnings are fed by a thinly disguised pessimism.

Hugo's next juvenile venture, *Bug-Jargal*, the story of a royal slave, is even more prefigurative and delineates even more sharply the dialectics of monster and revolution. Here, the wildly adventurous narrative has a definite political context and is enriched by motifs that will become increasingly important for Hugo: the role of the buffoon, the relationship of master and slave, and the possibility of brotherhood.

Bug-Jargal, though even more exotic than *Han d'Islande*, brings the themes of the monster and the revolution into an identifiable historical perspective. It is a colonial adventure story, set in Santo Domingo (Hispaniola) during the Slave Revolt of 1791. Hugo wrote the first version in 1818, when he was sixteen, and significantly expanded it in 1825, the year France recognized the independence of the island, which had taken the name of Haiti. There was thus something quite topical about this tale, which centers on three representative characters: a courageous French officer, who is the nephew of a rich planter; a heroic black slave of royal birth, who becomes a leader of the revolt; and a thoroughly evil mulatto dwarf, whose only motivation is vengeance.

Behind the remote setting and extravagant plot, the novel touches in more ways than one on issues that were uncomfortable ones for many nineteenth-century readers. The narrative describes a colonial defeat for the French. Moreover, seen in the perspective of 1826, during the reign of Charles X, these events were controversial; they pointed to many of the so-called evils brought about by the French Revolution. Echoes of the Revolution indeed fill *Bug-Jargal*. There is an explicit reference to the decree of May 15, 1791, promulgated by the National Assembly, which granted to free men of color an equal share of political rights with whites. Santo Domingo was a tinderbox that needed only a spark from Paris. In the novel, the violence of the slaves' insurrection is explicitly related to the fall of the Bastille, and politics seems to take precedence over the destinies of individuals: the French officer's wedding night is interrupted by the insurrection.

In *Bug-Jargal*, more clearly even than in *Han d'Islande*, Hugo's attitude toward revolutionary violence is ambivalent. The narrator—the young French officer—is distressed by the inhumane conditions on his uncle's plantation. He feels compassion for the slaves, who live in abject fear and hatred of the "absolute despotism" of their master, and is appalled to see them treated like chattel. His soldierly sense of honor tells him that, under such circumstances, there is logic and dignity in revolt. Hatred for the oppressor seems natural to him, and the cause of the oppressed a just cause. But revolt means chaos and cruelty. A people moved to frenzy is an ugly sight for a man trained to believe in law and order, in disciplined courage, and in the persuasive power of language. The horrors of the riot seem to him even greater than the horrors of the repression.

Violence is indeed the chief stumbling block for the young officer, as he considers the legitimacy of rebellious action. He is the witness of crimes committed against humanity in the name of human rights and liberation; the leaders of the insurrection compete with one another in refinements of cruelty. Hugo seems, however, less interested in specific details of the slave revolt in Santo Domingo than in those elements that refer specifically to revolutionary events in France, and more generally to the notion of revolution. This underlying concern with revolution rather than with colonial insurrection is confirmed by the incidents described in the epilogue, which take place after the events of 1791 and far from Santo Domingo—namely, in the somber year 1793, the year of the Convention and the Terror. This concluding note seems to anticipate by almost fifty years a scene in Hugo's last novel, *Quatrevingt-Treize*. It tells how, after a significant victory of the Republican troops, a political commissar known as a *représentant du peuple* confronts the divisional general and demands the heroic young officer's death on the guillotine.

Hugo's latent anxiety about the legitimacy of violence and revolt is further stressed by the presence in the novel of two opposing types of insurrectional leaders. Biassou, a historical figure, is described as monstrous in his combination of cunning and bestiality. The fictional Bug-Jargal, on the other hand, is a model of magnanimity—saving his enemies, protecting the defenseless, obeying a higher law of clemency. Through these two characters, history and fiction come into significant conflict. Biassou seems to confirm through his actions that history is violence. Bug-Jargal, in his ability to see beyond his race and serve a higher ideal, transcends the historical moment. The royal slave, in serving his people, aims at serving humanity.

The royal slave is a conventional figure in pre-Romantic literature. Aphra Behn's novel *Oroonoko, or The Royal Slave (1688)*, was translated into French in the middle of the eighteenth century.[24] What is symptomatic in Hugo's treatment of the slave of royal birth is not his noble and gifted nature. Bug-Jargal has musical and poetic talents, he is strong yet gentle, he loves deeply, and he is proud of his origins—but all this is to be expected. The truly remarkable feature of Hugo's slave hero is that he transcends all notions of class and race, that he affirms through his example the ethics of universal man. This effacement of all particularities and distinctions involves the ideal of a fraternity that is not a mere abstraction: the white officer and the black slave are linked by a deep friendship, and call each other *frère*.

This idealistic wishing away of all hatred and strife is, however, far from reassuring. The idyllic complementarity of black and white is disturbed by shady figures of mixed blood (*sang mêlé*), and more specifically by the villainous mulatto, Habibrah. And in the expanded version of 1826, the central presence of a white woman in the exotic setting not only introduces a sensuous note but creates an atmosphere of sexual rivalry. Bug-Jargal's love song is also a song of violence. There can be no doubt that the French officer sees the powerful, muscular Bug as the figure of the "phallic negro."[25] Sexual violence seems to be a constant threat. When the gigantic negro carries off the Frenchman's bride to save her from flames, the vision is that of abduction, if not of rape. There is even a hint that the officer secretly desires such a rape. He is obviously fascinated by the power of his black alter ego.[26]

A greater obstacle to dreams of fraternity and universal man is the presence of a third male figure, Habibrah, the evil jester of the plantation—a grimacing clown who is also something of a sorcerer, and an early embodiment of the monstrous buffoon whose avatars can be traced throughout Hugo's work. The description of Habibrah illustrates notions of the grotesque that Hugo would soon develop in his theoretical preface to *Cromwell* (1827). The misshapen dwarf has an enormous paunch and spindly legs, which fold up under him, when he sits, like the legs of a spider. His huge head is covered with woolly red hair, and his face seems to wear an eternal sneer. The moral traits, however, reveal the true monster. A favorite slave who enjoys special privileges, Habibrah is servile and cringing and incites his master to excesses of cruelty. When the insurrection breaks out, he kills his master, and later takes pleasure in describing the deed. Like Han, he is obsessed with vengeance; but in his case, the obsession is psychologically rooted in the ambiguous master-slave relationship that induces him to avenge his own servility. An accomplice of his master's tyranny, he wants at the same time to destroy and to imitate him. He represents the pathos as well as the threat of the oppressed. In a wider perspective, he is the incarnation of evil, of the monster in man. He symbolically tries to drag the "other" down with him as he takes his fatal plunge into the abyss. This death scene clearly foreshadows Frollo's demonic and visionary "fall" from the bell tower at the end of *Notre-Dame de Paris*.

Despite the rational nature of the officer's account, "visionary" elements pervade *Bug-Jargal*. The landscape is illumined by the fires of violence; entire forests are ablaze; the setting sun looks threatening; weird copper-red reflections can be seen on the granite faces of the mountains. These visionary effects are, however, for the most part internalized. The rhetoric of catastrophe is a function of the officer's traumatic experience during the bloody revolt. The word *vision* appears on the page that describes his most intimate fears after his bride has disappeared. From that point on, he lives as in a dream world in which a light, which is not the light of day, casts its uncanny glare on all manner of strange shapes. External events—voodoo practices, profanations of the Mass, naked hags dancing lascivious *chicas* while instruments of torture are being readied—confirm this *vision infernale,* to the accompaniment of scornful bursts of laughter.

Laughter itself, whether that of Biassou, Habibrah, or the witches, is perceived as a hellish sound, a *rire infernal.*[27] In *Han d'Islande,* the obscene laughter of Han and the diabolical laughter of the executioner were also associated with destructiveness. The difference in *Bug-Jargal* is that laughter takes on psychological as well as ideological significance. In what amounts to a tirade, the buffoon Habibrah explains with all the rancor of the downtrodden, and in a manner that looks ahead to both Triboulet and Gwynplaine, that the laughter of humiliation and revenge can counter the laughter of the tyrant, that it can become a weapon for vengeance and liberation. This revolutionary laughter announces, at a great distance, the grimacing stone *mascarons* of Hugo's poem "La Révolution," as well as the redemptive figure and central theme of his late novel *L'Homme qui rit.* Habibrah, too, wears his eternal grin as a tragic mask.

The more immediate link between laughter and ideological concerns in the two early novels is, however, located in repeated references to capital punishment. The executioner in *Han d'Islande* laughs hideously when he thinks of his victims. Likewise, it is with a laugh that Biassou, in *Bug-Jargal,* condemns men to death. And the condemned officer's sense of unreality as he meets his fate, as well as the mob's hysterical joy at the thought of exterminating fellow human beings, anticipates not only the Condemned Man's experience of the absurd in *Le Dernier Jour d'un condamné* but also the laughing, bloodthirsty crowd that has come to watch the spectacle of his execution.

The central images and motifs of Hugo's first mature novel can thus be seen taking shape in his early work. It is not a coincidence, after all, that the juvenile story set in the West Indies, far from France, concludes bitterly with the two words *guillotine nationale.* For the guillotine, as we shall see, casts its shadow across the pages of Hugo's first major work of fiction.

2

The Condemned Man

Mon esprit est en prison dans une idée.

H ugo the novelist found his voice in a book about death. *Le Dernier Jour d'un condamné* (1829), written in his twenty-seventh year, is a fictional confrontation with capital punishment. The Condemned Man's impending execution gives rise to an obsessive monologue cut short by the blade of the guillotine.

This sober and vehement book was vividly remembered by Dostoevsky the day he underwent the ordeal of his mock execution, and it came to haunt some of the most striking pages of *The Idiot*. Stripped of almost every anecdotal element, barely one hundred pages long, it is sparse and concentrated like the cell of the prisoner whose name and crime remain unknown. Hugo articulates the prolonged cry of anguish, the slow torture of human consciousness in its radical subjectivity, as it faces the horror of annihilation. *Le Dernier Jour d'un condamné* provides the grim record, the *procès-verbal* of agonizing thought, the "intellectual dissection" of a condemned human being (III, 664). In recording the death throes of an intelligence killed by the *idée fixe* of capital punishment, the novel also affirms, without didacticism, what Hugo in his preface calls "the sacredness of human life" (IV, 482).

This book of death is, moreover, a book of fracture and alienation. The compelling need to verbalize and communicate is thwarted by the fact that it is no longer possible to reach anyone through the spoken word. Well ahead of many nineteenth- and twentieth-century writers who imagined the prisoner's existential apprenticeship of the absurd, Hugo conceived of a prison-consciousness peopling its own solitude. The invasive first person singular fills the void that has been created. Like Shakespeare's Richard II, whose thoughts have become the minutes of time running out, Hugo's anonymous prisoner gives voice to his many different selves.

The Rift

Le Dernier Jour d'un condamné is an impassioned argument against capital punishment. As such, it needs to be historically situated. Ever since Cesare Beccaria in his 1764 work *Dei Delitti e delle pene* (Essay on Crimes and Punishment) had drawn wide attention to the question of penology, jails and penal reforms had become the subjects of much controversy. Hugo makes specific mention of Beccaria in his preface, and he continued throughout his writings to cite the Italian jurist's name with veneration. During his formative years, and as a beginning writer, he had heard a great deal about prison conditions and penal reforms. The death penalty in particular was a much-debated topic under the Bourbon Restoration.[1] After all the recent bloodshed in the wake of the Revolution, the question seemed to be: Does anyone or any group have the right, in the name of law and the collectivity, to put another human being to death? Must society be vindictive? In his preface, Hugo claims to have aimed his novel at all those who assume the right to judge (IV, 480).

Yet Hugo does not set up the problem in legal or legalistic terms. In the 1832 preface, he makes it clear that the question of life and death must be laid bare, without judicial verbosities and twistings, and that it must be placed where it can be seen in all its hideous reality: not among judges and in the law courts, but on the scaffold and in the figure of the executioner. The very word *bourreau*, even at the time of Hugo's early novel *Han d'Islande*, had a polemical resonance. Joseph de Maistre, devoted to the reactionary cause of the throne and the altar, had exalted the figure of the public executioner as the indispensable horror-link in the human association. What he proposed in *Les Soirées de Saint-Pétersbourg* was philosophically more far-reaching than the divine right of kings. The executioner was a necessary, mysterious agent in a political and metaphysical theory of evil that tied providential will to tragic expiation.

These notions, developed with somber eloquence by de Maistre, were bound to be intolerable to Hugo, who early in life felt drawn to a philosophy of universal forgiveness and came to relate the dream of abolishing all prisons to a rejection of the Christian notion of hell. The importance of de Maistre as a polemical adversary is made clear not only by textual references to the *bourreau* (on the day of the execution, the children cheer on the legendary executioner, Monsieur Samson), but by the obvious allusion, in the preface, to the clever dialecticians who make the "excellence" of capital punishment a pretext for paradoxes. Hugo concludes: "The executioner must go!" (IV, 495).

The sordid functionary of official murder is evidence of Hugo's lasting fascination with the world of crime and punishment. Hugo had read Vidocq's *Mémoires* with keen interest. This personal account by an adventurer-criminal turned police informant (he eventually became head of the Sûreté) provided a lesson in argot, the colorful language of the underworld, and confirmed Hugo in his horror for the guillotine. Vidocq describes what he himself calls the "scène horrible" of an old man's decapitation to the merry accompaniment of a military band and cries of "Vive la République!"[2] He also provides a vivid description of the way in which iron collars were riveted on convicts' necks.

Hugo was not satisfied, however, with indirect documentation. On at least two occasions, together with his friend David d'Angers, he had traveled to the Bicêtre prison to watch the riveting of iron collars and the departure of a chain gang. Throughout his life, he rarely missed an opportunity to visit jails. The convict scenes in *Le Dernier Jour d'un condamné*, the prison workshop in *Claude Gueux*, and the "punishment chamber" of the Force prison in *Les Misérables* all testify to his first-hand observations. As Pair de France, he repeatedly made use of his prerogatives to inspect jails and death cells, curious not only about the setting and physical conditions but about the behavior and psychology of the inmates.[3]

Much of *Le Dernier Jour d'un condamné* reads like a realistic document. The Condemned Man, having himself become an observer, describes what leads up to and follows the shackling of the convicts: the roll call and humiliating disrobing in the rain, the naked bodies shivering in the cold, the distribution of prison garments, the hammer blows during the riveting, and the departure of the fettered men in the open wagons, with their wet trousers clinging to their knees. But more significant than these picturesque scenes is the fictional elaboration of the Condemned Man's psychological and physical distress. Hugo imagines in some detail the pathology of fear, the anguish as the hour of execution approaches. The Condemned Man jots down the clinical symptoms: burning eyes, blurred vision, elbow pain, chills, violent headaches, excessive perspiration.

The more far-reaching psychological drama is the experience of otherness. Bereft of his past as well as his future, able at best to conceive of a future tense in terms of a head separated from its trunk, the man is, from the moment of his sentencing, aware of a barrier that isolates him. His own daughter fails to recognize him. Alienated from the other prisoners (the death penalty sets him apart from convicts who have been dealt less severe sentences), estranged even from himself, the Condemned Man projects his whole being as an already posthumous reality.

The imprisonment in a futureless present, the radicalization of a confined subjectivity, called for a special control of narrative technique.[4] Well before modern writers had developed a rhetoric of existential immediacy, Hugo in *Le Dernier Jour d'un condamné* created a disrupted yet associative mental discourse that allowed for no respite from the self. The slow-motion agony of the Condemned Man, caught in patterns of flow and discontinuity, might be seen as a literary venture in the direction of the interior monologue. The staccato stenography of anguish impressed Dostoevsky, as it had impressed Flaubert.[5] The breathless succession of short chapters corresponds to a time scheme totally without a hopeful dimension. Fictional technique and temporal perspective work hand in hand. The "diary" rhythm seems to point forward to the rhetoric of disjunction achieved by Sartre in *La Nausée*.

In the narrative and metaphorical rift produced by Hugo's literary devices lies the technical originality of the book. The unspeakable is written between the lines, as it seems to be written between the dismembered graffiti on the prison walls. Much remains unsaid. We are told nothing about the crime that was committed, the circumstances of the arrest, the former occupation of the Condemned Man, the kind of life he led. Chapter 47, entitled "Mon Histoire," which was to reveal the prisoner's biography and the history of his crime, remains a blank; these pages are supposed to have been either lost or never written. The reader himself is confined to the inexorable rhetoric of the present indicative.

The structural and rhetorical complexity of this apparently simple account is evident from the very first chapter, which is locked in on itself by the verbless exclamation "Condemned to death!" given at the beginning and at the end of the chapter, and repeated once more at its exact center. The locked-in structure of the entire novel is further indicated by the title, which begins with the terminal adjective "last" (*dernier*). The opening signals of chapter 1 set up a temporal opposition between "now" (*maintenant*) and "before" (*autrefois*), imposing a new sense of time. At the heart of the prisoner's "now" is the inescapable idea of a scheduled death, which has become his true prison. The nightmarish confrontation ("face à face") with this idea blurs all distinctions between object and subject.

A double metaphor transforms the image of captivity into an inner psychological space, as well as into the imaginary space of writing. The key metaphorical inversion, turning the prison image upside down, appears as early as the third paragraph: "my mind is imprisoned in an idea." The logic of this internalized enclosure implies that the so-called objective external reality acquires figural value. The imagination weaves intricate patterns into the rough fabric ("étoffe") of life. Thought itself becomes a tragic web, as prisoner status and the prison obsession are written into the dreadful reality of the oozing walls and into the weave or texture ("toile") of the coarse prison garb.

Law and Order?

The world of fetters, webs, and inscriptions is an alien world. The strategy of the text links the incarceration of the protagonist to the unease of the reader. Flaubert was not quite correct when he stated that only the preface—written several years after the novel—was didactic. For the text is reader-conscious, and reader-oriented, in morally committed terms. The Condemned Man explicitly hopes that the diary of his anguish will provide a memorable lesson ("profond enseignement") for all those who judge and condemn.[6]

Le Dernier Jour d'un condamné was clearly meant to upset readers and give them an uneasy conscience. It is a "frightful" book, a book that "makes one ill," complains the lady in the Molièresque dialogue-preface entitled "Une Comédie à propos d'une tragédie," which accompanied the third edition of the novel. A certain "Fat Gentleman" echoes the lady's indignation. No one has the right to shock readers with such atrocities: it is a book that gives one a "horrible headache"! The Fat Gentleman complains of having been laid up in bed for two days after reading it. Prisons and sewers may exist, but that is not a reason for writing about them. Who cares, moreover, about a nameless prisoner? Why be forced to concern oneself with somebody one surely does not care to know? Prisoners are no doubt justly condemned, and executions take place. Why make a fuss about them? What does it matter to society?

The truth, as Hugo saw it, comes out in this brief comic preface. It is spoken by the Chevalier when he expresses his nostalgia for the censorship of the Ancien Régime: books are weapons that can do a great deal of harm. The point is made even more forcefully by the anachronistic Elegiac Poet: "books are often a poison that subverts the social order." Who, indeed, asks another of the dismayed salon voices, would want to condemn a criminal after reading this atrocious book?

The imagined impact of the book may have been wishful thinking on Hugo's part, but the intentional thrust was clear. Formerly committed to the restoration and conservation of absolute monarchy, Hugo now was increasingly questioning, even challenging, the social order. Years later, he recalled how, at the age of sixteen or seventeen, he had one day watched, in front of the Palais de Justice, a very young woman—almost a girl—being branded for a petty domestic theft. The scream of the victim, he claimed, still filled his ears four decades later. It was from that day, when on a public scaffold a common thief was turned into a martyr, that Hugo dated his decision to fight forever the "evil actions of the law."[7] *Le Dernier Jour d'un condamné* was meant to convey the horror and terror of extreme punishment. It was, moreover, a testimony to the author's intellectual and moral evolution, as the social question began to take precedence in his mind over political considerations.

Hugo's desire to inspire in his readers a sense of social responsibility, even of guilt, casts light on the namelessness of the Condemned Man and of his crime. Hugo explains in his preface that the omission of the prisoner's name, as well as of anything special, individual, or contingent concerning the man, allowed him to plead the cause of *any* prisoner executed at *any* time for *any* offense; the plea was to be as universal as the cause (IV, 480). It is in the same light that one must understand the repeated shock effects achieved through an ironically appropriate gallows humor. Morbid puns and verbal playfulness regarding the head that is to be cut off stress, in prison argot, the split between the thinking head (*la sorbonne*) and the head as object (*la tronche*).

More aggressively alienating than either black humor or the refusal to provide anecdotal details is the presence of the gang of convicts. Their appearance in the novel dramatizes the choice between the death penalty and, equally horrible, a life of forced labor. There seems, at first glance, to be no other reason for their appearance in the text; the rebellious herd of *forçats* might even be deemed unessential to the Condemned Man's destiny. A digressive signal is in fact given when the protagonist, otherwise totally preoccupied by his eventual fate on the guillotine, becomes so absorbed by the spectacle of these convicts that he literally "forgets" himself (III, 673). Yet their centrality in the novel cannot be denied. Their shocking presence not only appalls the Condemned Man but forces the reader into contact with a world for which he probably has no interest and no compassion.

The reader is further unsettled by the reflection of an inverted and distorted microsociety that foreshadows the seditious underworld of the Cour des Miracles in *Notre-Dame de Paris*. The mirror-like quality of a situation in which the Condemned Man becomes a spectator makes him a mediating consciousness between social worlds radically hostile to each other. The Condemned Man himself is the object of class hostility: during his confrontation with a sardonic convict, whose bitter account of his petty crime and of society's vindictiveness anticipates Jean Valjean and the underworld of *Les Misérables*, he is scoffingly called *marquis* because of his educated speech and is physically intimidated into surrendering his coat. Hugo's digressive strategy forces upon the reader's attention the thoroughly unfamiliar world of outcasts and hardened criminals. In this sense, the Condemned Man functions as a guide and intermediary, leading to *Claude Gueux*[8] and ultimately to the derelicts of *Les Misérables*. The substantive *misérable* occurs indeed repeatedly in *Le Dernier Jour d'un condamné*.

The fact that the Condemned Man's crime remains unrevealed may signal more than collective social responsibility: it may well hide something that must remain nameless. We are told almost nothing about the personal circumstances of the Condemned Man. A striking feature, however, is the total absence of male figures in all the prisoner's intimate references. A father figure never once appears in the evocation of his family. Only female figures are mentioned—mother, wife, and daughter—who will, of course, be left without son, husband, or father. And in the detailed nightmare of chapter 12, in which the Condemned Man is visited by decapitated human figures, each carrying his severed head in his left hand, only the parricide fails to shake his fist at him.[9] Can we not assume that a tragic bond exists between the archetypal parricide and the prisoner? Such a reading would, furthermore, be politically charged, since the notion of parricide was in Hugo's time intimately bound up with the notion of regicide still haunting the collective consciousness in the wake of the Revolution.

A personal drama is thus dimly articulated within the broader psychodrama of history. Uneasy consciences, both private and collective, merge in a common sense of guilt that takes on the shape of the guillotine. The year 1828, in which *Le Dernier Jour d'un condamné* was written, happens also to be the year of Hugo's father's death. The scaffold obsession, ominously underlying the structures of family relations, points to a latent sense of being condemned without appeal. The image of the spider (representing *anankē*, or fate, in Hugo's work) significantly appears on the same page as the nightmare of the father killer carrying his own decapitated head.[10]

The silhouette of the guillotine is associated, throughout Hugo's life, with a triple fear: of the inexorable law of society or of any power group, symbolized by the executioner; of the irrational mob thirsting for bloody spectacles ("la populace avec son accordée, / La guillotine"—X, 271); and of the disturbing awareness of a personal complicity with irrational violence. This inner guilt, this grim intuition that somehow we are all murderers, was to lead Hugo to state quite literally, in "Le Verso de la page," that we are all involved when a fellow creature is put to death on some public square: "Nous sommes tous mêlés à ce que fait la Grève." And this self-condemnation, written many years later, still seems to hark back to a family crime—this time not to parricide but to fratricide, the perpetually reenacted crime of Cain. Man always kills his own brother, Abel: "l'homme est solidaire avec ses monstres même, / . . . il ne peut tuer autre chose qu'Abel."[11]

It is the first of these fears—of crimes committed coldly and legally in the name of society—that is overtly projected in *Le Dernier Jour d'un condamné*. The fictional representation of this society, which the preface condemns as a stepmother cruel to her disinherited children, stresses both coldness and oppressive politeness. The man-made terminal illness of the Condemned Man is the consequence of an inhuman administration of justice which Beccaria, half a century earlier, had already qualified as "cold atrocity" ("fredda atrocità").[12] The prisoner is impressed, upon his arrival in jail, by the civilities of the turnkey and the fiendish politeness of all those who have official dealings with him. Moments before his execution, he comments ironically on the extreme gentleness of the modern executioner.

In a strongly bureaucratized society, Hugo implies, evil can exist without even the need for powerful evil passions. Institutions and institutional functions take upon themselves, smoothly and efficiently, the ritualized vindictiveness of the group. Law courts, the rationally planned jail, the priest, the judges, the prison architect—all participate in a process of exclusion and retribution that leaves no room for hesitation or remorse. Prosecutors, jurymen, and defense lawyers alike can look serenely at the prisoner and continue eating with healthy appetites. If anything, the apparent gentleness of those who deal officially with the prisoner seems designed to make him feel more helpless and more hopeless. Society's cruelty feeds on complacency and indifference. It has a name: order; and a method: surveillance. Paperwork, proper channels, classifications, and numberings represent the more innocuous side of this "order." Real order is more sinister. It relies on police brutality, here taking the form of indiscriminate blows raining on the heads and shoulders of the convicts to put an end to their din and reestablish that external calm which—the word is ironically italicized—is known as *order* (III, 675). As for surveillance, it is graphically suggested in the figure of the sentry who stands night and day outside the door of the cell: the prisoner can never look toward the grating without encountering the sentry's eyes fixed on him.

Hugo obviously anticipates Michel Foucault's diagnosis of modern society's manifold prison and power controls. In *Surveiller et punir*, Foucault develops the idea that secretive, panoptic, and coercive techniques totally enfold the individual in what he metaphorically describes as a vast "carceral archipelago."[13] Hugo's indictment of the meticulous and furtive nature of penal processes is most explicit in the preface to *Le Dernier Jour d'un condamné*. Public executions in nineteenth-century Paris occur stealthily— "en tapinois." A sense of shame pervades the ideology of law and order.

Anachronism or Prolepsis?

As reader of his own novel, Hugo no doubt overstated its sociopolitical import when, some four years later, he set out to write the lengthy polemical preface for the 1832 edition. In still later years, having gradually moved to a thoroughly democratic and even prorevolutionary position, he continued to be proud of *Le Dernier Jour d'un condamné*, less from recognition of the literary and psychological merit of the text than from a desire to establish the life-long coherence of his moral vision. Intent on stressing his conversion to the cause of revolution, but equally intent on establishing the continuity of his political thought, he came to read his early novel as a subversive manifesto—not only as an indictment of capital punishment ("j'ai fait la guerre à la Grève homicide") but also as proof that he had been one of the earliest socialists ("un des plus anciens").[14]

Hugo was evidently determined to read *Le Dernier Jour d'un condamné*, retrospectively, as a direct political confrontation of the social order. This anachronistic perspective has much to do with Hugo's intellectual discomfort in the 1850s, after Napoléon-le-petit's coup d'état had definitely driven him into Republican opposition and after he had discovered, in exile, his vocation as visionary explorer of the mystery of revolution. He was keenly aware that as a spokesman for revolution, he was not taken altogether seriously in certain quarters—that his political conversion kept friends and foes remembering his ultraconservative, proroyalist days. Hence the recurrent desire to rewrite his own past. "Ecrit en 1846" (the title itself is a manipulation of chronology, as this poem was actually written in 1854) is clearly an effort to refute the view of him as unfaithful to his former beliefs and as politically unstable. While pretending, in this autobiographical piece, to give a diachronic account (his evolution from royalism to jacobinism), Hugo in fact projects a synchronic vision of his moral and political commitment: "depuis vingt ans, je n'ai, comme aujourd'hui, / Qu'une idée en l'esprit" (IX, 255).

What is this single idea, or singleness of purpose, which has occupied his mind for twenty years—that is, since 1826, as these lines were supposedly composed in 1846? All the verbs of the passage—*plaidé, réclamé, éclairé, affranchi, combattu*—point to a struggle for social and political progress. Hugo specifically prides himself on having pleaded for the underprivileged, rehabilitated the outcasts, defended women's rights, and called for schools instead of prisons to fight misery and crime. "Ecrit en 1846" proposes an image of a twenty-four-year-old Hugo totally committed to social reform and revolutionary ideals.

Even a quick look at Victor Hugo in 1826 tells, however, a somewhat different story. For in that year he published *Odes et Ballades*, a collection that contained many "royalist" poems, and still held largely legitimist convictions which he shared with the group of the "Muse Française." Even in 1828, the year in which *Le Dernier Jour d'un condamné* was written, the young Hugo was still very far from espousing a revolutionary, or for that matter "republican," position. In the winter of 1828–29, his play *Marion de Lorme* had not yet been prohibited by the king's censor; Hugo and his wife, in announcing their son's birth, had their names printed as "baronne et baron Victor Hugo"; and *Les Orientales*, appearing only a few weeks before *Le Dernier Jour d'un condamné*, could hardly be considered a political text.[15] A few months later, Charles X granted Hugo a most satisfying private audience and subscribed to fifteen copies of *Odes et Ballades* and *Les Orientales*. At the very most, Hugo might at that stage have been considered as leaning toward the liberal position. Certainly, the thought of revolution still filled him with dread.

To be sure, a steady evolution had taken place from the founding of *Le Conservateur littéraire* in 1819, to the invitation to the crowning of Charles X in Reims in 1825 (soon followed by the ode "Le Sacre de Charles X"), to what may be considered the pivotal year 1827—the year of *Cromwell* and "Ode à la Colonne de la Place Vendôme." Yet even in 1832, writing the polemical preface to *Le Dernier Jour d'un condamné*, Hugo was still far removed from a position sympathetic to revolution. He observed with bitterness that the "arbre patibulaire" (the gibbet) is the only tree revolution fails to uproot, that the scaffold is the only edifice it does not demolish.

In later years, Hugo argued that the Romantic literary revolution he had led in the 1820s had been charged with political significance, that his own early struggle against literary conventions had been a revolutionary political statement. This anachronistic equating of Romanticism and revolution is particularly pronounced in another poem of *Les Contemplations*, "Réponse à un acte d'accusation," likewise predated (this time to 1834), and which together with "Ecrit en 1846," also written in the fall of 1854, served as an ideological rewriting of Hugo's intellectual history. In a humorous but revealing manner, he sees himself in this poem as having unleashed the wind of literary insurrection, proclaimed the equality of all language, demolished the Bastille of conventional versification, ennobled plebeian prose, and altogether recreated in poetic terms the Terror of 1793. In a more serious vein, after comparing himself to the Revolutionary leaders ("Oui, je suis ce Danton! je suis ce Robespierre!"), Hugo sees his past writings, explicitly or at the "unfathomable depths of language," as committed to the "holy progress" ("progrès saint") of revolution (IX, 74–78).

The junctures between literary and political revolution continued to be problematized throughout Hugo's work. In the meantime, the militant preface of 1832, which tried to take a long-range view of *Le Dernier Jour d'un condamné*, was, in fact, closer to *Claude Gueux*, which appeared in 1834. Between 1828 and 1834, much indeed had happened: a revolution, a change of regime, popular insurrections, the undermining of Hugo's religious and political beliefs, and the prohibition of the play *Le Roi s'amuse*, which forced Hugo into open hostility with the government. The year 1834 was crucial in Hugo's political development; it was the year of *Claude Gueux* but also of his *Etude sur Mirabeau*, an exaltation of the great revolutionary orator, whom he saw, with a half-century's perspective, as the symbol of *le peuple*: the man of the Revolution who, in his anger and grandiose ugliness, embodied the force of events.

The propagandistic preface to *Le Dernier Jour d'un condamné* may have announced these developments. But it tended to misread the novel, whose political implications are first of all hallucinatory.

The Handwriting on the Wall

The central hallucination in *Le Dernier Jour d'un condamné* derives from the image of the guillotine, and more generally from the ceremonial of all public punishments. The horror and fascination inspired in Hugo by ritual contacts between executioner and victim was no doubt linked to his childhood visions of human limbs on trees, to Goyaesque early memories of men strung up along Italian roads during the Napoleonic wars.[16] His precocious obsession with the torn body, with physical torments, and with human degradation is certainly an important factor in his creative, visionary sense of horror.

Le Dernier Jour d'un condamné begins, indeed, on a visionary note. The Condemned Man is haunted by the terrible thought ("pensée infernale") of his violent end—an obsession that in his delirious dreams focuses on the image of a knife. He relives, in his mind, the "fantasmagorie" of the trial, with the spectators crowding the benches as ravens surround a corpse (III, 658). Inanimate objects become animate. The prison façade seems to suffer from leprosy; the prison itself is a "horrible being," half building and half man (III, 680). To the nightmare figures of his phantasmagoria the prisoner applies the word *grotesque*—a term that Hugo, in the preface to *Cromwell*, had recently endowed with poetic prestige. The mythopoetic potential of the grotesque is in fact constantly tapped in the novel, through incongruous puns about heads (the head-splitting, "à tue-tête" screams of the greedy street merchants near the scaffold—III, 709), macabre speculations on whether the head or the trunk will become the specter, and aggressive prison slang. The Condemned Man considers argot a pathology of language, comparing it to ugly warts and excrescenses; he is repelled yet at the same time strangely fascinated by those bizarre words that make him think of toads, the slime of snails, and the fateful image of the spider—words that possess a disquieting poetic force.

The oneiric vision is projected through specific nightmare apparitions, competing in horror with the image of the decapitated visitors: the comatose old witch in the closet, with one eye half-opened, who comes to life and bites his hand; the pale and bloody ghosts of former victims of the guillotine returning to watch the execution of the executioner. Surrealistic effects and spectral fears (the prisoner refers to a "chimère à la Macbeth") fill what the Condemned Man himself calls his "empty" and "convulsed" brain (III, 669). Fever is here a function of vacuity and the terror of nonbeing. The Condemned Man describes his dizziness in terms of a booming bell echoing through the hollow spaces of his brain. He associates this impression with the memory of a climb to the belfry tower of Notre-Dame—a climb that left him giddy and dazed with the enormous din and the fear of falling. The association of skull, bell, and precipice is particularly interesting because of the obvious thematic link with *Notre-Dame de Paris*, which was to appear only a few years later and whose genesis runs parallel, in a number of ways, to that of *Le Dernier Jour d'un condamné*.

If the central hallucination of the novel derives from the hideousness of the guillotine, it is because it involves the double image of skull and brain, as well as the specific violence of a decapitation-castration that assails consciousness itself. Throughout Hugo's work, the emblem of the skull corresponds to the privileged prison of poetic experience.[17] In a broader perspective, what appears to be involved is a drama: intelligence casting the image of its own thought back to itself. The novel can indeed be read as the account of a mind's self-awareness and self-scrutiny as it watches itself glide toward death, thought by thought. The incongruous gap between the thinking head and the head as object is thus not a simple matter of black humor. The fixation has its logic. What is at stake is quite literally the head. Puns and verbal conceits draw attention to the basic split; the head as external and internal reality—the glance of the subject and the glance of *the other*. Early in the novel, as the victim watches the departure of the chain gang, he is the observed observer. Later, he comes to view himself as the *seen* but unseeing object, as he imagines the mob gleefully watching his head fall.

His execution is thus conceived and feared as spectacle (the words *spectacle* and *spectateur* recur with an almost morbid insistence), while the tête-à-tête with the fixed idea of his death brings about a major metaphorical inversion. The obsession of imprisonment becomes imprisonment in an obsession. From that early point on, when the mind is seen as imprisoned in an idea, the development obeys its own logic: the prison-thought is seen written onto the walls of the real prison, while the text weaves its notion of writing into the massive metaphor of the Wall. The novel, at this level of interpretation, deals with the writer's obsession.

The handwriting on the wall is a literal reality, before it is turned self-consciously into a metaphor. The walls of the cell, on which can be read the prisoner's own destiny, are covered with signs, drawings, fantastic figures, fragments of thoughts, and disquieting names that intermingle and partially efface one another. The inscription of violence on the stone instills an almost primitive fear in the Condemned Man, who nonetheless pursues, totally fascinated, what he defines as the "reading" of his wall ("la lecture de mon mur"—III, 668). The underlying anxiety, it is easy to guess, involves writing itself. The prison space becomes the space of the writer. When the gap between doing and saying becomes widest, when speech no longer reaches anyone, the need to communicate becomes greatest. When nothing remains to be said, all remains to be told. Speechlessness itself asks to be revealed. Prison, with its graffiti, its mutilated scrawls on the walls, its pages of stone, becomes the space of writing. The walls, covered with traces—chalk, charcoal, carvings, black letters, forgotten names, dismembered sentences seemingly written in fiery letters—objectify the voice of silence.

The priority of the artistic sensibility is in fact clearly indicated on the first page of the novel, when the Condemned Man, evoking his former self, speaks of the steady "feast" of his imagination, of his youthful mind filled with "fantasies" weaving endless arabesques into the banal canvas of reality. Unlike Claude Gueux and Jean Valjean, who are illiterates at first, the nameless prisoner of *Le Dernier Jour d'un condamné* is a cultivated man, even an intellectual. He is "refined by education" (III, 662), knows Latin, seems to have read Pascal, has a bookish view of the world, recalls his study, asks for pen and paper, collects and annotates a *chanson d'argot*.

The prisoner's otherness is therefore not merely a function of the multiple rifts between him and society, the group of convicts, and his own family in the person of his daughter who no longer recognizes him. A still deeper separation marks the writer's experience. This deeper and wider gap of an absence-presence is, however, articulated precisely on the figure of the daughter—a most revealing fact in view of Hugo's own daughter fixation, which was associated throughout his life with the act of writing. In chapter 46, shortly after the frustrating visit of the little daughter, Marie, the Condemned Man explicitly states that it is for her and to her, but to a her-beyond-death, that he wishes to write these pages, "so that she may read them hereafter" (III, 706). The daughter as invisible reader becomes the *figura* of a literary afterlife. Inscribed into a posthumous order, writing is itself viewed as a rift that is not devoid of ideological consequences.

"The People Will Laugh"

The rift exists also, most dramatically, between the writer-prisoner and the common people who have come to watch his execution with obscene joy. The Condemned Man's animosity toward the populace (he states that he takes pleasure in seeing the crowd in the mud) carries sociopolitical overtones. The novel suggests, indeed, a far from happy relation with *le peuple*, whom Hugo, in the name of revolution, later celebrated yet continued to fear.

A few years before completing *Le Dernier Jour d'un condamné*, Hugo had written a poem entitled "Le Poète dans les Révolutions," in which the figure of the poet (the epigraph appropriately quotes André Chénier) is seen as the eternal victim of revolution: his head is destined for the executioner ("Il a . . . / Une tête pour les bourreaux!"—I, 810). The epigraph from Chénier, who was himself guillotined during the French Revolution, specifically refers to the hatred of political executioners—"bourreaux barbouilleurs de lois." Chénier's poem, written in jail as the last message from a condemned man, is thus the overt intertext for Hugo's own poem glorifying the writer's vocation as victim.

Hugo's denunciation of the political guillotine is, it seems, related in depth to his revulsion for the mob. The preface of the 1832 edition is explicit: "In revolutionary times, beware of the first head that falls. It arouses the mob's appetite for blood" ("Elle met le peuple en appétit"—IV, 484). This repugnance for the political scaffold is inscribed not only into the preface but into the body of the text. Referring to the famous trial of the four noncommissioned officers of La Rochelle, the prisoner writes: "for an idea, for a dream, for an abstraction, this horrible reality called the guillotine!" (III, 668). The novel seems to project the antirevolutionary specter of the guillotine into Hugo's much later "revolutionary" period. When, in "Le Verso de la page," Hugo insisted on the sacredness of life and denied the guillotine the last word—even though he had come to feel that revolution redeemed mankind—the images that imposed themselves came straight out of the stark pages of *Le Dernier Jour d'un condamné*: a pitiful victim awakened by the turnkey and the priest, while the infernal machine is being readied on the Place de Grève; the unspeakable procession through the crowd (X, 269, 284, 273).

The novel about the Condemned Man thus seems to have a proleptic function, echoing throughout Hugo's later texts which, especially during his long exile, confront as well as exalt the "monstre divin" of revolution. The heavily loaded image of the crowd, the *foule*, is perhaps the most revealing negative projection of *Le Dernier Jour d'un condamné*. Thirty years later, in "Le Verso de la page," Hugo would show how the ideal of the *peuple* is continually undermined by the reality of the *populace*, how the ferocious rabble is forever waiting and clamoring for the spectacle of public executions. But the model for the laughing, bloodthirsty mob is of course to be found in *Le Dernier Jour d'un condamné:* the "horrible foule buveuse de sang" (III, 694) and—more disturbing still, because of the striking later association of laughter with revolution—the image of the mocking crowd, the "horrible peuple qui aboie, et m'attend, et rit." Laughter seems indeed to be the ominous manifestation of the mob: "à des rires qui éclataient, j'ai reconnu que c'était la foule" (III, 707).

The association of laughter, cruelty, and popular masses acquires particular complexity in terms of the spectacle, whether it be the drama of the courtroom or the grim ceremonial performance on the scaffold. The hot breath of the crowd fills the courtroom as well as the public square; even young girls are corrupted by the collective avidity for violent sensations. The people relish the sight of scapegoats. Public torments are festivities. The Condemned Man's bitter remarks about the bloodthirsty spectator-crowd foreshadow the appalling merrymaking and hilarity of the Parisian mob watching Quasimodo the hunchback being whipped on the pillory in *Notre-Dame de Paris*. The prisoner's rage against the common people mounts in the final pages; and his ultimate cry, in the interrupted last sentence—"Ah! les misérables!"—is most revealing, not only because Hugo would later make the word *misérables* the title of a socially conscious novel but because this concluding cry of terror and hate embraces both the tormentors and the masses who have come to watch.

What further complicates this motif of laughter is that the hideous and pitiable convicts also laugh, and that their laughter is at once poignant and demonic. Faced with the somber and vindictive hilarity of these ragged men, the protagonist feels as though "petrified" by an unspeakable threat. Their spasms of angry joy make him weep and fill him with anguish. Their atrocious sneers, their imprecations, and their violent bursts of laughter seem infused with the idea of evil and destruction. In the confrontation scene between the Condemned Man and the brutal convict, the hoarse, rasping laughter of the hardened criminal is in fact described as a "râle"—a death rattle (III, 687). Ultimately, the bitterness of this laughter seems to contaminate the Condemned Man himself, as he moves toward the scaffold: "Alors j'ai ri horriblement aussi, moi" (III, 709).

A Hidden Wish?

The scoffing, jeering chain gang is clearly meant as an inverted image of the hideous crowd; the two laughters answer and oppose each other. It is around this opposition that the text builds its greatest ideological complexity. The substantive les misérables applies to both the populace and the convicts. That substantive, beyond its common usage, was to acquire a privileged status in the work of Hugo, who plays on two special meanings of the word: misérables are abject, despicable scoundrels, but also unhappy and potentially sublime victims of the social order. It is precisely from this latter group, the misérables condemned and excluded by society, that many years later in Hugo's most celebrated novel the new spiritual hero, Jean Valjean, will emerge.

But here is the point: the crowd and the convicts, despite the echo and the mirror effect of their laughter, are two very different collective realities. Side by side with the politically indifferent, irresponsible, and even repressive mob, Hugo places the victimized and rebellious herd of forçats who dream of vengeance (III, 675). The noble forçat, heroic challenger of authority, is a Romantic model. But the rebel forçat—as Balzac's Vautrin, a few years later, was to confirm—is also clearly of the devil's party. This satanic quality is, in Le Dernier Jour d'un condamné, intimately associated with the theme of laughter. The "masques de démons" become visible in the same paragraph in which are heard the fearful "éclats de rire" (III, 670). The old convict who laughingly shakes his fist at the sky becomes the emblem of blasphemous revolt—the hell imagery is unmistakable.[18] The episode of the riveting in the prison yard is translated into a tableau of grimacing humanity set in the underworld. It is presented as an experience that is at once visual (livid faces, burning eyes, convulsive movements, clenched fists raised in a gesture of defiance) and aural (rattling of chains, cacophony of voices, and—heard above the din of the "ronde hurlante"—curses and strident laughter). Thirty years later, this "echo of the demon's laughter" would be heard again in *Les Misérables*. When the convoy of chained men, the pitiable *cadène*, passes through the streets of Paris, the hallucinatory vision recalls the moral and physical hell of the earlier novel. Hugo is explicit: "Dante would have believed he had seen the seven circles of hell in motion" (XI, 651).

Visionary elements in *Le Dernier Jour d'un condamné* link the problem of evil to the social question. But the awareness of this link, as well as the conflicting manifestations of laughter that oppose the rabble and the victims of the social order, brings about an intellectual malaise. The Condemned Man is cast in a complex mediational role with regard to the two forms of laughter. The laughter of the crowd produces terror, whereas that of the convicts produces a keen awareness of moral and social discomfort. When the sardonic *ur*-Valjean appears in chapter 23, his "rire amer"— the laughter that sounds like a death rattle—is the signal for a social clash (III, 687). The convict's attitude toward the Condemned Man is clearly determined by class hostility, and his derision and slangy eloquence cause the latter to feel guilty about his own cultivated speech and refined education. The Condemned Man is, moreover, afraid of the physical force of the outlaw. He is, in this context, associated with the privileged classes.

This intellectual unease casts light on the Condemned Man's role as spectator. What he witnesses with such fascination and anxiety is of course what Hugo himself had witnessed, along with David d'Angers, in the Bicêtre prison. The theatrical nature of the episode creates a triangular situation, the pivot of which is the

Condemned Man, who will in turn soon become a spectacle for the "avid and cruel" mob, though in the meantime he watches the drama of the convicts from a cell that the turnkey compares explicitly to a private box at the theater: "Vous serez seul dans votre loge" (III, 670). The triangularity of the novel's structure is further stressed when the Condemned Man, on his way to the final act on the scaffold, joins in the laughter of vindictiveness and frustrated revolt (III, 709).

We are perhaps touching here on what is ideologically the most problematic and least conscious aspect of Hugo's early novel; for the mediation between the cruel laughter of the crowd and the pitiful yet defiant laughter of the convicts is insidiously related to the figure of the king, suggesting that the latent subject of the novel is indeed political in ways that the author may not have been willing (or able) to formulate explicitly. Chapter 40 begins with the curious remark, "Il est singulier que je pense sans cesse au roi" ("It is strange that I continually think of the king"). The ceaseless thought of the king is of course logical: the simple signature of the seven letters of his name, Charles, could mean pardon and therefore life. But the same ceaseless thought could also point in another, very different direction, associating the king not with life but with death. The spectator-spectacle inversion is in fact linked to a more basic reversal, for the supreme spectator is none other than the king. The cell from which the Condemned Man watches the riveting of the chain gang may be ironically described as a theater box, but the irony acquires quite another dimension when the turnkey's sentence is given in full: "Vous serez seul dans votre loge comme le roi" ("You will be alone in your box like the king"—III, 670). And it is here that the association of royalty and spectacle leads to another inversion, as well as to a disturbing substitution. For the king-spectator is also the king-spectacle. Behind Charles X, the king with the power to pardon, there is the vestigial memory-image of another king, Louis XVI, who was condemned and not pardoned, and who mounted another scaffold in front of another sea of heads.

The unformulated secret memory (or is it a dream wish?) hinted at by this substitution seems confirmed by the prisoner's revenge dream involving the execution of the executioner. The mob of victims will have its turn: "A notre tour nous ferons foule autour" (III, 702). A new time of laughter will come. And indeed there is in the novel an even more telling inversion, or conversion, substituting not merely one king for another but the figure of the king for that of the Condemned Man. As the screaming populace acclaims the arrival of the man to be guillotined, the victim comments that a king would not be greeted with a greater explosion of joy: "Si fort qu'on aime un roi, ce serait moins de fête" (III, 708). And on the following page, the analogue tends toward identity as the crowd reaches a climax of hysteria, "Comme pour le roi." More remarkable still is the link between king and laughter in the sentence that follows, as the Condemned Man, so far the victim of laughter, now in turn laughs aggressively: "Alors j'ai ri horriblement aussi, moi." Such a reading of an implicit wish for the king's death becomes even more convincing and complex if one recalls that it is, within the novel, figuratively wedded to the motif of parricide.

The death wish and the death guilt remain interlocked. They must, in fact, both be understood as part of the great nineteenth-century debate on history in the wake of recent social and political upheavals. Was the French Revolution a divine punishment to be understood in the light of the "reversibility of suffering," as Joseph de Maistre thought? Was it a sign of humanity's progress? Or was it perhaps the cause rather than the result of divine intervention?[19] Beyond the topical debate on history, the dialogue is primarily one that Hugo carries on tirelessly with himself. The nightmare-wish of violence in Le Dernier Jour d'un condamné has inescapable political overtones. But the underlying political thrust comes into sharp conflict with Hugo's articulated hostility to the notions of punishment, vindictiveness, and retribution, as symbolized by the specter of the guillotine. The word révolution does indeed appear in the text, though ostensibly with a nonpolitical, strictly psychological meaning: "A revolution had taken place within me."[20] The Condemned Man, after his trial, refers to the complete upheaval in his psyche. The notion of upheaval, extended to the social and political realm, will inform much of Hugo's later work. He will come to see the political revolution as a fundamentally traumatic yet also redemptive event. But the implicit justification of violence will be relentlessly countered, and even cancelled, by a denunciation of violent justice and of the horrors of history.

This denunciation, so powerfully delineated in *Le Dernier Jour d'un condamné*, will assume tragic proportions in the novels to come.

1. Octopus. *Pieuvre*.

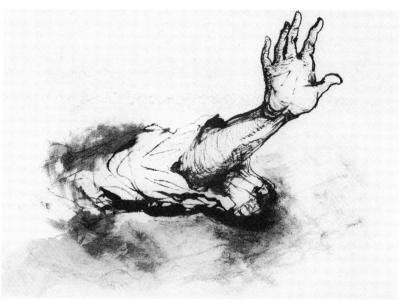

2. Conscience in front of an evil deed.
La conscience devant une mauvaise action.

3. The judge. *Judex*.

4. The executioner. *Le bourreau*.

5. The Vianden ruin seen through a spider web.
   La ruine de Vianden à travers une toile d'araignée.

6. Town near a large body of water.
   Ville au bord d'une large étendue d'eau.

7. Gavroche at the age of eleven. *Gavroche à onze ans*.

8. Gavroche dreaming. *Gavroche rêveur*.

9. The chain. *La chaîne*.

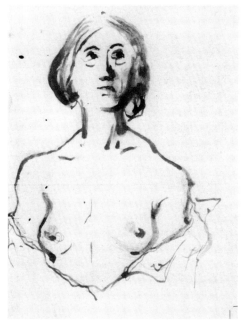

10. *Miseria*.

11. The king of the Auxcriniers. *Le roi des Auxcriniers*.

12. The Dover reefs. *Les Douvres*.

13. The octopus. *La pieuvre*.

14. Old St. Malo. *Vieux St. Malo.*

15. The haunted house. *La maison visionnée.*

6. The devil-ship. *Le bateau-diable*.

7. The Durande after the shipwreck. *La Durande après le naufrage*.

18. The toilers of the sea. *Les travailleurs de la mer*.

19. The last buffoon thinking of the last king.
Le dernier bouffon songeant au dernier roi.

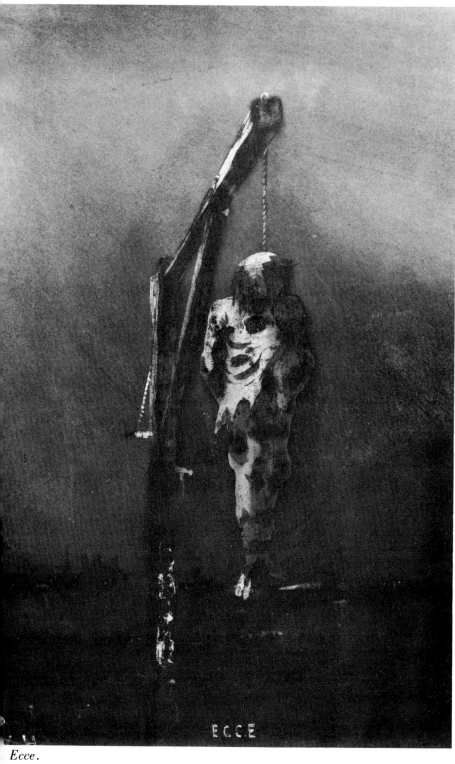

Ecce.

21. The Eddystone lighthouse. *Le phare d'Eddystone*.

22. The Casquets lighthouse. *Le phare des Casquets*.

23. Tourgue castle. *La Tourgue*.

24. Cannon. *Canon*.

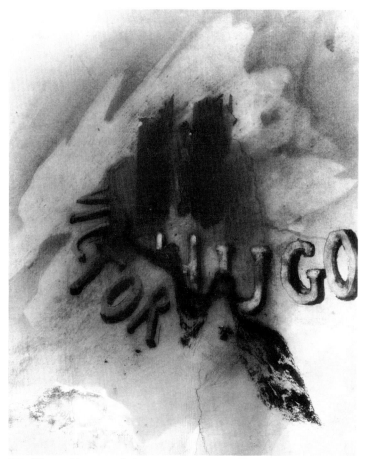

25. Victor Hugo and the ruins of a fortress.
Victor Hugo et les ruines d'un bourg.

26. Ruins of Gros Nez castle, Jersey.
Ruines du Gros Nez.

27. My fate. *Ma destinée*.

3

The Living Stones
of Notre-Dame

*Les révolutions transforment
tout excepté le coeur humain.*

There are subjects enough for several novels packed into *Notre-Dame de Paris*. Beyond the cathedral itself, the title points to the city that was to haunt Hugo's imagination for the rest of his life. Notre-Dame, the edifice, stands symbolically at its topographic and historical center. The melodramatic plots develop a number of individual dramas, all linked in some way to the architecture of the cathedral and to the labyrinth of the city: the gargoyle-like hunchback, whose soul is confined in the double prison of deformity and deafness; the passion-ridden priest, victim of his own evil, who seems to come straight out of a Gothic tale; the persecuted virgin-orphan, who succumbs to the love she feels and inspires. And around these central characters a variety of marginal figures evolve, occasionally usurping the center of attention: the mischievous, riot-prone student; the leaders of the mob; the ironic writer-beggar; the bereaved mother driven to ascetic reclusion and to madness; the cunning old king whose terminal illness announces historical change.

The wealth of themes is even more impressive than the variety of human dramas: the encounter of the Beauty and the Beast; the symbolic political rivalry of the lovers (the sinister Priest, the frivolous Soldier, the coarse People); the dawn of the modern world under the sign of the recently invented printing press; knowledge and the will to power; the politically explosive anger of the underworld; a nostalgic glorification of ancient monuments; an implicit theory of the grotesque that challenges all forms of conservatism. And above all this hovers the notion of *anankē*, announcing destruction and death.

Notre-Dame de Paris is indeed a novel about death; and *anankē*, the Greek word for fate, which the author claims to have seen engraved inside one of the cathedral towers, is according to him the foundation of the book: "C'est sur ce mot qu'on a fait ce livre." Hugo, however, translates this abstract notion into a vivid and disturbing symbol. For *anankē* is close in sound to *arachnē*, the Greek word for spider; and the recurrent image of a fly caught and destroyed in a spider's fateful web becomes one of the unifying metaphors of the novel.[1]

Perhaps more important still is the central image of stone, present both concretely and metaphorically in the title. The houses and the monuments of the city are a creation in stone—a "rêve de pierre," as Baudelaire was to put it.[2] Walls, statues, paving blocks, gargoyles, gables, towers, and buttresses invade the setting. The metaphorical presence of stone is even more pervasive. Frollo, the somber archdeacon, is repeatedly represented as a man of stone, vaguely recalling the Commendatore of the Don Juan legend. When he falls to his death, he rebounds like a tile on the pavement. Quasimodo, the hunchback, is not only stone deaf, but his "psyche" is described as imprisoned within stone walls. *Notre-Dame de Paris* can be read as an elaborate series of variations on the themes of oppression and incarceration.[3]

The stone metaphor extends even to ideas, to abstractions. There is petrification through fear, but there is also the more frightening petrification through dogma. The symbolic range of the image includes political violence and the dynamics of history. *Notre-Dame de Paris* was written in the immediate aftermath of the July Revolution of 1830. Hugo repeatedly alludes to the function of the paving blocks during the insurrection. His personal notes, as he considers his novel, are filled with stone images: "Depuis Juillet, le trône est sur le pavé"; "Le plus excellent symbole du peuple, c'est le pavé." More significant still is the conviction that the Parisian street is the revolutionary setting par excellence: "le mot terrible de la révolution de 1830, c'était *le pavé*."[4] These partly disquieting, partly hope-filled revolutionary associations become more meaningful in terms of the larger symbolism of the novel, if one keeps in mind that Hugo came to view Paris not only as the capital of the nineteenth century but as the civilizing center of the world, the city of ideas and ideals, whose steady change and growth and whose forest-like "vegetation of framework and stone" suggest live roots and *living stones,* in an almost religious sense.[5]

Hybrid Forms

Hugo's Paris, that "chronicle of stone," is thus the city of fixity as well as of change. The narrator is at once the antiquarian crusading to preserve[6] and the historian concerned with mobility, progress, and transitional situations. The notions of permanence and transformation seem to intermingle, as they do in the preface to *Les Feuilles d'automne,* written only a few months later, in which the poet tersely states that revolutions transform everything except the human heart (IV, 369). It is hardly surprising that side by side with stones and stone metaphors, *Notre-Dame de Paris* insistently proposes hybrid forms and figures, suggesting mixture, incompleteness, and processes of becoming.

Architecture itself is affected by hybridity. The Place de Grève, the setting of many dramatic scenes, offers a simultaneous display of architectural evolution, blending in the same field of vision the semicircular Roman arch, the Gothic ogive, and the square window of the emerging new style. Centrally located stands a "hybrid construction" symbolically carrying three different names (IV, 59). But it is not only the sinister Place de Grève, the traditional site of public executions, that appears as one of those weird "intermediary beings" Hugo spoke of in his preface to *Cromwell*. The cathedral, too, looms as an extraordinary composite in time and space. Unlike other constructions, which correspond to a moment in history or represent a perfect type, Notre-Dame, in which several styles exist and commingle ("se mêlent"; "s'amalgament"—IV, 96), is no longer a Romanesque and not yet a Gothic structure. It is an edifice in transition, the product of a grafting process.

The stress on hybrid forms appropriately extends to the writing of the novel itself. A historical novel is by definition a problematic mixture of "fiction" and "fact," raising moreover the subtler question of history as fiction. The generic blendings, as well as the need to reconcile the artist's and the historian's concerns, are explicitly mentioned by Hugo in a prefatory note. The reader is asked to unravel that which belongs to the realm of the historian from that which is part of the artist's aim (IV, 22). The uneasy relation of fiction to history—this at a time when Walter Scott's fame was at its peak—was in fact discussed by some of the best minds of the age. Pierre-Simon Ballanche, who saw the poet in a prophet's role, insisted that poetry and fiction were entering into alien territory and were in danger of discrediting themselves as soon as they invaded the domain of history. Hugo himself, an attentive reader of Ballanche, asserted that he preferred to "believe" in fiction rather than in history, that he was more concerned with "moral" than with "historical" truth.[7] In a Hegelian perspective, it is not historical fiction alone that is characterized by hybridism: the novel as a genre is a hybrid form—one of those *Zwitterarten* in which "prosaic" circumstances and "poetic" longings intermingle.[8] For Hugo, such hybrid status corresponds to the highest promise of modern art. In an early critical text, he praises this "new genre" capable of combining narrative and dramatic elements (II, 435). Later, after completing *Les Misérables*, he was to maintain even more pointedly that the novel, "cette merveilleuse nouveauté littéraire," is a remarkable fusion of epic, lyric, and dramatic components (XII, 204).

It is not surprising that in *Notre-Dame de Paris* hybridism extends to the characters themselves. Gringoire, the parodistic alter ego of the poet-dramatist, is an "esprit essentiellement mixte" (IV, 67), an indecisive, complex composite of all human passions and propensities. There is more than a hint of incompleteness in Frollo's observation that this half-sage, half-madman is but a rough sketch of something or other—a "vaine ébauche de quelque chose" (IV, 275). Incompleteness and approximation are, of course, inherent in the name of Quasimodo the hunchback. The first two syllables (meaning "in part" or "almost") are made explicit in the remark that this deformed being is but an "*à peu près*" (IV, 117). Quasimodo's hybrid nature is what makes him a monstrous creature; he is neither a beast nor a complete human being. He refers to himself as distressingly indeterminate, a "je ne sais quoi."[9] Popular superstition sees him as the "bastard" progeny of the archdeacon and the devil. The hilarity he provokes is more than a manifestation of heartlessness; it betrays a fear of the unknown. He has come to be associated with the Mardi Gras, the occasion of all travesties and of coarse farces and grimaces. He cohabits with monsters of stone, and at a distance he could be mistaken for the gargoyles that serve as mouths through which the gutters of the cathedral disgorge themselves. He is the animate brother of the grisly, laughing gargoyles, the yelping gorgons, the fire-breathing salamanders, the sneezing griffins—to all the stone monsters that occasionally awaken from their sleep of stone and appear to come to life (IV, 290).

This life of the stones cannot be dismissed as a simple matter of "grotesque" sensationalism. The name Quasimodo harks back to the First Epistle of Peter, whom Christ compared to a rock ("Tu es Petrus . . ."), and who, in his Epistle, compares those he addresses to newborn babes in search of the "living stone" of God. "Quasimodo geniti infantes . . ." is the introit of the Sunday Mass following Easter. "Quasimodo" is thus at once the linguistic signal of a figure of speech (comparison, metaphor) and a triple reference to innocence, petrification, and spiritual renewal.[10]

Hugo's notion of the grotesque cannot, in any case, be reduced to facile picturesqueness. The famous preface to *Cromwell* (1827) developed a theory of the grotesque involving broad issues: the stages of civilization, the imitation of nature (mimesis), the relation between ugliness and the sublime, the anguish of modern man. If, in *Notre-Dame de Paris*, the Cyclopean eye of Quasimodo corresponds to the Cyclopean rose window of the cathedral, if animals look like men and human beings like animals, it is because all limits, all boundaries, seem to be erased in what Hugo conceives as the pandemonium of a total vision. For such a vision necessarily implies transgression. What are ultimately transgressed, beyond the sterile canons of "good taste," are the conventional lines of demarcation between ugliness and beauty, between evil and good. Transgression, in Hugo's view, serves to span the widening rift that in modern man separates body from soul. That is why, in the preface to *Cromwell*, Hugo called for a new poetic vision, capable of bringing about a "fertile union" of opposites. "Tout se tient," he proclaimed (III, 50–51). But if all is related, and ultimately connected, this also means that the writer must help break down all rigid systems, while maintaining and even glorifying a sense of mystery and incompleteness. In his theater, Hugo consistently undermined the monolithic nature of neoclassical tragedy, and in so doing eventually challenged the tragic code.[11] In his poetry and in his fiction, he did not cease to stress the double motif of decipherment and incompleteness.

In *Notre-Dame de Paris*, the affinities between hybrid constructs and incompleteness characterize in particular one form of architecture: writing. The edifice of literature, according to Hugo, always remains unfinished ("toujours inachevé"—IV, 144). All the ages of mankind are busily at work in his synoptic vision. Each word and each text, like every stone brought to a building, means not just an addition but a transformation. Typically, the graffiti on the cathedral wall—the Gothic, Hebrew, Greek, and Roman scripts—blend by effacing one another. Hugo's preoccupation with language and literature as a composite effort at endless becoming helps explains the powerful presence of the Tower of Babel imagery, here and elsewhere in his work. The chapter about the relentless labor of writing concludes with the image of the "seconde tour de Babel du genre humain" (IV, 144). Hugo had only recently written his visionary poem "La Pente de la rêverie," in which the tower of the many languages occupies an enigmatic central position. *Notre-Dame de Paris* relates architecture to scripture, no less than vision to history. The emblem for architecture as well as for writing is Babel. It is both a disturbing and exhilarating emblem, if only because neither edifice nor text is ever complete. They are works of transition: "Pendent opera interrupta." To describe the cathedral, Hugo significantly refers to a literary monument, Virgil's *Aeneid*.[12]

The transition motif also affects the text of history. The choice of 1482 as the historical setting for the novel is highly significant. Louis XI, whose shrewd reign helped dismantle the feudal edifice, is about to die, and the Middle Ages appear to be coming to an end. The late fifteenth century is thus a pivotal point, a transitional moment in the larger drama of history, whose sequential progression also seems to be subject to the fateful rule of *anankē*. Centuries, explains Hugo, are the inscrutable and often self-contradictory sentences in a much larger text that tells of a steady progression.[13] Along this linear time scale of history, each moment is both a transition and an effacement. Political systems and power structures replace one another. This very special concern for historical mutation, this transitional perspective on both past and future, explains the cultural anachronisms that stud the novel (references to Montaigne and to Régnier, for example), as well as the number of political allusions to the far-distant fall of the Bastille.

The year 1789 looms both as a projected future in relation to the narrated time (1482) and as a relevant past for the author and his reader from the perspective of the writing time (1830). The French Revolution, which is not the overt subject of *Notre-Dame de Paris*, is nonetheless its mythical time: it lies both behind and ahead.[14] But if the mythical time is 1789, the actual or psychological and political time is 1830—the year Hugo wrote the novel, a year that was itself perceived as a period of transition. The July Revolution marks a historic interruption; it signals the end of the Bourbon Restoration and the beginning of Louis-Philippe's constitutional monarchy. There is little doubt that Hugo, like many of his contemporaries, viewed the events of July 1830 as an articulation in a deeper change. It represented a gap, an ellipsis. The many topical allusions to contemporary events (the July street violence, the riots of December and of the following February, the sack of Saint-Germain l'Auxerrois, the National Revolution of Belgium, the debates on the death penalty) all stress the transitional and hybrid nature of the times. Together with his generation, Hugo is haunted by the revolution of 1789. The discontinuities of 1830 are understood to correspond to the larger discontinuities of the Restoration. Thus Hugo maintains from the outset that the "hybrid royalty" of Louis-Philippe is but a "useful transition": the time for the Republic is not ripe—but it will come (IV, 1191). In the meantime, the revolution of July 1830 is an aborted revolution; just as in the novel, the underworld's assault on the cathedral is a failure. The populace is not ready; it is not yet aware of its historical mission. Symbolically, Quasimodo does not understand who his natural allies are. Hunchback and vagabonds engage in a fratricidal struggle.

The Printed Edifice

Is Hugo himself ready for revolution? There can be little doubt that, in selecting the cathedral as a subject, Hugo obeyed in large part what must be called a "conservative" impulse. In the prefatory note of 1832, he claims that one of the chief aims of the novel— and of his life—is to "conserve" ancient monuments. *Conservateur*, however, denotes someone who protects and preserves (the curator of a museum) as well as a person committed to the defense of the social order and of the institutions of the past. (*Le Conservateur littéraire* was the title of an ultraroyalist review launched in 1819 by Victor and his brothers, Abel and Eugène). There is a latent (or is it residual?) political significance in the narrator's claim to have "repaired" the cathedral by describing its condition in 1482, to have restored it to its status before barbarians of all sorts—including revolutionary barbarians—disfigured it. The article "Guerre aux démolisseurs," the companion piece to *Notre-Dame de Paris*, is even more explicit. The monuments of the past represent the "venerable book of tradition." Hugo even calls for laws that would protect the "sacred" nature of the past (IV, 499–509).

Yet the one pointed message in the novel is that the "book of tradition" will necessarily, and providentially, be replaced by a new kind of book. For the future is even more sacred than the past. The chapter that most powerfully betrays Hugo's ideological tension concerning permanence and change has death inscribed in its title: "Ceci tuera cela" ("The One Will Kill the Other"). It is an apparently digressive chapter, which for various reasons Hugo withheld until the 1832 edition. The setting is melodramatic, but the thrust is clearly didactic. A mysterious visitor, who is in fact the king of France in disguise, accompanied by his physician, has come one evening to consult the learned archdeacon in his cell. The light is dim, and the cell is ominous in its very simplicity. The subject of the consultation ranges from medicine to astrology, to alchemy. The powder in the flasks, the old king's quest for health and power, Frollo's hermetic language—all suggest Faustian motifs and satanic influences. Through the window, the black silhouette of the cathedral looks like an enormous two-headed sphinx. It is in this setting that Frollo, looking in turn at the silhouette of the great church and at a recently printed book he owns, sadly states that "ceci tuera cela"—terse words he immediately glosses: the book will destroy the edifice.

Hugo devotes an entire chapter to the development of this idea. Architecture used to be the book of mankind; with the advent of the printing press, writing has become the new architecture, both more powerful and more durable. The alphabet used to be of marble, and pages were of granite. The Gothic cathedral is a late and supreme illustration of a text made of stone. Its façade is described as one of the most "beautiful architectural pages"; each of its stones is termed a "page" in the history of the nation and in the history of arts and sciences (IV, 92, 95). Much like the pages of any text, however, they demand to be "read," and therefore deciphered. Frollo is fascinated by the emblematic portico of Notre-Dame, which he decodes like a "page de grimoire" out of a dark book of spells (IV, 125). The metaphor of hieroglyphs is a recurrent figure suggesting inscription in stone, as well as a revelatory and initiatory decipherment.

Priest and narrator do not, however, interpret the relation of writing to architecture in the same manner. They both view the invention of the printing press as a pivotal event. But for Frollo, the press signals the undermining of sacerdotal power and the erosion of dogma, an essentially anticlerical enterprise. Through him speaks the fear of the priestly caste, aware that a new power is about to replace the church. For the narrator, on the other hand, the monuments of the past—the columns and obelisks of Karnak, the pagoda of Eklinga, the temple of Solomon—were the stupendous structural manifestations of total ideologies. But their "visible majesty" (elsewhere Hugo refers to architecture as the "art-roi") ultimately calls for dethroning (IV, 22, 144). Architecture was "la grande écriture" of mankind; it was the product of entire peoples, a "collective" achievement. But it did not speak for and to the people. Its theocratic nature was fundamentally undemocratic; its signs spoke to the initiated; its forms, dedicated to the principle of immutability, resisted any change, any progress. The rigidity of dogma is, as it were, inscribed in the stones; it is petrification to the second degree. Even the more mobile transitional styles, like the Gothic, can only tend toward "mouvement perpétuel" (IV, 140).

For the narrator, Gutenberg's invention signified a major shift from theocracy to democracy. What is feared by Frollo as the end of a world is really the beginning of a new one. The printed logos, thanks to the printing press, will not only be more durable but will mark a redemptive victory. Years later, in *William Shakespeare*, Hugo was still exalting the untearable book. Gutenberg was a "redeemer": he had freed thought from perishable matter and had launched an unstoppable process (XII, 67, 219–220). The edifice of literature is intelligence in action. As Hugo explains in a text that recaptures the spirit of the 1830 revolution, the word (*la lettre*) must never be allowed to petrify.[15]

This dynamism of the literary text, this liberating vocation of the writer, explains why Hugo, though a nostalgic preserver of old monuments, extolled the ideological implications of the printing press, and did so precisely to the extent that "the one" was bound to kill "the other." The novel about a cathedral is thus also a novel about the political—and by implication revolutionary—responsibility of the printed word. The narrator of *Notre-Dame de Paris* calls Gutenberg's invention "the greatest event in history." It is more than a technical revolution; it is the matrix of all revolutions—"la révolution mère" (IV, 141).

It is significant that the metaphor to suggest the feverish printing activity of postmedieval man remains architecture, and specifically the Tower of Babel: "C'est la seconde tour de Babel du genre humain." These last words of the chapter can be read as the emblem of an inner contradiction that all of Hugo's work aims to resolve. In a highly personal document of the exile years, "Philosophie. Commencement d'un livre," which he himself thought of as a general preface to his works, Hugo was to state: "This entire world is a phenomenon of permanence and transformation" (XII, 16).

The long concluding paragraph of "Ceci tuera cela" suggests, however, an even greater malaise. For Hugo transmutes the Biblical image of the Tower of Babel into a positively charged metaphor: the tower that was to reach unto heaven is the symbol of a magnificent human thrust; the confusion of languages with which God punished man's overreaching ambition is the evidence of a fertile variety, of the underlying harmony of contraries; the apparent chaos is the hum of a gigantic beehive of human creativity.[16] Yet the same image of the Tower of Babel continues to imply transgression, and even aggression against God. The printing press, in Hugo's context, has indeed a more far-reaching subversive destiny than mere anticlericalism or the demolition of theocracy. Writing ultimately involves a competition between *author* and *auctor*, between two creative principles.

Metaphysical anguish is thus never absent from the act of writing. On the very same page on which the printing press is seen as *la révolution mère*, humanity's self-renewal is compared to the change of skin of the "symbolic serpent," which, ever since Adam's time, has stood for human intelligence. Similarly Frollo, in his quest as an intellectual, is struck by the age-old symbol of the "serpent biting its tail" (IV, 124). The repeated reference to the serpent is interesting evidence that the points of view of the narrator and of Frollo, while seemingly distinct, overlap disturbingly. "Ceci tuera cela" is a key chapter because it suggests to what extent this novel about dead and living stones is fundamentally concerned with the difficult relation between the letter and the spirit.

The Empty Space

Two characters in the novel live out their destiny in intimate contact with the stones of the cathedral: the hunchback foundling, Quasimodo, and his adoptive father and master, the archdeacon Frollo. Quasimodo's association with the edifice goes beyond intimacy; it is symbiotic, even incestuous. He not only speaks with the stone figures, but lives in a "mysterious and preexistent harmony" with the cathedral. This harmony takes the form of "cohabitation"; Hugo even uses the sexually more suggestive word *accouplement*—mating (IV, 118). The strong sexual charge of this love relation is nowhere more apparent than in the elaborate description of Quasimodo's ecstasy as he rings the bells. The choice and the sequence of verbs (*flatter, commencer, s'ébranler, palpiter, frissonner, déchaîner, saisir, étreindre, éperonner, hennir*) unmistakably suggest an orgasmic crescendo. Fifteen bronze bells make up Quasimodo's "seraglio"; but his favorite concubine is the big bell called Marie. The incestuous intimacy is brought into even sharper relief when Hugo explains that the bells are what Quasimodo loves most in the "maternal edifice." The womb becomes the figure of the world. As the foundling has grown up, the cathedral has successively been "his egg, his nest, his home, his country, the universe." Yet this maternal space is also "possessed" and "filled" by Quasimodo (IV, 118–122).

The symbiotic process is, of course, also a process of identification. Just as Quasimodo's grimace *is* his face, so he becomes a "living chimera," threatening—according to popular superstition—to change other human beings into stone (IV, 291). Hugo's metaphor for Quasimodo's monstrous shape is that of a grotesque stone building: his deformed back has the shape of a dome, his bandy legs are like spiraled columns. Ultimately, his entire body is viewed as a prison—a "boîte de pierre"—confining his atrophied yet yearning psyche (IV, 119, 168).

Petrification, in *Notre-Dame de Paris*, is always related to the dialectics of a spiritual absence-presence. Quasimodo communicates life to the stones of the cathedral precisely because his deafness allows him to hear with his eyes; his somber figure radiates a strange light. The misbegotten reality of his being is converted into a poetic force. It is because his deafness separates him from ordinary language that the Beast finds the mediating symbolic language of poetry and flowers with which to address Beauty. His contemplative disposition—the precondition of the poet's vision, according to Hugo—is bought at the heavy price of a mutilating imprisonment in the self. But the most important spiritual signal associated with the hunchback is that of his name, which not only recalls the living stones of Saint Peter's Epistle ("Quasimodo geniti infantes . . .") but links his mortal destiny to a hope for resurrection. The foundling infant, left near the church door, was discovered by Frollo on so-called Quasimodo Sunday, the Sunday after Easter, and his name is thus quite literally patterned on the words ("quasi modo") with which the introit of that special Sunday Mass begins.[17]

In the case of Frollo, the symbolism of the living stone is more ironic and more disturbing. Whether motionless or agitatedly wandering through the streets of Paris, he is repeatedly described as a living statue. He himself feels that he is changed to stone, petrified by the horror of his own being, by his complicity with death. The image of the walking statue unavoidably brings to mind Don Juan's avenger-antagonist, the marble statue of the Commendatore. As Hugo himself was quick to point out in another context, Don Juan's damnation complements the damnation of Faust.[18] There is no doubt that the legend of Faust, as well as the

Don Juan–Commendatore motif, informs *Notre-Dame de Paris* thematically. Power as eros and eros as power—each is the obverse of the other; they are interchangeable conceptual forces at work. Frollo, in his study cell, is devoured first by "an appetite for science," by a libidinous desire for knowledge, and next by a fever of the senses, a boundless and frustrated appetite of the flesh: the two appetites feed each other. The image of Faust is equidistant from that of the Commendatore; this is made perfectly clear by a reference to an engraving attributed to Rembrandt, depicting Doctor Faustus in a dark cell exactly like Frollo's (IV, 115, 191).

The irony of such allusions and references is that they tend at the same time to amplify and to reduce Frollo, who belongs to the demonic tradition of the Gothic novel; he is a sibling of Matthew G. Lewis's and E. T. A. Hoffmann's accursed monks. But he is also a caricature of the intellectual, a fictional projection of the prematurely aged, sexually repressed scholar cloistered with his books. The irony is compounded by suggestions of self-caricature, which hint at an uneasy awareness of deficiencies and guilt. Frollo as a studious child and later as a young priest—austere, grave, serious, ardent in his pursuit of knowledge—has much in common with the image Hugo has of himself as an adolescent. Hugo moreover perceived his writing activities, at the time he settled to work on the novel, as a form of self-willed imprisonment. The biographical text published by Hugo's wife, and substantially "dictated" by Hugo himself, makes the following analogy: the poet about to begin the novel, shortly after the July Revolution, bought himself a bottle of ink and a heavy woollen sweater, locked up his suits so as not to be tempted to go out, and "entered into his novel as into a prison."[19] And it is revealing that Hugo goes to the trouble of informing his reader that Frollo's cell, on top of the tower, among the ravens' nests, has been built many years earlier by one Hugo de Besançon—a doubly meaningful signal, since the homonym (Hugo) is coupled with the name of Hugo's own birthplace.

These autobiographical elements become even more telling in a psychothematic perspective. The figure of Cain casts its shadow over Frollo's relation with his young brother Jehan, for whose death he feels ultimately responsible. "Cain, what have you done with your brother?" he accuses himself aloud (IV, 323). The fratricidal obsession, recurrent in the work of Hugo, may well have been particularly strong in those years when his brother and former literary rival Eugène was confined in the insane asylum of Charenton. It is, to say the least, noteworthy that Frollo, having lost his parents when his brother Jehan was still a nursling, entrusted him to a nurse in Bicêtre—a place famous for its prison already evoked in *Le Dernier Jour d'un condamné*, as well as for its asylum. Guilt and spiritual emptiness characterize Frollo's more lucid moments. Fire and ice, the traditional extremes of hell, alternately symbolize the priest's state of mind. Self-diagnosis amounts to a lament over loss of faith. In the chapter carrying the Dantesque title "Lasciate ogni speranza" ("Abandon All Hope"), Frollo laments that he carries the prison chill of despair within him: "J'ai la nuit dans l'âme" (IV, 233).

This darkness in the soul, this spiritual emptiness that extends to the cathedral itself, seems to subvert and negate the symbolism of the living stone. Religion in *Notre-Dame de Paris* is at the same time a negative force and an absent faith. All stones tend to form walls; all walls suggest prisons; and prisons, while confining, also generate the age-old dream to "go beyond," to achieve transcendence. There are indeed many places of confinement in *Notre-Dame de Paris*: the Trou aux Rats where Sister Gudule, the recluse, has buried herself alive in an anticipated tomb; the dungeon where Esmeralda languishes after being tortured; the penal cave in the Bastille where the bishop of Verdun has been shivering for fourteen years in one of the iron cages contrived by Louis XI; Frollo's cell; and the cathedral itself, which in this novel functions more as a fortress than as a place of worship. The peculiarity of these carceral spaces is that their transcendental potential is minimized. Walls, even church walls, seem at best only to recall the memory of an absent yearning.

Put into other terms, the many religious signals in the novel (the "Saint Peter" or *petrus* motif; the link established throughout between the gallows and the Cross; the name of Quasimodo; his public flagellation, including the crowd's laughter and the soiled sponge thrown in his face), precisely because they point to a spiritual void, function in a negative and negatory manner. Quasimodo's deafness symbolically keeps him in the dark. As for Frollo, it is not so much the melodramatic elements—his alchemical activities, his attempt at rape, his satanic laughter, which echoes the rasping laughter of Sister Gudule—that suggest the absence of God, but his poetic and tragic vision. Looking at the sky reflected in the waters of the Seine, he has the "terrible vision" of the reflected abyss. He tries to flee, in vain. The vision of the abyss is inside him.

The tragic counterpart to this vision is Frollo's symbol for fate: the fly caught in the transparent web. Fly and spider become a metaphysical emblem, a "symbole de tout," not because the fly is caught and destroyed but because it is caught and destroyed while trying to reach light and freedom. The spider's web is compared to a glass window, and more specifically to the rose window of the cathedral ("rosace fatale"), which interposes between the light beyond and the fly the cruel obstacle of a transparent wall (IV, 201). Even the religious Gothic construct is thus seen in a nonreligious and even antireligious perspective, confirming the priest's conclusion about the vanity of religion, the "inutilité de Dieu."[20]

This sense of spiritual vacuity spreads to the entire novel, affecting the various characters and, from all the evidence, the young author himself. Did he not confess as much in a contemporaneous poem, "La Prière pour tous," addressed to his daughter, in which he refers to his soul as empty of faith—"vide de foi"?[21] His friend and critic Sainte-Beuve in fact greeted Les Feuilles d'automne, the volume containing this poem, with the sad comment that the poet "no longer believed," that a dismal skepticism had invaded his great lyric inspiration. About Notre-Dame de Paris, Sainte-Beuve was even more outspoken, lamenting that all the sumptuousness of the novel could not hide a fatalistic view that deprived the great cathedral of celestial light. Montalembert—another friend who later turned against Hugo—similarly bewailed the "void" made manifest beneath the brilliance of the text.[22]

The emptiness in question is not, however, a conceptual flaw. As the narrator himself observes, it is precisely intellectual activity that undermines faith. Yet the cathedral, a stronghold of religion, seems an empty shell. It is almost everything: an architectural landmark, an observation tower, a fortress, a place of refuge. But it is not a place of worship. Quasimodo seems to be its only true life-spirit. With him gone, the cathedral will stand deserted, inanimate, like a gigantic skeleton (IV, 122). But even while he fills the immense edifice with his Cyclopean presence, its function seems to be that of a monstrous carapace. The dark and deserted nave, where hardly anyone ever seems to move about, is a place of mourning. Notre-Dame is a church without candles and without human voices—"sans cierges et sans voix" (IV, 245). Even worse, it is a prayerless church. The only religious service described in the novel has to do with the grim punitive ceremony in which Esmeralda, stripped to her shift, barefoot, and with a rope about her neck, does public penance before mounting the gallows. Prayer, later so important in Hugo's understanding of religion, seems altogether absent or undermined by irony. The old king even prays to the Virgin Mary to justify having Esmeralda put to death.

The religious edifice is not merely empty; it is downright threatening. Through the open portal, the length of the church looks like a cavern or the dark entrails of a mythological monster. The rose window, at once Cyclops' eye and fateful spider, seems to cast an evil spell both outside and inside the cavernous space. A sepulchral light communicates to everything the complexion of death. It is as though the entire edifice were given over to evil practices.[23] Frollo's hallucinatory vision transmutes the livid arches into mitres of damned bishops. But even the supposedly "objective" narrator describes the cathedral as a harmful construct whose great portal "devours" the populace under the relentless eye of the rose window.

Discontinuities

The year 1830, in which *Notre-Dame de Paris* was written and in which Hugo achieved his great theatrical triumph with *Hernani*, was also a year of spiritual crisis for him. The symbolism of the living stone was not only religious in nature; it concerned poetic creativity itself. Did Hugo not later proclaim, in "Les Mages," that poets are high priests and prophets who are especially aware of the living stones—"Ceux qui sentent la pierre vivre"?[24] By the time he wrote the poem "Les Mages," in exile, Hugo had gained a new religious and political faith. But this highly personal set of beliefs, which had little in common with any doctrine or established religion, might never have come into being without previous immersion in a spiritual night.

Many factors, besides the obvious political discontinuities, contributed to Hugo's doubts and uncertainties in 1830. There were, to begin with, some psychological and familial disturbances behind the façade of self-control and success. His wife's difficult pregnancy increased her resentment of his constant physical demands. Did Hugo guess that his daughter Adèle (named for her mother), the fourth child to survive, was an unwanted baby? What seems certain is that his wife, as of July 1830, avoided sexual relations with him. And there was the double betrayal of Sainte-Beuve, as a literary friend and intimate of the household. Did Hugo suspect that Sainte-Beuve and his wife were having an affair? He did know, at any rate, that Sainte-Beuve was in love with her, which impaired their mutual trust.[25] Other still more intimate matters, some of them partly subconscious, no doubt contributed to a sense of disorientation and frustration in 1830. There was the recent death of his father, somehow related to the haunting themes of orphanhood and parricide that informed *Le Dernier Jour d'un condamné*. There was, like a living reproach, his brother Eugène's insanity— a source of guilt as well as a warning. And there was also the inner turmoil of an unusually vigorous young man of twenty-eight undergoing a period of abstinence. Of this sexual repression and of its psychic dangers, Frollo became the fictional projection.

From a strictly intellectual perspective, the most important development during this period was a growing political disorientation: Hugo was losing his old political faith, but had not yet been able to replace it with a new one. In 1825, as a celebrated young ultraroyalist poet, he had been invited to the coronation of Charles X at the cathedral in Reims. It is revealing that in the plot of *Notre-Dame de Paris* Reims remains the place of origin of the lost children, and that in the historical context of the novel it is precisely in the Reims cathedral that Louis XI was crowned.[26] Since 1825 Hugo had, however, broken with his old royalist beliefs. Many factors, including his friendships with Sainte-Beuve and the sculptor David d'Angers, brought him closer to democratic views. But it is interesting that, in the aftermath of the July Revolution, Hugo refers to the abandoned ideology almost as to a lost faith, linking his former political views to the metaphor, as well as the substance, of a religion: "My old monarchist and catholic conviction of 1820 has crumbled piece by piece during the last ten years . . . Something of it remains in my mind, but it is no more than a religious and poetic ruin." This "ruin" of his former beliefs remains a place his memory can visit, but it is no longer a shrine: "je n'y viens plus prier."[27]

Hugo's ideological crisis was bound to affect his views on the function of art. His waverings, his temptations, and his regrets around 1830 must be read against a general tendency (illustrated by writers such as Sainte-Beuve and Pierre Leroux) to stress the social and political responsibility of the artist.[28] Hugo remains ambiguous. On the one hand, Pierre Gringoire, the ironically treated poet-philosopher in *Notre-Dame de Paris,* takes a rather detached view of events, considering himself aloof from the civil strife and uninvolved in the "tempête civile" (IV, 305). And Hugo himself, as late as 1833, inveighed in the name of artistic integrity against the demeaning militancy of "l'art enrôlé."[29] Yet the social mission of art was one of his earliest convictions.[30] *Les Feuilles d'automne,* which belongs to the same period as *Notre-Dame de Paris,* clearly echoes this ambiguity. The preface to this collection of poems maintains that the "human heart" is a more lasting reality than political concerns, that art must above all remain faithful to itself; while the last piece in the volume, carrying an epigraph from a political poem by André Chénier, has the poet sit in judgment over kings, announcing that his muse—the "muse indignée" concerned with human rights—will soon place his art in the service of political ideals.

The Forward Glance

To serve the cause of profound transformations and to help give birth to the future became eventually, for Hugo, the chief functions of the poet. For the time being, he only dimly perceived the full thrust of his own ideas. *Le Dernier Jour d'un condamné* had ideological implications that reached beyond apparent intentions. A sense of historical and political necessity, it seemed, was at work beneath the controlled literary surface. This deeper sense of an ideological drive, of an emerging yet still largely repressed commitment, may explain Hugo's fascination with the notion of *anankē* around 1830. The preface to *Les Feuilles d'automne* does speak of the hidden work of revolutionary ideas still buried in potentially explosive "underground passages."[31] The metaphor suggests a revolutionary undermining of tired and corrupt societies, as well as the sense of a fated subconscious elaboration.

A curious feature of Hugo's work is that his tropes and literary imagination tend to act out sedition and to subvert the established order long before these tendencies are conceptualized and translated into political terms. In later years, Hugo was to insist, somewhat anachronistically, that his early literary efforts had had a revolutionary motivation, that he had made the nine muses sing the Carmagnole: "Je fis souffler un vent révolutionnaire. / Je mis un bonnet rouge au vieux dictionnaire."[32] But the anachronism is only on the surface, and the ideological thrust of his early texts reaches far beyond mutinous syntax and versification, or flamboyant imagery. It is moreover significant that, in Hugo's own view, literary insurrection should have given the signal. For such a view of his own political evolution casts an even brighter light on the narrator's comment, in *Notre-Dame de Paris*, that the invention of the printing press is the matrix of revolutions.

Revolution appears thematically as a constant prophecy in *Notre-Dame de Paris*. An ineluctable forward movement of history seems

to carry from Louis XI's dismantling of the feudal edifice to Mirabeau's work in favor of the people, and, beyond 1789, to the still
unattained goal of revolution at the time Hugo is writing. The
"hour of the People" will come, prophesies the Flemish delegate
Coppenole; it will come, he ominously tells the king during their
interview in the Bastille, when the tower of the king's fortress falls
(IV, 310).

These somewhat facile prophecies are made more meaningful,
in the context, by constant references to repressive social, judi-
ciary, and political conditions. Justice, in the form of the presiding
magistrate during Quasimodo's trial, is quite literally deaf. Penal
inhumanities—floggings, the pillory, torture, public executions—
pervade the text. Even the gentle aristocratic ladies derive cruel
pleasure from humiliating a gypsy. As they torment Esmeralda,
they are compared to young Roman ladies, amusing themselves
by having gold pins thrust into the breast of a beautiful slave (IV,
181). But it is the king's despotic bent, his tyrannical sense of
decorum (he has the pavement speedily washed after the massacre),
and above all his hubris in trusting his own strength and the
strength of the Bastille that underscore the prerevolutionary motifs
of the novel.

The iconography and legend of the fall of the Bastille are at the
heart of *Notre-Dame de Paris*—both as a memory and as a projection. The old fortress can be seen at a distance, as a sinister
counterstructure to the cathedral; its gloomy bell can be heard far
away. The king uses it as his residence, preferring its austere
walls to those of the Louvre. It is the stronghold of monarchy. And
the most dramatic action in the novel is mob action, when the
Truands—the hordes of the Parisian underworld—arm themselves
and assault that other symbolic fortress, the cathedral. The collective event is like a general rehearsal for July 14, complete with
pillage of weapons, mob anger, a procession of frightening phys-
iognomies, and chaotic exploits, while the tocsin lends the event
a fierce solemnity.

The account of this assault upon a symbol of authority has
mythical grandeur. The advancing mob of *argotiers* is seen as an

awesome procession of dark and silent figures, a "river" of humanity, a frightful herd of men and women in rags, armed with scythes, pikes, and halberds. In the torchlight, the black pitchforks project like horns over the hideous faces (IV, 285). The huge beam serving as a battering ram is transformed into a hundred-legged mythological beast butting against a giant of stone.

This figuration of joint action and communal assault derives directly from the iconography of the French Revolution.[33] The epic grandeur of the event is further enhanced by references to the *Iliad* and to Homeric epithets (IV, 292). But the combination of myth and historicity proposes a bidirectional perspective: the event still to happen has already occurred. The French Revolution, by the same token, is a matter of the past, yet remains to be accomplished in the future—depending on whether one looks at history from the standpoint of 1830 or of 1482. This ambivalence clearly bespeaks a political dilemma. On the same page, the reader is told that the hour of the people is not yet ripe ("l'heure du peuple n'est pas venue") and that this hour will come ("Vous l'entendrez sonner"—IV, 310). The two sentences have a different ring, depending on whether they are read from the fictional point of view of 1482, or from the writer-reader point of view, after the unfinished business of the July Revolution of 1830.

The narrator's attitude toward the *peuple*—one of the most highly charged words, politically and emotionally, of the nineteenth century—is even more ambivalent. The mystique of the idealized lower classes is inscribed in the revolutionary tradition. *Le Chant du départ*, one of the best-known revolutionary marching songs, proclaims the regal dignity and irresistible force of the new sovereign—the People. "Le peuple souverain s'avance." In the context of *Notre-Dame de Paris*, the people's sense of dignity is still a "vague" and "indistinct" potential (IV, 46). Their forward march is, however, overwhelming. Recurrent water images—river, ocean, tides—suggest relentless flux and ineluctable historical processes. The opening pages describe the crowd in front of the Palais de Justice in terms of sea, waves, swells, and currents that ceaselessly assault the "promontories" of the houses. This human flood tide knows no ebbing. Its force is a constant threat of violence. Hugo speaks of the "flot irrésistible" of the crowd, of its providing a spectacle of "terror" (IV, 284).

The threat is in the flood's destructive power. A poem dated May 1830 warns the king to pay heed to the oceanic high tide of popular forces ("la haute marée / Qui monte incessamment") if he wants to survive in this century of violent change.[34] What complicates and enriches the image of these oceanic forces is the association of Paris with the ocean. Quasimodo, we are told, dreams of no other ocean than Paris, which roars at the feet of the cathedral's colossal towers (IV, 120). A personal note by Hugo, jotted down years later, is quite explicit: "I have had two passions in my life: Paris and the Ocean."[35] In *Le Rhin*, where he refers both to the living stones and to the flood tides of the capital, he specifically makes Paris the theater of violence and of civilization.[36] This eruptive civilizing process is a constant promise and a constant threat. In an image that appropriately combines flux and rock-like solidity, the oceanic city becomes a crater spewing the "lava of events."[37]

It is revealing that the *peuple* so intimately associated by Hugo with the oceanic and volcanic city imagery should be presented, and magnified, in a grotesque perspective. Quasimodo becomes horribly beautiful as he challenges the society that made him an outcast (IV, 247). In the act of saving Esmeralda from the hand of "justice," the Beast becomes the Beauty. Later, during the siege of the cathedral, in the weird nocturnal light, the deformed bell-ringer looks like a hoary old king out of some legend (IV, 293). Hugo's ideology of the grotesque and the dialectics of ugliness and the sublime, which he discussed in the preface to *Cromwell*, were to him obviously not a simple matter of picturesqueness and artistic license. In offering the view that the grotesque was a predominantly modern manifestation, corresponding to the increasing rift between the physical and the spiritual, Hugo had in mind renewed possibilities of a *total* vision. He thus anticipated Mikhail Bakhtin, an attentive reader of Hugo, who proposed that the grotesque and the *carnavalesque* are elements of a collective ritual, a liberation from the established order.[38] The Mardi Gras, with its roots in folklore, stands at the center of this carnival atmosphere. It is significant that Phoebus, having forgotten Quasimodo's name, remembers only that it is the name of some religious holiday, something like Mardi Gras, the merrymaking day before Lent (IV, 180).

Riotous heterogeneity characterizes the grotesque and the *carnavalesque*—two notions overtly linked in Hugo's text. The spectacle of aggressive variety begins in the early pages of *Notre-Dame de Paris*, during the election of the Pope of Fools. All possible shapes and forms, all possible human expressions, are displayed in this competition of ugliness. In setting up his "théâtre des grimaces," Hugo deliberately refers to the notion of the grotesque ("grotesque échantillon des deux sexes"). And he associates this grimacing parade with the masks of the Venice carnival, as well as with the grimaces of the sculpted *mascarons*, the grotesque stone heads of the Pont Neuf (IV, 50–51). Stones remain at the center of the novel. There is something of the petrified nightmare in Hugo's theater of grimaces.

Theatricality and the awareness of the theater are significant features of *Notre-Dame de Paris*. They no doubt reflect some of Hugo's preoccupations and stage battles of 1830. But they also go beyond such professional concerns. The novel begins with a spectacle. The opening chapter describes a crowd in the great hall of the Palais de Justice, before and during a performance of an allegorical mystery play. The spectacle is multiple: the mystery play, the crowd of spectators, and the dignitaries on their platform are all jarring actors in a vast performance. The narrator himself refers to a "spectacle of spectators" (IV, 27). And the "spectacle" of the dignitaries—the Cardinal de Bourbon, the Flemish delegation—has political implications. So does the allegory of Gringoire's mystery play: Nobility, Clergy, Trade, and Labor are interlocked in an apparently endless drama. These political-theatrical signals prepare a whole network of thematic and symbolic associations. History, politics, social injustice, and the dialectics of the grotesque all have in common a theatricalization that intensifies the ideological complexity of the novel. The Palais de Justice, where Gringoire's unsuccessful mystery play is performed, is the same place where Esmeralda, after emerging from the torture chamber, is condemned to death before an impatient crowd that is compared to an audience in a theater. The "theater of grimaces" disturbingly blends expressions of savage mockery and pain. Problematic laughter echoes throughout the book. Even in Hugo's early novel *Le Dernier Jour d'un condamné*, the fierce laughter of the convicts and of the sensation-hungry crowd had social and political implications. But the range of laughter is far more impressive in *Notre-Dame de Paris*, preparing the grand thematics of laughter and revolution that inform *Le Roi s'amuse*, the poem "La Révolution," and above all the late novel *L'Homme qui rit*. Some of the laughter in *Notre-Dame de Paris* is light-hearted, joyful, teasingly irreverent, boisterously contagious: the laughter of the students, and the impish *fou rire* of Jehan, Frollo's dissipated younger brother. But *fou rire*, in Hugo's work, is never innocent. The *fou rire* of the rabble comes in cruel response to the naked horror of Quasimodo's body on the pillory. This kind of laughter is at the same time cruel and obscene. "Chanson obscène" and "gros rire" are wedded in the same sentence. Cruelty and sinister moods are in fact almost automatically signaled by fits of laughter—a carry-over from the Gothic novel and from melodrama: the "rire sinistre" that greets Gringoire in the Cour des Miracles, the "rire lugubre" of Sister Gudule, obsessed by the idea of revenge, the collective laughter of the mob as the tormented Quasimodo begs for water, the "bestial" laughter of the hangman, the "abominable" and even "demonic" laughter of the fallen priest. With Hugo, however, laughter has ideological implications, and Bakhtin was surely wrong when he stated that for Hugo laughter was mostly a "negation," a degrading and destroying principle.[39] Hugo's laughing rabble in *Notre-Dame de Paris*, although not yet the dignified *peuple*, is compared to Homer's laughing gods on Olympus (IV, 51). The hierarchical inversions proclaiming the majesty of the buffoon, which were to receive their most elaborate mythopoetic expression in the great poem "Le Satyre," are founded on the dissolving, subversive, but also affirmative laughter from below.

This, no doubt, is the full meaning of the bond established between the grotesque and the sublime—a bond that involves a radical inversion of values. As Hugo explains in one of the most moving poems of *Les Contemplations*, the sublime is to be sought not at the lofty heights but among the victims and sufferers down below: "Le sublime est en bas."[40]

In this perspective, it is significant that the only *peuple* to be represented in *Notre-Dame de Paris* is the Parisian underworld: the tribe of beggars, vagabonds, and criminals crowding the slums of the Cour des Miracles—a terrifying and alienated city within the city, with its own laws of lawlessness. This Kingdom of Slang is an urban figuration of hell, a labyrinth inhabited by what Hugo himself defines as the "lowest stratum" of the population (IV, 171). But this throng of outlaws is potentially prerevolutionary in its vindictiveness toward the social order. Trouillefou, the king of this grotesque realm of argot, explains that the cruel laws of society— in particular, capital punishment—must be turned against society itself (IV, 78).

These pages on the underworld, in which the real and the fantastic intersect, are among the most striking in the novel. Their power was much admired by Flaubert.[41] Their grossly realistic yet nightmarish and visionary quality brings to mind a fusion of Breughel, Franz Hals, Callot, and Goya. Hugo himself repeatedly mentions names of painters. The prosaic and brutal realities of the tavern are accompanied by a reference to Callot, and the horrors of prison suggest "l'oeuvre extraordinaire de Goya."[42] The poetry of hell— a human hell—is perceived as a form of hallucination, a "rêve horrible," as Gringoire penetrates into the Truands' violent and parasitic world.

This asocial and essentially apolitical (or prepolitical) proletarian mass may have its strange appeal: vitality, love of excess, black humor, verbal inventiveness. Argot, ever since *Le Dernier Jour d'un condamné*, was a fascination that ultimately led to the brilliant pages on the language of crime in *Les Misérables*. But no matter what its virtues, the "lowest stratum" represented by the Truands is seen in a negative, pathological perspective. These ruffians follow their worst instincts. Lazy, debauched, and cruel, they are collectively depicted as a lower form of animal life (swine, snails in the mire, crabs, insects, spiders) or as a huge wart on the city. Hugo compares the entire Cour des Miracles to a vast sewer. These living masses of real and false afflictions, these limping, shuffling wretches—lame, one-armed, one-eyed, covered with festering sores—are like sinister actors forever preparing to play their part in the comedy of theft, prostitution, and murder that is enacted day and night on the streets of Paris. (The theatrical metaphor extends even to crime.) The picture is certainly not flattering to the lower classes. Hugo is quite outspoken: the "good people of Paris" (the "bon populaire parisien"—IV, 171) are hardly less cruel and bestial than this horde of beggars and criminals.

The point seems to be that if the "hour of the people" has not come yet, it is because the *peuple,* except as a utopian notion, does not yet exist. Certainly it did not in 1482. But did it exist in 1830? That is the larger question. The reference to the stone *mascarons* has a direct relevance. Hugo was later to associate himself with the "somber genius" of Germain Pilon, to whom he attributed the *mascarons* of the Pont-Neuf. He exalted the "mage statuaire" for having sculpted these grimacing stone masks of suffering and revolutionary vengeance and for having thus created the image as well as the ideal reality of the *peuple:* "tu fis le peuple, toi."[43] This idea of creating through artifact the as yet nonexistent but potentially ideal *peuple* remained dear to Hugo, who believed that this was the specific task of the writer and, more specifically still (at least in 1830), of the dramatist. The nineteenth-century playwright, in Hugo's view, had to create his audience, and this act of creation had far-reaching political implications.[44] From creating an audience to creating a new political conscious-ness, there is only one step. As Hugo himself was to put it in *William Shakespeare,* discussing the theater as a crucible of civ-ilization, "the masses become the audience, which in turn becomes the people." *William Shakespeare* in fact elaborates on this creative political function of the writer, who is destined to transfigure the rabble—the *canaille*. The prime mission of the creative intellect is to metamorphose the brutish mob: "construire le peuple."[45]

The corollary is self-evident: if the *peuple* remains to be created, that is because what exists in reality is the rough and unsavory rabble that Hugo himself had seen in action. *Notre-Dame de Paris* betrays a malaise toward the lower classes that was evident earlier in *Le Dernier Jour d'un condamné* and that, ironically, was to grow as his political evolution led him to embrace their cause. A feeling close to revulsion lurks behind the surface picturesqueness. The worst is not the looting and the drunken rampages of the criminal gangs, nor even the inherent filth and depravity of the crowd. More loathsome still (here, too, Hugo drew on personal memories) is their taste for the spectacle of human suffering. The vile throng relishes the sight of physical punishment and public executions; it indulges, without compassion, in collective voyeurism. A fundamental love of destruction quickens the multitude. In the brief preface to the novel, alluding to revolutionary violence, Hugo even suggests that the *peuple* has a taste for destroying churches: "puis le peuple survient, qui les démolit."

It is a fitting irony that Hugo put the finishing touches on *Notre-Dame de Paris* during the month of riots that led to the sack of Saint-Germain l'Auxerrois and the archbishop's palace. Contemporary events seemed to echo the Truands' "à sac!"—a threatening cry already heard coming from the mob of impatient spectators at the beginning of the novel. According to his wife, Hugo watched the populace throw into the river the books of the archbishop's library—an act of vandalism that surely must have made a lasting impression.[46] But there was something more troubling still. For it was the common people who, in December 1830, had vehemently demonstrated against the abolition of capital punishment for political crimes. Hugo again was an appalled witness: he heard the throng roar outside the House of Peers.[47] For Hugo, who prided himself on having recently written *Le Dernier Jour d'un condamné* in order to provoke the "horror" and the "terror" of capital punishment,[48] this roaring crowd clamoring for the death penalty could hardly have been a less discouraging sign than the destruction of books—including the ones he used as documents for the writing of his novel. This discouragement affected not only the intellectual's possible relations with the working classes; it affected the historical novelist, so taken with transitional forms and historical becoming, but who also suspected that history's march forward was a chancy affair, that faith in horizontal, linear progress did not correspond to the most probing vision.

The Vertical Perspective

The most persistent spatial metaphors in *Notre-Dame de Paris* are, indeed, of a vertical nature. The chief features of the cathedral are its lofty height seen from below and its plunging view of the city from above. A privileged perspective is repeatedly attributed to the ravens perched on the tower and to birds in flight. "Paris à vol d'oiseau" is the title of the virtuoso chapter presenting an overview of all the districts of Paris. The Parisian topography, with its tight network of streets, is perceived along combined vertical and horizontal axes: on the one hand is the circumscribed, "imprisoned" web of streets, with its many ramparts, walls, and enclosures; on the other are the thousands of houses that spring up (again the image of the living stone) "comme toute sève comprimée" (IV, 97). At about the same time, *Les Feuilles d'automne* proposed a city poetry in which the figure of the poet, who always loved heights, dreams of being lifted to a supreme tower from which he might stare into the city's abyss: "Oh! qui m'emportera sur quelque tour sublime / D'où la cité sous moi s'ouvre comme un abîme!" (IV, 441). Later, in his Guernsey exile, Hugo characteristically wrote standing up in his "lookout" atop Hauteville House, blending in his imagination the inner vision of the absent city with the visible turmoil of the sea.

Notre-Dame de Paris, much like the contemporaneous *Les Feuilles d'automne*, betrays a powerful ocular temptation. The novel is unusually rich in references to the eye, the glance, the view. "Tout vous prenait aux yeux": this total visual seduction of the "spectator" at the top of the cathedral tower is strengthened by the metaphor of his glance's getting "lost" in the labyrinth beneath him (IV, 100). The *eye* in fact becomes personified. Conversely, the rose window is changed into a Cyclops' eye.[49] The eye ultimately invades the other senses, even substitutes for them. The sound of the bells can be *seen*, as can laughter. Quasimodo's deafness heightens the general keenness of his visual perceptions; he listens to Esmeralda's songs with his eyes (IV, 262). This libido of seeing was characteristic of the young Hugo. Staring into sunsets was one of his favorite pastimes as a Parisian *promeneur*. The poem "Soleils couchants," which evokes the mobile archipelagoes of clouds, carries as epigraph a line from a tale by Nodier that links sight to the life of ideas.[50] Even the theater was for Hugo a "point d'optique," just as versification—which he considered of primary importance in the theater—was the "forme optique de la pensée."[51] But this optical fascination, this concupiscence of the eyes, did not go without accompanying fears. The possibility of blindness was very much on Hugo's mind, especially as he suffered from intermittent eye afflictions. He liked to bring up the examples of Homer, Milton, and Ossian. More threatening than the somewhat romantic fear of such a glorious infirmity was the fear of a sensuous visual addiction that might interfere with true vision. Eyes, in the sordid song of the procuress, are compared to windows opening on the spectacle of obscenity and cruelty (IV, 253). Windows are dangerous invitations, not only to reverie but to voyeurism of all sorts. It is through a window that Frollo first glimpses Esmeralda performing her enticing dance.

The frequency and intensity of the voyeuristic impulse in *Notre-Dame de Paris* has much to do with repressed sexuality. A frustrated Gringoire, peeping through a keyhole, delights in looking at Esmeralda, in her nightshirt, getting into bed. Frollo likewise watches Esmeralda being made love to in the room next to his, while his "lascivious" glance is compared to that of a beast of prey. The aggressive and transgressive glance from room to room is, however, described in terms of verticality: "Son oeil plongeait avec une jalousie lascive sous toutes ces épingles défaites" (IV, 213). More strikingly still, his first visual awareness of Esmeralda dancing in the square is from the top of the tower, while he himself is watched watching from down below: "Son oeil fixe plongeait dans la place." And again: "le poids du regard redoutable qui tombait à plomb sur sa tête" (IV, 178, 184).

The dynamics of lust, no less than the aesthetics of a bird's-eye view of Paris, seem to imply a vertical perspective. The vision of the city is remarkably consistent. The snake-like meanders of the Seine ("qui serpente"; "plus changeante qu'une robe de serpent"—IV, 184, 110) are dramatically transformed into a vision of verticality: dreams of suicide, lyrical reveries, phantasms of inverted depth and height—inverted, because the visual perceptions seem to open up a double abyss below and above. The quays of the Seine, with their nocturnal flux of lights and shadows, provide what Hugo describes as a background worthy of Rembrandt: "Rembrandt a de ces fonds de tableau" (IV, 318).[52] It is in this nightmare setting that Frollo has his terrifying vision. The Tour de Nesle's reflection in the water and the singular effect of its obelisk-like shaft shooting up into space create a two-directional impression—a sense of an abyss that extends both infinitely high and infinitely deep.[53] The inverted promontory-tower seems to want to reach up to heaven like the Tower of Babel, at the same time as it appears as an inverted steeple of hell.

This remarkable page clearly suggests that the perspective of verticality in *Notre-Dame de Paris* cannot be accounted for simplistically in terms of repressed sexuality or as a strictly aesthetic option, a device to intensify the network of horizontal lines.[54] Hugo's originality, in the chapter "Paris à vol d'oiseau," is that he provides a cartographic surface description together with the view of a bird in flight, thus combining the flatness of a "plan géométral" with a mobile aerial perspective. The dramatic result of this fusion of perspectives is that the maze of streets appears not merely as a surface labyrinth but as a depth to be plumbed, a nether region filled with mysteries and revelations: "Le regard se perdait longtemps à toute profondeur dans ce labyrinthe" (IV, 100). The special value attributed to vertical movement—to the sense of depth, falling, loss, reemergence—obviously implies a broader vision.

This vision depends on a double inversion, one that is both social and poetic. Hugo makes the point that in the Middle Ages, when a building was complete, there was almost as much of it underground as aboveground. Each palace, fortress, and church had a "double fond." The foundations of a building were thus *another* building, to which one descended instead of ascended. This two-directional verticality is a metaphorical reversal, which Hugo elaborates by analogy with landscape mirror effects. The architectural inversion is likened to the way in which mountains and woods "appear reversed in the mirror of the lake" beneath them (IV, 227).

Years later, in *Les Travailleurs de la mer*, Hugo was to translate this simile into dramatic and visionary terms, describing at length the cathedral-like underwater architectures created by the relentless toiling of the sea. But it is clear from the outset that the architectural and natural inversions also function as metaphors for social and moral phenomena. In *Notre-Dame de Paris*, the social analogue for the architectural "double fond" is the countersociety of the underworld. The parodic nature of this countersociety is obvious: Gringoire is judged by three "sovereign" judges; Clopin Trouillefou, presiding over the assembled vagabonds, is compared to a doge in the senate, a king in parliament, a pope in conclave. Even Arthurian legends are invoked: the assembly of thieves, beggars, and rogues is defined as a "table ronde de la gueuserie" (IV, 79). Parody is a direct challenge. What is inverted—or rather subverted—is the sense of social hierarchy, the established law and order of the society "above." The enthronement of the rogues, which parallels the carnival election of Quasimodo as Pope of Fools, implies thoughts of radical dethronement. (The verb *détrôner* appears in relation to architectural and historical change—IV, 59). The inverted society turns laws upside down. Yet this reversal is not simply a matter of subversion or perversion. Hugo's subsurface metaphors relate to his utopian vision: the moral and political salvation is to come from below. This will be the central message of *Les Misérables:* the world of suffering and of criminality is redemptive. Hence the elaborate metaphor of the mine as figuration of the vast underground activity destined to achieve gradually a quite literal upheaval: "qui transforme lentement le dessus par le dessous." The vertically conceived upheaval is, however, part of the forward march of humanity. The same passage in *Les*

Misérables concerned with the *mine révolutionnaire* proposes the image of an underground linear progression: "Les utopies cheminent sous terre dans les conduits."[55]

Yet there is another, perhaps more important vertical structure recurrent in Hugo's fiction and poetry—one that has nothing to do with historically conceived progress, and even tends to negate it. This is the downward movement associated with pure contemplation, the descent into reverie, a contemplative mode that transcends chronological and historical time. Gringoire, penetrating into the dream-labyrinth of the Cour des Miracles as though guided by some Ariadne's thread, in fact loses the thread of his memory and of his reason: "le fil de sa mémoire et de sa pensée était rompu" (IV, 75). The descent into the world of fantasy makes him oblivious to the real world, as he moves deeper and deeper into the shadowy regions of daydreams. "Enfoncé de plus en plus dans sa rêverie": the mental processes involved suggest an immersion, a sinking deep below the surface. The timeless "espaces imaginaires" are reached not by flight but by a gradual and terrifying descent. Thus, Frollo's hallucination of an inverted cityscape also marks a moment out of time. Dream-declivity is indeed a striking feature of *Notre-Dame de Paris*. In one of the book's most nightmarish moments, Esmeralda, even though she is being led by Frollo on rising ground, has the distinct sensation of walking downhill: "Il lui semblait cependant qu'elle descendait une pente" (IV, 321).

The choice of terms and images unavoidably brings to mind Hugo's early visionary poem "La Pente de la rêverie" which describes the vertiginous and revelatory descent below the surface of the "monde réel" down toward the "sphère invisible" where the poet, sounding the double sea of space and time, glimpses the abyss of eternity, History, embraced in total simultaneity, is here deprived of its historical becoming. "La Pente de la rêverie," conceived and written at about the same time as *Notre-Dame de Paris*, initiates a mode of vision that weds metaphors of verticality to somber and grandiose meditations on atemporality. Over thirty years later, in *Promontorium somnii*, Hugo will repeat: "La rêverie est un creusement." The same idea is expressed in *William Shakespeare*, where poetic genius is depicted as staring into darkness. And in *L'Homme qui rit*, meditation is described in terms of a miner's descent into the mineshaft.[56] In all these cases, the vertical insight corresponds to the transhistorical vision of the prophet, whose atemporal perception is radically alien to the chronological, linear, progressive time of history.

Effacement, Displacement, Occultation

To the extent that Hugo's imagination is drawn downward along the "spirale monstrueuse" that he associates with Dante's vision,[57] *Notre-Dame de Paris* is less a historical than a visionary novel. In this transfigured world, objects come to life while human beings become monsters and even turn into stone. If one considers that Frollo is not alone in experiencing the external world as an "apocalypse visible" (IV, 255), one can perhaps better appreciate what Hugo meant when, years later, in a letter to his publisher Lacroix, he maintained that he had never written a historical novel.[58]

A statement such as this, surprising as it may seem, could be understood in several ways. For even when read in a historical perspective, *Notre-Dame de Paris* looks as much forward as backward, forcing the reader—especially the reader of the 1830s—to think about history as a *problem,* rather than as an account of figures and events. In *L'Homme qui rit,* Hugo would speak of history as a "reflet de l'avenir sur le passé."[59] The willfully anachronistic, proleptic, and prophetic elements, determining a multiple temporality, moreover set up a structural model that would allow Hugo to question the meaning of events. This questioning was to become increasingly intense as the problem of revolution, already so persistently written into *Notre-Dame de Paris,* loomed larger and larger in Hugo's thought. Finally, the resistance to sequential temporal schemes and the resistance to the historical notion of surface linearity would also mark a latent resistance to the *fait accompli,* as well as to the naïve trust in a melioristic progression.

Hugo's proud assertion that he had never written a historical novel, coming as it did some forty years after *Notre-Dame de Paris* and shortly after the completion of *L'Homme qui rit,* betrayed the poet's lasting hostility to history. It echoed Ballanche's conviction that a poet, as soon as he speaks the language of history, debases his Orphic calling, which is to fathom the "causes profondes" and proclaim deeper truths.[60] Had not Hugo stated unequivocally, in an early essay on the historical novel, that he preferred moral to historical truths?[61] History itself, he increasingly came to feel, was a vile flatterer of worldly power, submissive to facts, indifferent to principles.[62] It could even be argued that Hugo's literary strategy, perhaps in an only partly conscious way in *Notre-Dame de Paris,* was to subvert the genre of the historical novel by constantly counteracting that genre's overt commitment to historicity.[63]

Hugo's preference for the visionary mode did not go unnoticed by perceptive contemporaries. Sainte-Beuve, for instance, commented in *Le Journal des Débats* (it was, of course, a left-handed compliment) on the "visionary" sense of fate that hung over the novel. Interestingly enough, Sainte-Beuve associated, in one and the same sentence, the words *fantastique* and *vertical.*"[64] But one must go further. Hugo's visionary tendency was not merely a matter of escape into haughty and picturesque fantasy, as Sainte-Beuve would have one believe. The fantasy in question meant an attraction to the darker side, if not to darkness; it implied a denial of the sensuous glance. At a certain level, the theme of petrification in *Notre-Dame de Paris* signals the guilt of excessive attachment to form and matter. The temptations of the glance and the fascination with visual delights have as their counterpart the latent motif of blindness, which was to become explicit with Bishop Myriel in *Les Misérables* and was later to achieve its full poetic statement with the figure of Dea in *L'Homme qui rit.*

In *Notre-Dame de Paris* the dangers of the seeing eye, implicit in the pervasive voyeurism, are worked out in striking images. Frollo, speaking of Esmeralda's visual effect on his senses, evokes the black circle that afflicts the eye imprudent enough to gaze at the sun (IV, 232). Elsewhere, the glaring sun is metaphorically associated with love of gold and sinful alchemical practices (IV,

133). True insight is never sight but vision. It requires darkness, and comes from darkness. Hugo defines *rêverie* and *contemplation* as a glance able to stare into darkness until it brings forth light.[65] The fear of blindness is accompanied by a secret wish for blindness. Many years later, in a curious document, Hugo recalled that around 1828 he had been worried about recurrent "black spots" in his field of vision, yet had felt drawn to the "venerable" infirmity of blindness as an elective sign of genius (III, 1375). Once again, "La Pente de la rêverie," dated 1830, appears as a crucial text. It depicts the descent to vision as a blurring and blending of shapes, a fading away ("les formes disparurent"), an immersion in the dark unknown. Effacement will remain for Hugo a prime condition of visionary occultation.

Effacement is in fact one of Hugo's favorite words. The short prefatory note to *Notre-Dame de Paris*, which describes the narrator's encounter with the word *ananké* engraved on the cathedral wall, stresses the fact that the inscription has since disappeared. And not only has the word been effaced, but so has the man who traced it—as the cathedral itself may well be effaced some day. Three times the verb *effacer* is repeated in the same sentence. It is as though the entire edifice of the novel were meant to rise on a multiple erasure. The final line of the prefatory note stands apart, a one-sentence paragraph: "C'est sur ce mot qu'on a fait ce livre"— a founding affirmation as well as the affirmation of a void.

The principle of effacement in Hugo's work has far-reaching implications. It not only signals a steady displacement of the historical center of gravity but corresponds to the dynamics of undoing that Hugo reads into the processes of nature and of creation. It also denies the priority, and even the status, of the historical event. History itself—both as event and as discourse on the event—must ultimately be effaced in favor of transhistorical values. To be historically committed is a moral responsibility. But more important still is the need to understand that beyond history's inability to provide meaning, there is history as evil. What is involved is not a banal inventory of history's horrors—the brutalities, contusions, fractures, mutilations, and amputations attributed to man throughout history by the narrator of *Notre-Dame de Paris* as he considers the historical ravages that disfigured Gothic architecture. More fundamentally, evil is linked to the very notion of sequentiality. Hugo even inverts the proposition. Not only is history evil, but evil is to be defined by its historical status: "Le mal . . . est essentiellement successif." The corollary follows: ultimate values are outside historical time. "Rien de successif n'est applicable à Dieu."[66]

Resistance to sequential schemes continues to subvert and enrich Hugo's historical fictions. The poem "Ponto" in *Les Contemplations*, written with the chronicles of Tacitus, Froissart, and Montluc in mind, is a chronological list of horrors—"crimes de la gloire" as well as crimes committed in the name of religion— that make up history from Alexander to modern times.[67] The chronology of history is a journey to the end of the night. "L'histoire, c'est la nuit"—that is the gloomy definition in *L'Homme qui rit*.[68] In reaction to this linear path of infamy, Hugo typically introduces a cyclical reading, which, at the end of his career as novelist, will thoroughly problematize his most patently historical novel, *Quatrevingt-Treize*.

The seeds of this subversion of historical time, as well as the underlying need for transcendence, are already clearly at work in *Notre-Dame de Paris*. As a historical novel, it is consistently sensitive to the problems of transition and becoming that are implicit in Hugo's choice of historical period. In its subtle parallels and topical allusions, it is powerfully alert to the political issues of the day. But even though it appears committed to history as a meaningful progression, with the French Revolution looming as the messianic event, *Notre-Dame de Paris*, by means of a rhetoric that denies linearity, also seems to point to an exit from history, thus foreshadowing the ultimate vision of Gauvain in *Quatrevingt-Treize* and, earlier, the moving speech of Enjolras in *Les Misérables*, as he prophesies, from atop the revolutionary barricades, humanity's liberating exit from the "forest of events."

But what precisely are the terms in which one can move past history after the experience of the Revolution and the Napoleonic adventure? *Les Misérables* will face this question.

4

Les Misérables:
Salvation from Below

Se totaliser dans un livre complet . . .

The Waterloo episode in *Les Misérables*—consisting of nineteen colorful chapters—may well be the most provocative digression in all of Hugo's fiction. Tangential as it may seem, no digression could be more central. There are other long digressions in *Les Misérables*, monumental assertions of the poet-novelist's ego and of his prerogatives of total vision. But the lengthy discussion of convents deliberately entitled "Parenthèse" and the description of the Parisian sewer system (to take but two examples) are at least bound up with the adventures of the ex-convict Jean Valjean, as he moves from dereliction to salvation. No such claim could be made for the Waterloo episode. Jean Valjean never even comes close to the battlefield. Yet there is every reason to approach this novel from the perspective of this military disaster.

For Waterloo also meant victory. In the late spring of 1861, on the forty-sixth anniversary of the battle, Hugo decided to visit the battlefield. He settled in a small hotel in the village of Mont-Saint-Jean, whence he could glimpse the commemorative statue of the lion. This is the site he chose to finish the novel he had begun some sixteen years earlier, before the events of 1851 drove him into prolonged exile. The importance of the site is tersely inscribed at the end of the manuscript, immediately following the description of Valjean's nameless grave: "Fin/Mont-Saint-Jean 30 juin 1861 à 8 h. $\frac{1}{2}$ du matin" (XI, 997). The completion of the book under the sign of Waterloo ("le dénouement est écrit, le drame est clos . . ."; XII, 1651) harks back, however, to the opening pages of the novel. And this not only because at some stages of writing he had considered placing the Waterloo episode at the very beginning (thus introducing the epic note at the outset),[1] but because the text as we now have it opens with an immediate reference to the fateful year 1815. This temporal signal is repeated at the beginning of book 2, which describes Valjean's arrival in Digne: "In the first days of October, 1815 . . ." The text thus insistently situates itself historically, in the post-Waterloo context of the Restoration.

But Waterloo was also a literary challenge, as indicated by Hugo's choice of that battleground to complete his novel. To Auguste Vacquerie, he wrote on that momentous June 30, 1861: "It's on the plain of Waterloo and in the month of Waterloo that I have fought my battle. I hope not to have lost it" (XII, 1121). As for the episode itself, Hugo referred to it in terms that underline its structural and thematic importance. From Mont-Saint-Jean where he had just written the word *Fin*, he explained to his son Charles: "The structure is up; here and there, some part, some architrave has to be sculpted, and the porch of Waterloo remains to be built" (XII, 1651–52). The word *architrave*, connoting a temple-like construction, suggests monumentality and ample vision. But the key image is the "porche de Waterloo," leaving little doubt that, even though he had written it after all the rest and had placed it at the heart of his text, Hugo considered the Waterloo episode as the spiritual gateway to his novel.

The section on Waterloo appears well after some three hundred pages of dense text, and seems doubly incongruous since it opens part 2, which carries the diminutive title "Cosette." Part 1 (the novel is made up of five massive parts) has described the saintly bishop of Digne, Monsignor Myriel (or Bienvenu, as he has come to be known); the dramatic arrival of the ex-convict Valjean in his house, Valjean's theft of some silver, and his redemptive confrontation with the bishop; a further crime committed by Valjean against a child; his subsequent rehabilitation, under the name of Monsieur Madeleine, in the town of Montreuil-sur-Mer, of which he becomes benefactor and mayor; and his heroic surrender to justice to save a vagrant, falsely accused of his own former identity and crimes. It is at this point, as Valjean again disappears into the anonymous world of prison, that Hugo chose to locate his Waterloo digression, which represents an eight-year leap back in time.

The tie-in with the story line is almost fortuitous, as though to suggest some mysterious convergence of pure chance and necessity. Hugo provides well over fifty pages of elaborate descriptions of battlefield and battle and indulges in meditations on history, before he launches the reader, *in extremis*, after the battle has been fought and lost, into a dream-like sequence: the moonlit, war-torn landscape is visited by an ominous, prowling figure come to rob the dying and the dead, who lie in heaps—some of them buried alive—in the ravine where the French cavalry met its doom. The prowler is the infamous Thénardier, who in the process of stealing the watch, the silver cross, and the purse of the heroic Colonel Pontmercy, unintentionally saves his life. And this Colonel Pontmercy, we later learn, is the father of Marius, the young hero of the novel.

Some preliminary remarks are in order. Since Thénardier, it turns out, is the very individual to whose cruel guardianship young Cosette has been entrusted, the Waterloo episode, blending chance and necessity, also prefigures symbolically all manner of unpredictable conjunctions.[2] At the literal level, the encounter of father and stepfather on the battlefield prepares for the conjunction in love of Cosette and Marius, for which Hugo provides the telling subtitle "La Conjonction de deux étoiles" (XI, 517). At the level of metaphor, the confrontation of heroism and villainy signals the permanent interaction of good and evil, an ambiguous system of inversion and conversion. Private obsessions do not suffice to account for Hugo's insistence on the horror of whole battalions buried alive in the ravine. The emergence of Colonel Pontmercy from among the dead, thanks to an act of villainy which, against the perpetrator's will, turns out to be an act of mercy (the pun of the Colonel's name is part of the ambiguity), participates in a larger saga of rebirth. And in this saga, Waterloo itself—a mass slaughter and a calamitous defeat—retrospectively appears as an illumination, or at least as what Hugo, with reference to Marius' political education, calls an "élargissement de l'horizon" (XI, 497).

From Montenotte to Waterloo

On the arm of Valjean's fellow convict, Cochepaille, is the tattoo *1815* (XI, 238). This inscription in the flesh confirms the structural and symbolic importance of the date. Not only does it mark a problematic turning point in history (is it the beginning of a new world or a relapse into the old order?), but the emperor's dramatic return from Elba and his subsequent defeat correspond ironically to Valjean's emergence to social existence from out of his spiritual prison-death. They also correspond, in time, to the confrontation between good and evil in the bishop's house—to the beginning of Valjean's spiritual rebirth.

Dates, always important in Hugo's system, signal far more, however, than coincidence or contrast. The juxtaposition of Napoleon's fall and of Valjean's spiritual ascent takes on further significance when set against the precise duration of Valjean's imprisonment: 1796 to 1815. This nineteen-year hiatus in Valjean's life spans precisely the years of Napoleon's glory, between the brilliant military campaign in Italy and the Hundred Days. A concrete detail reinforces the parallel: the fastening of Valjean's chain in the prison of Bicêtre, before the departure of the chain gang, occurs on the very day (22 April 1796) that Bonaparte's victory at Montenotte is proclaimed in Paris (XI, 109). The young general's triumph is thus from the outset ironically contaminated. The link between ignominy and glory suggests the bitterness of a victory that was to signify a reign of tyranny and violence. The choice of Montenotte (Hugo had other Italian victories at his disposal: Millesimo, Lodi, Castiglione, Arcola, Rivoli) allows Hugo to play out etymologically the dialectics of victory and defeat, for Montenotte contains both the suggestion of ascension (*monte*) and of the darkness of night (*notte*).[3] What lurks behind these complex articulations of victory and defeat is not only a discrediting of traditional heroic modes but an affirmation of a nonmilitary kind of heroism.

A similar dialectic affects another crucial date, 1832. For the glorious hours of the revolutionary barricades, even though Hugo invokes Homer, Troy, and the Titans, are marred by the awareness that what is occurring is civil strife and police repression. The words "héroïsme monstre" sum up the last stages of the carnage (XI, 869). Once again—this time quite literally—an exalting downward movement transcends and negates the sordid heroics of war. The deeper heroism of Valjean, whose apolitical role on the barricades is that of a courageous conscientious objector, manifests itself as he rescues the unconscious Marius by lowering him through a manhole, and becomes a saviour-hero in a perilous descent into the labyrinthine sewers.[4] The Fall-Ascent is tersely announced by the subtitle, referring to salvation in the mud: *"La Boue, mais l'âme."*

The Passer-By

By disclaimer, preterition, and open statement Hugo multiplies the digressive signals in the Waterloo episode. He begins by referring to himself as a visiting tourist-narrator, walking across the terrain, forty-six years after the battle. This transient figure, this *passant*, takes delight in the bucolic landscape. Self-indulgently, he connects Hougomont—site of one of the fiercest battles—to a putative ancestor, the name *Hougomont* supposedly deriving from *Hugomons*, the name of a manor built by one Hugo, Sire of Somerel. This leisurely, digressive opening is part of a broader discursiveness leading to the appearance of a local peasant, who for three francs offers to explain "la chose de Waterloo"—and who is in turn supplanted by the historian-narrator. This ambling pace is in deliberate contrast to the violence of the battle. But passer-by and bucolic landscape are not merely delaying tactics or ironic commentaries on the futility of war; they function metaphorically, linking the battle to the larger context of the book.

First, a general comment on the word *passant* by which Hugo, as intruding narrator, refers to himself in the opening section of the Waterloo episode. The same substantive is curiously also used to describe an obscure general, Cambronne, who became famous for having defied the enemy, in a hopeless last stand, with the scatological exclamation *Merde!* The unknown officer Cambronne is a "passant de la dernière heure." More significantly still, the returning convict Jean Valjean, when he first arrives in Digne, is also referred to as an anonymous *passant*. But anonymity, in the novel's context, is not a derogatory notion. One of the most moving figures on the revolutionary barricades is a nameless workman ("un passant héros, ce grand anonyme) who speaks up in favor of total sacrifice (XI, 282, 93, 829).

"Un Passant" is a title Hugo considered for part 1 of the novel.[5] Did he give up the idea when he realized that this figure would cast its shadow over the entire work? The recurrent trope of the passer-by is in fact wedded to the larger themes of passage, transition, effacement, and becoming. Toward the end of the novel, at the time of the ultimate sacrifice, Valjean understands that as Cosette's adoptive father, he has been a *passant* in her life and must now disappear ("Jean Valjean était un passant . . . Eh bien, il passait"). If, as Marius puts it, Valjean has been a saviour "en passant," it is because as an outsider he is already partially beyond this world. "Je suis dehors" is echoed a few pages later by "je suis hors de la vie" (XI, 967, 990, 958–959). All of *Les Misérables* describes a process of transition in which every threshold is marked by obliteration. Valjean's tombstone, in accordance with his wishes, carries no name. Even the four anonymous lines written on the stone, concluding with an image of departure ("le jour s'en va"), have gradually become illegible—"effaced." And effacement, for Hugo, is always part of a process of transformation.

There is a thematic link between the transient wayfarer and the bucolic Waterloo landscape forty-six years after the battle, for this landscape presents itself in a state of wave-like mobility. The plain is a vast undulating sweep of ground ("vaste terrain ondulant"— XI, 262). A clump of trees "disappears" gracefully ("s'en va avec grâce"). Water images correspond to this undulating landscape. In one of his notebooks, Hugo refers to the "immobile waves" of the terrain (XII, 1533). The text of the Waterloo episode mentions in close proximity the flowing of water and the disappearing clump of trees, as well as the "enormous waves" made by the rolling countryside. This liquid imagery is further exploited, as early as the very next paragraph, by a reference to a "flotilla of ducks" in a nearby pool.

Water and liquefaction are, of course, appropriate in the historical context of Waterloo. The unseasonal rain of the night of June 17–18 was in large part responsible for Napoleon's defeat. The French artillery, bogged down in the mire, could not be brought into decisive action early enough. The treacherous landscape, neither solid nor liquid, helped disintegrate the world's most powerful army. When the sun finally appeared, it was a setting sun, whose sinister glow was in contrast to the rising sun of Austerlitz, ten years earlier. The reign of water must further be understood as a signal of catastrophe if one recalls that the chapter describing Valjean's spiritual shipwreck in prison is entitled "L'Onde et l'ombre" ("The Waters and the Shadow"—XI, 116).

The metaphorical alliance of water and defeat is sustained throughout the episode. The rout is called a "ruissellement." The last remnants of the Old Guard stand like rocks in "running water." The disbanding army is like a "thaw" (XI, 278, 280). Flight and panic liquidate the day. Beyond these images of undoing, a larger principle is at work. Disintegration is part of the dynamic process of transformation. Not only is the landscape physically and historically transfigured (Wellington, returning to the site, does not recognize his battlefield), but the battle itself, in its chaos and mobility, becomes the enactment of the *truth* of change. The fixity of a mathematical plan immobilizes movement. "Geometry is deceptive," explains Hugo—and he calls for a painter who would have "chaos in his brushes" (XI, 269, 264). The ceaselessly erosive and destructive movement of the sea becomes the model of the battle: the shock of army meeting army creates an "incalculable ebb," the battlefront waves and undulates, regiments form "capes" and "gulfs" and "reefs" as they advance and withdraw. Or rather, it is the battle that becomes a metaphor for the endless toiling of the sea. The mobility of war and the mobility of landscape come to be metaphors for a deconstructive reality of which the sea is Hugo's favorite symbol. One is reminded of the transformational vision, in "La Pente de la rêverie," of huge continents perpetually "devoured" by the oceans.

Disintegration in its diverse manifestations (flowing, melting, thawing, vanishing) is the chief image for the catastrophe of Waterloo. Yet disintegration, for Hugo, is always wedded to reconstruction. The wild grandeur of the abandoned garden on the rue Plumet—the happy enclosure of Cosette and Marius' secret love—provides "unfathomable ecstasies" to the contemplative mind, by revealing "decompositions of forces resulting in unity" (XI, 636–637). These laws of constructive decomposition are made manifest throughout Hugo's work, whether in the metaphorical virtuosity of *Les Travailleurs de la mer*, where infinitely changing sea architectures illustrate the principle of constructive effacement, or more explicitly in "Philosophie. Commencement d'un livre," which was planned as a general preface to his works. "Les désagrégations sont des germinations" (XII, 35)—this pithy affirmation sums up a development on endings that are beginnings, on beginnings that relate to completions, on death which is birth.

This alchemy of decay and vitality is also the mystery of Waterloo. The wayfarer at Hougomont conjures up visions of petrified horror made visible. The narrator-*passant* on the battleground, like Virgil on the plain of Philippi, experiences the hallucination of catastrophe: lines of infantry undulate; trees quiver; whirlwinds of specters exterminate one another. Yet 18 June 1815 also marks a fresh start. And like all pivotal dates it is Janus-faced: it looks ahead, but also glances back to the past. This double perspective on the military disaster is further complicated by the deliberate epic framework of the episode.

The End of the Sword-Wielders

The battle of Waterloo was an ideal pretext for a bravura piece. Ten years earlier, Hugo had already met the challenge with the poetic tour de force "L'Expiation." In *Les Misérables*, the picturesque elements became ampler, as Hugo indulged in massive evocations of armies of the past and of their paraphernalia. Busbies, floating sabretaches, crossbelts, and hussar dolmans—all in motion—occupy the field of vision. The sheer pictorial exuberance is confirmed by the reference to Salvator Rosa, a painter who specialized in battle scenes (XI, 264).

The literary register is that of the epic tradition. Both sides are glorified, for these are neither ordinary Frenchmen nor ordinary Scotsmen. "These Scotsmen died thinking of Ben Lothian, as did the Greeks recalling Argos" (XI, 274). In this modern reenactment of the *Iliad*, every soldier has something of the heroic stature of his general. Every act of valor, every individual death, is a collective event. The death throes of the French army transcend the historical moment. In a typical figure of speech, the agony of the last units is made to signify the death of the great Napoleonic victories: Ulm, Wagram, Jena, Friedland.

The figural pattern remains deliberately epic. So does the process of amplification. The hideousness of the wounds, we are told, has probably "never been seen anywhere else." The military formations are not battalions but "craters"; the cuirassiers are no longer cavalrymen but a "tempest"; each unit is a "volcano"; lava contends with lightning (XI, 274). The mythical nature of such amplifications is made still more explicit by reference to legendary archetypes. The cavalry squadrons are transmuted into "giant men" on "colossal horses." The metamorphosis is completed when horses and men become centaurs. Hugo in fact provides an epic reading of his own text: "These narrations seem to belong to another age. Something like this vision appeared, no doubt, in the ancient

Orphic epics which told of centaurs, the old hippanthropes, those Titans with human heads and chests like horses, whose gallop scaled Olympus" (XI, 272).

These epic references and devices are not a self-indulgent literary game. They function in a complex manner, serving ambiguously both to magnify and to discredit the historical moment. "The epic solemnifies history," Hugo had written in the famous preface to his play *Cromwell*—making clear, however, that modern times required a dramatic rather than an epic perspective (III, 57). But the historical line of demarcation is never clearly drawn. Much like his young hero Marius, Hugo had been entranced by Napoleon's battle proclamations, the bulletins of the Grand Army, "those Homeric strophes written on the battlefield" (XI, 472). It was through the recorded exploits of the preceding generation that he discovered the link with a privileged past when Action and the Word were seemingly not at odds.

The immediate though troubling link—for Hugo, as well as for Marius—is the father. General Léopold Hugo ("Mon père, ce héros au sourire si doux" of *La Légende des siècles*) is the intercessor between the royalist adolescent and the revolutionary and postrevolutionary glory he came to associate with the figure of Napoleon and with filial piety. In the ode "A mon père" ("Je rêve quelquefois que je saisis ton glaive, / O mon père!"—II, 487), the twenty-year-old anti-Bonapartist but patriotic poet had already celebrated the imperial army. Soon this celebration was to extend to the emperor himself, and eventually to the political ferment of the revolution which the emperor helped spread across Europe.

But filial piety is also the sign of a feared inadequacy. The "romantic" generation, having reached the age of manhood once all had been played out on the battlefield of Waterloo, exhibited recognizable symptoms of frustration and impotence. Marius, Hugo's contemporary, knows that he can never equal his father's military prowess. The pen, proposed as a glorious rival, was in fact recognized as a not altogether adequate substitute for the sword—at least in the early years. ("Quoi! toujours une lyre et jamais une épée!" the young Hugo wrote in the same ode to his father.) Hugo eventually translated the anxiety of weakness into a vindication of nonbelligerent virtues. But it is noteworthy that his work, even though increasingly committed to a philosophy of progress, consistently suggests generational regression, if not decadence. The son rarely achieves the stature of the father.[6]

The chronologically regressive shift from Napoleon to revolution is at the heart of this nostalgia for epic grandeur. In his early review of Walter Scott's *Quentin Durward*, Hugo, while outlining a theory of the modern novel, betrayed anxiety in the face of a never-to-be-equaled greatness. In an obvious allusion to the French Revolution, and in contradiction to his overtly antirevolutionary fervor, the young poet-critic extolled "the generation that has just written with its blood and its tears the most extraordinary page of all the pages in history" (II, 433). As for Napoleon, whose ties with the Revolution are constantly evoked, Hugo's reception speech at the Académie Française, in 1841, explicitly stated that Napoleon in his imperial excessiveness had the secret of "transforming history into an epic" (VI, 147).

By the time Hugo wrote *Les Misérables*, Napoleon had become for him the embodiment of epic action. He had been a despot, yes; but the masses had worshipped him. For them he was *l'homme-peuple*, as Jesus was *l'homme-Dieu* (XI, 472). Balzac's *Le Médecin de campagne* illustrates, in another mode, how deeply rooted the myths of Napoleon's invincibility and immortality were in the popular mind. Hugo himself sees Napoleon as the prodigious architect of a collapse, as a dark genius committed to violence, destruction, and ultimate catastrophe. The terminology is revealing. Napoleon is a fearsome athlete ("sombre athlète du pugilat de la guerre"), a fateful destroyer of men ("grand bûcheron de l'Europe"), an "archangel" of war (XI, 261, 256, 498). But this archangel, in whom good and evil coexist in almost superhuman doses, is above all a genius. He appears—the pun is only half-involuntary—as the "Michelangelo" of war. The comparison is typical of the romantic tendency to juxtapose and blend prophetic, artistic, and political figures. Thus Hugo evokes the "mighty power" by which one becomes Moses, Aeschylus, Dante, Michelangelo, or Napoleon (XI, 284, 88).

Shaper and conqueror of Europe, Napoleon is the man of destiny. Hugo sees him in symbiotic complicity with events, treating destiny as his equal. Mythical images work their way to the foreground. Napoleon is the "titanic coachman" of destiny. Yet he is also destiny's victim (a "condamné du destin"), or, more precisely, he is part of a larger design that the author glimpses when he conceives of Napoleon as an "involuntary revolutionary" and elaborates the metaphor of a defeated Robespierre on horseback, whose defeat prepares the future (XI, 270, 261, 85, 287).

The Epic Counterpoint

The year 1815 thus marks for Hugo the point of intersection between the heroic enterprise and a superior design. It also marks the end of the military epic and the beginning of a new spiritual adventure. The symbolic parallelism and contrast between Napoleon's and Valjean's itineraries cannot be overlooked: the convict returns from the Toulon galleys, in October 1815, by moving north though Digne and Grenoble. It is the same road that Napoleon had taken on his short-lived return to power from the island of Elba seven months earlier. Just as the fall of Valjean in 1796 coincided with the rise of Bonaparte, so now the fall of the emperor corresponds to the reemergence of the convict. The contrapuntal motif has distant roots. Years earlier, Hugo the tourist, after visiting the *bagne* of Toulon, meditated at length along the *route Napoléon*, and associated the figure of Jean Tréjean (the original name of Valjean) with the destiny of the emperor.[7] The symbolic contrast is further stressed in the text. Valjean shakes his fist at the church in Digne, in the same square where Napoleon's new proclamations had been printed (XI, 99). The convict-*passant* enters the city by the same street the emperor had come through: "la même rue qui sept mois auparavant avait vu passer l'empereur Napoléon" (XI, 93).

Marching, passing, and progressing are all related to the image of an itinerary, and quite specifically to the painful but redemptive road of suffering, the *via dolorosa*. The nightmarish landscape in which Valjean experiences his total abandon—the low hill resembling a shaved head, the dark sky, the sinister light, the one deformed tree—unmistakably brings to mind Golgotha and the Passion of Christ (XI, 98). The agonizing crossing of the sewer, much later in the novel, is further proof of Hugo's obsession with Christ's Calvary. The Valjean-Christ parallel is clearly indicated in the chapter entitled "Une Tempête sous un crâne," which describes Valjean's great moral crisis culminating in the decision to turn himself in to save the falsely accused tramp. Valjean yields to the same "mysterious power" that some two thousand years earlier had impelled another condemned man to "march on." The chapter concludes with a renewed reference to the Man of Sorrows in whom were summed up all the sufferings of humanity, and who also at first had thrust aside with his hand the terrible cup brimming over with darkness (XI, 205, 212).

The allusion to Christ is related to a deeper literary intention. The images of inner struggle and spiritual itinerary are part of a deliberate program to displace the traditional hero in favor of a new conception of the epic. As a preamble to the key chapter "A Tempest in a Brain," Hugo writes: "To create the poem of human conscience, were it only in reference to one human being, were it only in connection with the lowliest of men, would be to blend all epics into one superior and definitive epic." The prism in this moral perspective is, however, not that of analysis but of enlargement and universalization. Hugo retains more than the term *epic*; he conceives the locus of this inner struggle as a mythic battleground. "There, beneath the external silence, battles of giants as in Homer are in progress; skirmishes of dragons and hydras and clouds of phantoms as in Milton; visionary spirals as in Dante." The systematic evocation of the great epic poets further stresses the specific elements of a literary tradition that Hugo wishes at once to emulate and to subvert, as he sets out to explore that "infinity which every man bears within him" (XI, 201–202).

The expression "every man" (*tout homme*) points to an anonymous, collective humanity. The epic dimensions of such a collectivity were no doubt already on Hugo's mind when, in his early twenties, he published the article on Walter Scott in *La Muse*

Française (July 1823) in which he called for epic novels ("grandes épopées") to suit the poetic needs of the modern age (II, 433). By the time of *Les Misérables*, he had developed the theory of an epic concerned with the great adventure of mankind, in particular with the destiny of the oppressed, redeemable, and ultimately redeeming *peuple*, toward whom his deepest reactions remained, however, characteristically ambiguous. In Hugo's view, all the social and political struggles of the nineteenth century, including mob violence and police repression, occurred within "the great epic field where humanity is struggling" (XI, 867).

This collectivization and universalization of the human drama implies that the conscience of a single human being, even the "lowliest," mirrors and reenacts the drama of humanity's "conscience"—and beyond this of the conscience of the world. Hugo repeatedly thinks and writes in terms of an "enlargement of the horizon" (XI, 497). Napoleon is impeached by divine judgment, against the backdrop of infinity ("dénoncé dans l'infini"—XI, 273). The cosmic scene is indeed, according to Hugo, the chief subject of his novel. The important digression on monastic life begins with a clear statement of purpose: "This book is a drama whose main character is the Infinite." And in a letter to Frédéric Morin, written a few weeks after the completion of *Les Misérables*, Hugo referred to his novel as an "espèce d'essai sur l'infini."[8]

The Death of the Hero

The ambivalent attitudes toward the epic must be read in this ambitious context. Nostalgia for epic virtues is offset by an uncompromising denunciation of martial horrors. Napoleon is an "archangel of war" because the notion of crime remains attached to his enterprise, and this crime of violence calls for expiation. Imperial glory no doubt sounded a "Titan's fanfare" throughout Europe. But the word *fanfare* also makes one think of *fanfaronnade*: empty boasting. Marius' "epic effusion" is easily deflated by his politically more mature friends, who convert him to revolutionary ideals (XI, 498–499).

Demystification of the epic idiom and of conventional epic values was to be carried out more systematically, by means of parody and association with archaic violence, in Hugo's last novel, *Quatre-vingt-Treize*. The undermining process is, however, already at work in *Les Misérables* and is one of the elements that accounts for the central importance of the Waterloo episode. Popular nostalgia for Napoleonic grandeur was no doubt quite affecting; Hugo himself felt vulnerable to its appeal. But such nostalgia, no matter how justified by the republican origins of the Empire, was an error; it implied the glorification of war. And war is carnage. Even the barricade fighting, though legitimized by revolutionary fervor and explicitly compared to the exploits at Troy, was ultimately nothing more than a "grand slaughter" ("tuerie grandiose"). There is more than a measure of irony in the authorial remark that "the epic alone has a right to fill twelve thousand lines with one battle" (XI, 866).

The epic length and the epic tone of the Waterloo section thus find their deeper ironic justification. The military defeat signals not only the end of Napoleon and a turning point in history but a major shift in the moral and intellectual perspective. A new page of the larger text has been set before the collective consciousness: "Les sabreurs ont fini, c'est le tour des penseurs" ("The sword-wielders have had their day, the time of the thinkers has come"— XI, 287). And the end of the *sabreurs*, the discrediting of the sword, also means the death of the traditional hero. There still is room for physical courage, of course, provided it serves a humane cause. In contrast to glorified acts of warfare and to the "stupid slaughter of the battlefield," Hugo sets up the unsung bravery of the great servants and visionaries of humanity.

Hugo's own most sustained commentary on the demise of the hero is to be found in *William Shakespeare* (1864), a wide-ranging discussion of the nature and destiny of genius. Shakespeare appears in this key text as the symbol of the genuine conquerors: the thinkers and the poets. The pen is destined to outlive and vanquish the sword. For Hugo, this is a transcendental reality, as well as a matter of historical evolution. The ascent of the seer means the downfall of the power-hungry, the annihilation of *hommes de force*. But this hoped-for twilight of the violent conquerors and this liberation from hero-worship ("le prophète anéantissant le héros") have their own sad grandeur. Irreverent rejoicing would be out of order; the hero deserves worthy funerals: "Let us not insult that which was great. Jeers would be unseemly at the hero's burial" (XII, 322–323).

The end is thus also a beginning. Napoleon misjudged the vast dawn of ideas which, according to Hugo, characterized the nineteenth century. Napoleon's unredeemable error, in a sense, was not military or political. By adopting the derisive term *idéologue* to discredit philosophers, he became symbolically guilty of the most fatal imprudence: he mocked the future (XI, 283, 288).

The Bridge

If the end is also a beginning, then the catastrophe of Waterloo serves as a vital transition. This paradox of a constructive defeat draws its strength from the interplay of rupture and continuity; it centers on the themes of paternity and temporal progression. For paternity in *Les Misérables* relates both to an origin that has to be found and to a hiatus that must be spanned. The need for a historical continuity is structurally inscribed in the Waterloo episode. The deceptive artificiality that links the episode to the main plot only draws attention to the question of articulation and juncture. The signals speak for themselves. Thénardier, the criminal prowler, and Pontmercy, the wounded hero he robs and saves at the same time, are bonded. The meeting of the "fathers" foreshadows the meeting of the children, the "conjunction of the stars" Marius and Cosette. The digression ends on an ironic yet deeply meaningful note. The wounded colonel gives his name, *Pontmercy*, the two last syllables of which are recorded as an expression of gratitude for a criminal action that turns into a blessing, while the entire name later provides the link with the son. The generational theme is in fact woven into the fabric of the Waterloo digression by means of a wordplay, as the narrator explains that one of the "generative scenes" ("scènes génératrices") of his story is tied in with the great battle (XI, 261).

Other wordplays, especially of an onomastic nature, suggest the notion of a gap to be bridged. Paternity and the image of spanning are, as it were, built into the name of Pontmercy. If the last two syllables point ironically to gratitude, the first one (*pont*, meaning bridge) unmistakably denotes a crossing over. There is further evidence that the bridge is symbolically related to Marius' father. Pontmercy, after the Restoration, retires to the small town of Vernon, which is known for its "beautiful monumental bridge" (XI, 457). The metaphor of the bridge would indeed seem to be at the conceptual origin of this father image. A note in the manuscript indicates that Hugo, in choosing the name for Marius' father, hesitated among the following: Pontchaumont, Pontverdier, Pontbéziers, Pontuitry, Pontverdun, Pontbadon, and Pontflorent.[9]

The implied trajectory is not, however, a simple matter of genetic or historical continuity. In a sense, what is being spanned is precisely Pontmercy himself, as well as the historical moment he represents. For the father figure has been hidden from view, forgotten, dismissed. Marius is first presented to the reader in a section entitled "The Grandfather and the Grandson." The title points to a gap: Where indeed is the father? The answer is that, after the fall of Napoleon, he has quite literally been made to disappear. A family sense of scandal (Pontmercy was not only a professional soldier but a fervent follower of the Usurper) forces the ex-cuirassier to keep himself out of sight and to renounce any role whatsoever in the upbringing of his son. This cancellation of the father-presence symbolically reflects a political desire to erase the entire 1789–1815 period as a criminal and irrelevant interlude.

Once again, Hugo plays on the image of the bridge, as the Ancien Régime grandfather Gillenormand assumes the role of father-substitute in lieu of the repudiated son-in-law. So long as the grandfather successfully influences the political opinions of his grandson, they both meet "as on a bridge" ("comme sur un pont"— XI, 473). But this bridge is a delusion; it is projected over a void. History cannot be denied with impunity. The Revolution and Napoleon cannot be juggled away. Once Marius awakens to the historical reality, when he discovers his father and what he stood for, the false bridge collapses and the void appears: "Quand ce pont tomba, l'abîme se fit" (XI, 473).

There is pathos in this discovery. Marius reaches Pontmercy's deathbed when it is too late; father and son were not destined to make contact in life. But this frustration only heightens the value of a legacy that transcends death. Marius finds a written message— a terse spiritual testament—which he will devoutly carry on his person. The reactionary grandfather's act of father-usurpation must be understood in the light of this newly affirmed spiritual bond with the Empire, and, beyond it, with the Republic. When Gillenormand discovers the note Marius carries religiously like an amulet, and which refers to Pontmercy's elevation to the barony on the battlefield of Waterloo, this leads to a violent confrontation. To Marius' defiant statement "I am my father's son" Gillenormand categorically replies "*I* am your father" ("Ton père, c'est moi"— XI, 478).

The eclipse of the fathers in favor of the grandfathers is a recurrent feature in the work of Hugo.[10] Valjean, who at first appears as a grandfather figure in relation to Cosette, becomes her surrogate father after the death of Fantine. In a sense, Fantine must die so he can assume this role. The accession to paternity, signifying also a new life for Valjean, takes place exactly nine months after the death of Fantine. The narrator's language is strong: fate "wedded" ("fiança") these two uprooted lives (the symbolic Widower and Orphan); their two souls meet in a close embrace ("s'embrassèrent étroitement"—XI, 341–342).

Much could be said about the latent incestuousness of Valjean's feelings for Cosette: guilt about their drawn-out seclusion; his surveillance and possessiveness; the exclusive nature of his affections; his sense of terror at the sight of her growing beauty; the jealousy he experiences when he suspects her of having fallen in love; his hatred for Marius, which can be overcome only by an act of total self-sacrifice; the fetishistic attachment to her clothes; his animal-like protectiveness ("C'était un dogue qui regarde un voleur"—XI, 641, 646). The explicit exoneration from incestuous feelings ("Poor old Jean Valjean certainly did not love Cosette otherwise than as a father") only points up the equivocal nature of his feelings for her. On the same page on which Hugo takes the trouble of clearing him from any possible suspicion, he goes on to say that Jean Valjean was a "strange" father indeed—"a strange father in whom there is something of the grandfather, the son, the brother, and the husband" (XI, 810).

The incest motif, as André Brochu has shown, subtly reappears in Gillenormand's relation to his grandson, a relation that seems overdetermined by an affective transfer.[11] Marius is the son of Gillenormand's favorite daughter, now dead. The hostility to the son-in-law, Pontmercy, can in fact be explained in terms of jealousy. The transfer to Marius is, so to speak, made visible: Gillenormand is struck by the resemblance between his daughter's portrait and Marius. The text is even more outspoken: "He had never loved a mistress as he loved Marius" (XI, 728).

Intimations of incest have an autobiographical resonance, reminding one of Hugo's sense of loss and guilt after his daughter's death by drowning. But the father-substitution, on which the incest motif appears grafted, also signals a symbolic political crime. Gillenormand, the grandfather, is a typical man of the eighteenth century, shaped by, and faithful to, the mores of the Ancien Régime. His assumption of paternal authority corresponds to the return to power of the monarchy in 1815. The problematic link with the father is thus not a matter simply of tradition (the tie with the past) but of allegiance to history's forward movement. The bridge leads in both directions. The discovery of the heroic father is bound up with the discovery of history as progress. Pontmercy's example reveals to Marius the historic mission of the Republic and the Empire in forging national and revolutionary ideals.

The father emerges as a mediating figure between past and future. Once properly understood, he becomes a principle of conversion. It is significant, however, that the political revelation, though inscribed in a continuum, does not depend on a filiation in direct line. The conversion process requires an outsider: the father comes to the family as a son-in-law. This principle of a dramatic conversion allowing freedom of choice, rather than of a socially or atavistically determined political consciousness, was to be featured even more sharply in *Quatrevingt-Treize*.

The idea of progress, coupled with the account of a personal political evolution, is thus articulated in a complex manner on the bidirectional date 1815. The young man's political education requires first the rehabilitation of the father, just as it requires the rehabilitation of Napoleon. In reading history and studying documents, "the veil that covered Napoleon from Marius' eyes gradually fell away." What is unveiled in the process is an even more important historical reality: the French Revolution. Marius begins to understand its true significance with regard to the anachronistic world of the grandfather. Where he formerly deplored the fall of the monarchy, he now sees the advent of a new order: "What had been the setting was now the rising of the sun" (XI, 471–472).

But this inner revolution, these regressive discoveries and rehabilitations of the father, of Napoleon, of the men of the Revolution, precisely because they reveal the truth of progress require ultimately the effacement of the father figure. This would explain not only the self-sacrificing disappearance of Pontmercy but the even more systematic vanishing process that leads Valjean on his earthly journey to a nameless grave. The image of effacement and self-effacement ("Le jeune homme arrivait, le bonhomme s'effaçait") must be read against the other figuration of mobility and transitoriness—the passer-by. Valjean, we have seen, qualifies himself as a *passant* in Cosette's life. He knows he must make room for Marius, and for the future (XI, 930, 957, 967).

Marius' moral and political apprenticeship is thus determined by a double movement, regressive and progressive, that first reads (leads) back to the Revolution via the Empire and the Bonapartist adventure, and then proceeds forward to transcend the paternal example. When his fervent readings into the past reveal to him the vitality of the revolutionary figures (Mirabeau, Saint-Just, Robespierre, Camille Desmoulins, Danton), he at first recoils, blinded by the light. But the movement back in time actually represents a steady advance. His dazzlement is a symptom of spiritual progression. He is an "esprit en marche" (XI, 470).

Marius' political evolution is seen by Hugo as typical; it is the "story of many minds of our time." The interest in collective history does not, however, account for the detailed evocation of Marius' childhood. There is little doubt that if Hugo took the trouble to retrace step by step all the phases of Marius' political education, it is because he was moved to recall the political climate in which he grew up and to describe his own gradual detachment from royalist views. The personal note appears clearly in the pious chapter "Requiescant" ("Let Them Rest")—a farewell to the past, as well as an evocation of the ultraroyalist days of his adolescence, which are associated with the mother image. The important autobiographical poem "Ecrit en 1846" at the beginning of book 5 of *Les Contemplations* (entitled "En Marche"), which describes his gradual awakening to history and his understanding of the providential role of the Revolution, significantly begins with the memory of his mother ("Marquis, je m'en souviens, vous veniez chez ma mère") and ends with a reference to his mother now in the grave. This is paralleled in *Les Misérables* by the absence of the father in the adolescent life of Marius, and by the early feelings of gloom and resentment associated with him: "il était sombre à l'endroit de son père" (XI, 466).

Waterloo, Good or Bad?

A historically symbolic father who is first eclipsed, then found, and later transcended; a political apprenticeship that moves backward to the Revolution and then sweeps forward to the ideal of progress; a stress on pivotal dates (1815, the year of Waterloo; 1789, the year of the Revolution; 1830, inaugurating Marius' participation in the historical struggle; and, beyond the narrated events of the novel, 1851, the year of Louis Napoleon's coup d'état, which sent Victor Hugo into exile)—all these crisis signals betray an uneasy view of the linearity of history. For if history is a movement forward—and Hugo was committed to the notion of progress—how then is one to explain discontinuities and tragic relapses such as the Restoration and the Second Empire? Waterloo becomes symbolic of the dilemma.

The essential ambivalence of Waterloo is reflected in the title of the didactic chapter 17: "Faut-il trouver bon Waterloo?" Hugo explains in what sense Waterloo can be considered both bad and good. Objectively speaking, Napoleon's defeat marks an interruption in the forward march of history. It means an oppressive and repressive return of the past. The clock has been set back. The event is a counterrevolutionary victory. The monarchies of Europe have seemingly crushed the rebellious, liberating spirit embodied by France. This, several years after the return of Louis XVIII, remains the commonly accepted opinion: "the era of revolutions was forever closed" (XI, 132).

But another perspective was possible, in the light of which Waterloo appears as a major turning point on the mysterious road of progress. His mission accomplished, the seed of new ideas having been disseminated throughout Europe, the tyrant had to go. More profoundly, Napoleon's defeat could be interpreted as a victory in the larger battle of which God is the supreme general. Hugo invokes a cosmic battlefield: "Waterloo is not a battle; it is the change of front of the universe." What is involved is nothing less than global destiny. The privileged vision of the author-seer embraces the grand mission of the nineteenth century in the human adventure. Napoleon's victory at Waterloo was simply not "within the law of the nineteenth century" (XI, 273). Waterloo was a providential event because it made room for what Hugo calls the "grand siècle" (a polemical expression, since these two words are usually associated with the reign of Louis XIV) and the dawn of new ideas ("vaste lever d'idées"—XI, 283). The mission of this new century is later preached by Enjolras, the young political idealist, from atop the barricades. It is to be "Promethean" in its liberating drive.

The day of Waterloo, 18 June 1815, defined as a "catastrophe," is thus also a day of destiny; more precisely, it is the "hinge"

("gond") of the nineteenth century. It marks the historical articulation in a providential drama which begins with the French
Revolution and which, despite apparent setbacks, is not to be
arrested. For the Revolution cannot be defeated. Hugo, speaking
of the work of the Revolution and of the devious paths of history,
plays on the multiple meanings of the word "fateful." The Revolution is "providentielle et absolument fatale" (XI, 286); it brings
ruin and death, but is destined ultimately to transcend the violence
of history. The apocalypse of Waterloo foreshadows the end of
violence in history, and, better still, of history as violence. Hugo's
dream, here as elsewhere, is quite literally an exit from what
Enjolras describes, in his utopian sermon on the barricades, as
"the forest of events" (XI, 835). The ideal of such supreme freedom
casts light on the uncommon adjectival turn with which Hugo sums
up the bewildering significance of the great defeat: "To us, Waterloo is but the stupefied date of liberty" ("la date stupéfaite de
la liberté"— XI, 286).

The Victory of Cambronne

Who, under these circumstances, won the battle? History books,
according to Hugo, fail to give the right answer. For the victor is
neither Wellington nor Blücher. They were mere beneficiaries of
chance, and that chance—quite trivially—took the form of water.
Had it not rained during the night of June 17–18, the future of
Europe might have been different. Yet this chance is hardly of an
ordinary sort. The narrator, referring to the "marvelous cleverness
of chance" ("prodigieuse habileté du hasard") hints at the intentionality of an invisible plan. *Hasard* is here the mask of con-
catenation. The text indeed proposes the oxymoronic "enchaînement
de hasards." The peculiar "chain" of chance events, before and
during the battle, points therefore not to contingency but to necessity. This is sharply signaled by the even more pointed oxymoron "hasard divin" (XI, 285, 261, 283).

The conclusion is self-evident: Waterloo is the victory of God.
This is implicit in the relation between the infinitely small (the

deceptive sign of the peasant-guide) and the fate of the world. It is made explicit in the affirmation that the part played by men was nothing, that all was stamped with "superhuman necessity." Hugo does not hesitate to cast God in the role of supreme protagonist: "Was it possible that Napoleon should have won that battle? We answer: no. Why? Because of Wellington? Because of Blücher? No. Because of God" (XI, 283, 273). Hugo has alluded, a few pages earlier, to the "mysterious frown" that became perceptible in the depths of the heavens. There is even a hint that God might have become jealous of the "excessive weight" of Napoleon: "Il gênait Dieu." Napoleon, guilty of hubris, was unconscionably jovial the morning of the battle. The "supreme smile" is God's alone (XI, 270–271, 273, 266).

Yet God is not the only victor in this catastrophe. There is also a *human* victor ("l'homme qui a gagné la bataille de Waterloo"— XI, 281): the aforementioned General Cambronne, who, when the ammunition ran out and the last units were summoned to surrender, went down in history by defying the enemy with a resounding *Merde!* Lamartine, deploring the occasional "filth" ("saletés") of Hugo's language in *Les Misérables*, specifically protested against Cambronne's obscenity flung in the face of destiny—"Better to die in silence."[12] But what Lamartine failed to understand is that by challenging the power of guns with the lowliest of words, by refusing to be silent, Cambronne-Hugo affirmed not the prestige of the latrine but the power of the word.

Nor is it a minor detail that Cambronne should also be called a *passant*—the very term Hugo as narrator applies to himself as he tours the old battlefield. Cambronne, the unknown hero, is a "passer-by at the last hour," an insignificant participant in the historic event, who, by dint of a single word defying the thunder of war, attains "Aeschylean grandeur." The infinitely small achieves Titanic status, just as the basest word in the French language ("le dernier des mots") becomes the finest word ("le plus beau mot") ever pronounced. In the face of the nothingness of brute force, Cambronne finds an "expression" (and Hugo a pun): he expresses "excrement." That which is ex-pressed comes, verbally, from what

Bakhtin calls the "lower stratum of the grotesque."[13] But this grotesqueness is not the negative pole of an antithesis; it remains altogether positive, even lofty. The coarse expletive is qualified by Hugo as "sublime." The scatological utterance here comes from the soul: "il trouve à l'âme une expression, l'excrément" (XI, 281–282).

The reference to the soul or spirit (âme) is not in the least ironic. Cambronne, faced with imminent annihilation or surrender, seeks a word the way one looks for a sword; and the word he finds comes to him, Hugo explains, by inspiration from above ("par visitation du souffle d'en haut"—XI, 282). The divine afflatus lifts him to the heights of epic irreverence.

This epic irreverence conveyed by the most plebeian of utterances further undermines the epic sense of hierarchy and distance. Bakhtin's observations on Rabelaisian laughter and carnavalesque profanities apply to Hugo's Cambronne, who has the laugh on his side. Such transformational laughter not only exorcises fear and challenges authority; it contains huge regenerative power.[14] Interestingly enough, there is an allusion to Rabelais in the Cambronne chapter, and it is accompanied precisely by a reference to the carnival, the Mardi Gras. More interesting still is the link, in Hugo's mind, between Cambronne's terse exclamation and the title of the novel, with its sociopolitical connotations. In a note found in his papers, Hugo characterizes the word merde as the "misérable des mots," and again as the "misérable du langage."[15]

The symbolic victory of merde is of course not simply a linguistic matter. In concrete, literal terms, all battles, Hugo would say, end in mud, excrement, and putrefaction. That is the outcome of all violence. The pattern is structurally repeated later in Les Misérables. The heroic butchery at the barricades quite logically leads to a descent into the sewers—an immersion that is clearly regenerative.

Cambronne's personal victory is of course also symbolic. At one level, it is a victory against the English general: by uttering the "last of words" (le dernier des mots), Cambronne, by a mere dropping of the particle, has the final word (le dernier mot). At another level, his is the victorious laughter of defeat which truculently denounces the mockery of meaningless survival ("cette dérision, la vie"—XI, 282). The transcendental, prophetic nature of such a denunciation of the sin of senseless living is illumined by the extraordinary passage in *William Shakespeare* in which the prophet Ezekiel is glorified as an eater of excrement ("il mange des excréments.")[16] According to Jean Massin, Hugo's Ezekiel is the Cambronne of the prophetic mode.[17]

The less obvious victory, however, is achieved against the commander-in-chief, Napoleon. This is implicit in the confrontation of two types of laughter—a confrontation that recurs throughout Hugo's work: the arrogant laughter from above and the grotesque, buffoonish laughter from below. The grin of the satyr forever challenges the laughter of Olympus. Napoleon, still riding high, also laughs. On the morning of the battle, confident that he can still treat destiny as an equal, that this privileged complicity lends him a manner of immortality, he defiantly displays a jocular mood. The chapter entitled "Napoléon de belle humeur" describes the Emperor in high spirits, full of verve, indulging in *bons mots*. At breakfast, before the battle, he has repeated fits of laughter ("accès de rire"), unaware of the divine frown. This Napoleonic laughter connotes not merely hubris and tragic irony; it is related to Napoleon's worst sin, that of having held thinkers in contempt and thus having denied the future. Laughter, in Hugo's work, is almost always politically significant: the oppressive laughter of tyranny is countered by the liberating laughter of the downtrodden—the slave, the faun, the lackey, the clown, the redeeming victim. The gross, plebeian laughter associated with Cambronne's exclamation corresponds to the dynamic laughter of the oppressed who say *no* in order to reaffirm *yes*. Such laughter is revolutionary in nature.

The harsh comedy of street language and the resilient locution of the marketplace do indeed have a rebellious potential. The word *merde* contains the seed of revolt. Cambronne's vigorous utterance links him, in Hugo's mind, to the rebel figure of Prometheus: the single word thrown into the face of the enemy has a "grandeur eschylienne." But Prometheus translated into modern terms means revolution. Nothing could be more telling than the association, in the chapter on Paris entitled "Railler, régner," of the names Danton, Prometheus, and Cambronne. The chapter ends with the elliptical remark that the same fearsome lightning darts from the torch of Prometheus to the clay pipe of Cambronne: "Le même éclair formidable va de la torche de Prométhée au brûle-gueule de Cambronne."[18]

From Cambronne to Gavroche: Salvation from Below

Cambronne answers the enemy's ultimatum with the most democratic word in the French language. Hugo himself, assessing his linguistic contribution, claimed to have revolutionized the literary idiom. ("Je fis souffler un vent révolutionnaire. / Je mis un bonnet rouge au vieux dictionnaire"—IX, 75.) It is hardly excessive to suggest that Cambronne's pungent exclamation corresponds to Hugo's personal intention, as well as to the larger themes of *Les Misérables*. These themes, in particular the political implications of popular speech and popular laughter, are illustrated by one of Hugo's most striking creations, the slangy street urchin Gavroche—and beyond him, by the personalized figure of Paris, the city of revolutions. Gavroche, the vagrant boy familiar with thieves and prostitutes, the *gamin* who sings obscene songs and has a poet's mastery of argot, is truly a child of the big city: "Le gamin de Paris, c'est le nain de la géante" (XI, 432). And of course Paris, the gigantic parent, is the *figura* of the people. The metaphor works both ways. The capital is the populace, and the populace is the *gamin*—with his teasing lightheartedness and irrepressible laughter, but also his grim love of freedom and courage. "To depict the child is to depict the city." If the city populace is comparable to a child, it is because it still has to be formed morally and politically. The mob, the masses, have a potential that needs to be educated, elevated, or as Hugo puts it, "sublimed" (XI, 443).

Yet the political potential is there, and laughter is its manifestation. The laughter of Gavroche is the laughter of the city, and the laughter of the city—likened to that which might issue from a "volcano's mouth"—is the laughter of revolution. This laughter is ominous. Gavroche himself may think that he is carefree. He is not. Always ready for a prank, he is also "ready for something else." He will in fact die, singing a mocking song, while gathering cartridges for the outnumbered fighters on the barricades. The imp becomes a hero (XI, 442, 433, 439). The merrymaking populace of Paris is likewise capable of epic anger. But this threatening laughter is not merely a signal of courage and violence; it ultimately serves to build the utopian city of justice. Paris, the capital of revolutionary anger, is also the capital of revolutionary revelation, and as such is destined to become a new Jerusalem. In pages written while in exile to serve as introduction to *Paris-Guide* at the time of the Exposition Universelle of 1867, Hugo denounced the smug and doomed materialism of the Second Empire: "Paris, lieu de la révélation révolutionnaire, est la Jérusalem humaine" (XIII, 591).

From laughter to epic anger, from argot to the sublime, from *fex urbis*—the dregs of the city—to revelation: Hugo is not interested in irreconcilable antitheses but in the spanning of apparent opposites. The excremental motif reappears in the *gamin*'s warning that the police are coming, which is the signal to escape through the sewage drain: "Ohé, Titi, ohéée: y a de la grippe, y a de la cogne . . . pâsse par l'égout!" (XI, 438). It appears even more clearly in the expression *fex urbis*, which etymologically equates the city populace with fecal matter. We are back to the word of Cambronne. Only now the excremental motif is permeated with the realities of social conditions and fraught with revolutionary hopes and ideals. It is the signal that salvation is to come from the filth of the lower stratum, from the depths of misery and crime, from the social *inferi*.

Not surprisingly, the first reference to the *égout* is associated with an image of escape. Salvation is to be found below. Hugo, the polished bourgeois, instinctively apprehensive of mob ignorance and mob violence, here faces some of his most difficult inner contradictions, as he deals with the salvational virtues of the social cloaca. This helps explain another digression, one dealing with the criminal gang called Patron-Minette. The appellation derives from *patron-minet*, which in old slang means early morning—a reference to the crepuscular hour when the gang's night work is done and they disband. But it becomes clear that Hugo is playing on the word *mine*, phonetically contained in the word *minet*, and that this word connotes the reality below the surface, the nether regions, the bowels of the earth, with further suggestions of the hellish abyss where the "social Ugolino" (a clear reference to Dante's hell) indulges in vice and crime. Here is the great "cave of evil," oozing with physical and moral pollution (XI, 532, 533).

The image of the mine also connotes arduous work and the extraction of precious ore. The verb *piocher* (to dig with a pick), metaphorically associated by Hugo with the substantive *idée*, means to work or study very hard. The first chapter of the digression on Patron-Minette is entitled "Les Mines et les mineurs." Its idealistic and redemptive overtones are intensified if one remembers that, early in the novel, Bishop Bienvenu extracts saintly pity from what Hugo calls the "mine" of universal misery: "L'universelle misère était sa mine" (XI, 91). Salvation from below is indeed the message of the Patron-Minette episode. Hugo reminds his reader that the first Roman Mass was said in the catacombs. Similarly, the new social gospel, the new religion of progress, will spread through the communion of social suffering. The lowest stratum of society is also the revolutionary mine where utopias are elaborated: "Les utopies cheminent sous terre dans les conduits."[19]

This underground imagery remains ambiguous. The figure of Christ is disturbingly coupled with the abhorred figure of Marat, who embodies, for Hugo, all the terror of mob violence. The *fex urbis* can, no doubt, be elevated; that is precisely the mission of the new social prophet. But this prophetic calling first implies a plunging into mud and putrescence. Prophecy and salvation from below are central to Hugo's personal religion. For Hugo's God is no longer the authoritarian divine principle hierarchically and sublimely situated above, but emerges from subterranean darkness, from chaotic and dynamic human suffering and human becoming. That is what police inspector Javert, who lives by the faith that God is allied with law and order, is made to discover through Valjean's magnanimity.[20] The discovery that God rises from the lower depths comes as a great shock to the relentlessly righteous Javert, and leads directly to his suicide. But this same association between God and the dregs of the earth also makes far more meaningful the narrator's somewhat surprising comment that Cambronne's historic cry, which so profoundly shocked Lamartine, came to him by divine inspiration—"par visitation du souffle d'en haut" (XI, 282).

The Language from Below

Slang reflects this paradox at the level of language. Hugo devotes to argot another of his lengthy digressions. His colorful observations may not be of great philological value, but they take on a thematic function and impose a parallel between popular language and the ambivalent nature of the underworld. The first word of the digression is the Latin *pigritia*, from which Hugo derives the French *pègre*, designating the world of thieves considered as a social class. The link between argot and the world of crime suits Hugo's structures. Like the underworld, slang is a pathological "excrescence" ("excroissance maladive"—XI, 702), but at the same time it implies vitality and constant evolution.

The many references to argot as a pathology of language (Hugo calls it a "pustulous vocabulary," a wart-like, ulcerous idiom) are significantly associated with the excremental motif (XI, 697). Slang is compared to a horrible beast made to inhabit the darkness of the cloaca. It is also compared to an underground edifice, collectively built by the accursed race of *misérables*. Willful crime and dehumanizing punishment are inscribed on its walls. The prison imagery is inescapable. The shameless tropes of slang seem indeed to have worn the "iron collar," the *carcan*. The words of this special language appear as if shriveled under the red-hot iron of the executioner. The sense of shame associated with the underworld idiom explains why Eponine, once her love for Marius has illuminated her crime-ridden existence, refuses to speak that "horrid language," argot (XI, 721).

Yet Hugo is fascinated by the forcefulness and vitality of slang and links it to the revolutionary spirit. This vitality, to be sure, remains repellent ("vitalité hideuse") and mirrors the hideousness of criminal faces in the prison and the galleys. Hugo defines argot as the "verbe devenu forçat"—the word become a convict. The double suggestion of force and action implicit in the terms *verbe* and *forçat* reinforces the contention that argot is the language of rebellion and militancy, a "langue de combat" (XI, 705, 699). The speech of the underworld expresses the subterranean and perhaps subconscious utopian yearnings associated with the sufferers in the mine.

The power of such a linguistic code is valued by Hugo for strictly poetic reasons. Henri Meschonnic quite rightly sees Hugo's interest in argot—an interest already displayed in *Le Dernier Jour d'un condamné*—as part of a broader reflection on the nature of language and on the poet's will to control it.[21] The "hideousness" of slang, according to Hugo's theory in his preface to *Cromwell*, constitutes a source of aesthetic value: "Beauty has only one type; ugliness has a thousand" (III, 55). The digression on slang in *Les Misérables* is quite explicit. Slang is essentially a poetic construct because of the steady displacement of meanings and the ensuing masquerade of words. Argot's mask-words ("mots masques") serve as camouflage. But conversely, this metaphorical inventiveness brings about a cratylic immediacy, which results in an idiom rich in *mots immédiats*. Argot thus joins poetry in the elaboration of a language designed at once to conceal and to reveal ("tout dire et tout cacher"—XI, 703). In a note accompanying the manuscript of *William Shakespeare*, Hugo elaborated on the relationship between popular language and poetry: "Figurative language is essentially popular language" (XII, 351).

The victory associated with the lowliest of words thus transcends praise of Cambronne's indomitable spirit. It does more than hint that salvation comes from unexpected quarters. It signifies the victory of the word as poetic manifestation, the victory of language as poetry—and, by extension, the victory of the supreme master of language, the poet. For the word is more than a sword transforming the vanquished Cambronne into a victor. It is more beautiful than what it represents and has its own opaque reality ("les mots sont des choses," Hugo writes in the poem "Suite," in *Les Contemplations*). The word's action is militant ("le mot s'appelle Légion"), yet the word's power lies less in its revolutionary potential than in its divine auctorial origin. The concluding line of "Suite" proclaims this all-powerful logos: "Car le mot, c'est le Verbe, et le Verbe, c'est Dieu" (IX, 81).

The link between the excremental and religious motifs is suggested repeatedly at the level of metaphor. The Petit-Picpus convent, into which the ex-convict forces his way to escape the manhunt and in which he finds refuge and expiation, is defined by Hugo—together with all monastic enclosures—as a place of putrescence (XI, 392). Conversely, when Valjean, in his ultimate escape, descends into the Parisian sewers, his involuntary memory resuscitates the powerful sensation he experienced when he "fell" from the street into the convent. Spirituality and filth are once again dialectically related.

The revelation of this bond between spirituality and the underworld is in itself a powerful religious experience. The shock turns out to be too much for Javert. His one-track mind, coupling justice and authority, is incapable of accepting the sublimity of the wretch, of assimilating the paradox of a beneficent malefactor, a hideous moral hero, an inverted moral order in which the criminal is redeemable and haloed. When he becomes aware of the superior abyss (the "gouffre en haut"—XI, 915), when he realizes that God is *below* at least as much as above, Javert's machine derails (the section is entitled "Javert déraillé"). He destroys himself, testifying to an intolerable truth.

Les Misérables, in Hugo's mind, grew to be an increasingly religious book. All of human destiny, the narrator explains, is summed up in the dilemma: loss or salvation. In the episode of the barricades, he describes the subject of the book as the unrelenting movement from evil to good, from night to day, from nothingness to God (XI, 713, 865). The *misérables* are in fact the victims of a social damnation, dwelling in what the preface refers to as "hells" on earth. But Hugo rejects the notion of eternal damnation. Satan himself, according to a famous line in *La Fin de Satan*, will be reborn as the angel of light: "Satan est mort; renais, ô Lucifer céleste!" (X, 1762). Hugo clearly conceives of himself as a modern Dante—but a Dante who is the prophet of a new religion of liberation. His God is not chief jailer. "No eternal hell!" proclaims the voice from the dark in *Les Contemplations* (IX, 387). Instead, Hugo announces movement toward a higher consciousness through suffering. Redemption, in these terms, implies the transcendence of the prison image.[22]

The Leading Figure: The Infinite

Hugo's most substantial commentary on the religious significance of *Les Misérables* is to be found in a text of 1860 known as "Philosophie. Commencement d'un livre" (XII, 13–72), which was originally planned as a preface to the novel, before it evolved into a lengthy introduction to his entire work. It can perhaps best be described as a spiritual testament. The first sentence sets the tone: *Les Misérables* is meant to be a religious book ("Le livre qu'on va lire est un livre religieux"). The text dwells on some of Hugo's most dearly held notions: dynamic undoing and ceaseless reconstruction, the vitalism of natural forces, the intimate solidarity of the universe, the dialogue with the unseen, the paradox of the irreducible identity of author and God.

But the most interesting aspect of this "philosophical" preface— though it is not so obvious at a first glance—is its polemical intentionality, which illumines the point of intersection between Hugo's religious and political convictions. Hugo writes: "misery being materialistic, the book about misery must be spiritualistic" (XII, 71). This somewhat facile opposition of matter and spirit, of subject and literary treatment, takes on its proper meaning only if set against the backdrop of Hugo's private quarrel with his fellow "socialists," at a time when French socialism, abandoning earlier utopian and spiritualistic leanings, tended to link revolutionary virtues with impiety. Pierre Albouy has convincingly argued that Hugo's real enemies, around 1860, were not at all, as one might believe, conservatives and reactionaries but socialist atheists, who had by then become the predominant force in the socialist movement.[23] Hugo's profession of faith must therefore be read as a protest against what he himself calls "intestinal socialism"—that is, a socialism too exclusively preoccupied with economic realities and economic solutions. Man's needs do not consist merely of filling his belly. The soul is hungry, too, and cannot live on meat and nothingness (XII, 65–66). Radically opposed to the notion that religion is the opiate of the masses, Hugo attempts instead to associate atheism and conservatism. This is the point of an early chapter in which the bishop confronts the smug, sacrilegious senator. Hugo sees an essential tie between religion and democracy, not simply because republican fervor is compatible with faith but because belief in the Supreme Being legitimizes the principles of equality and justice. In Hugo's metaphysical perspective, infinity is identifiable with progress. Thus, he can assert, in a sociopolitical context, that the greatest political misfortune would be generalized atheism: "Le plus grand de tous les malheurs, ce serait tout le monde athée" (XII, 69).

There is ample internal evidence of the religious thrust of *Les Misérables*. Some of it is obvious, such as the narrator's declaration, at the beginning of the digression on convents, that the novel's chief protagonist is the infinite ("Ce livre est un drame dont le premier personnage est l'infini"—XI, 389). The dimension of infinity is, however, most often internalized, as during Valjean's first great moral crisis ("A Tempest in a Brain") when it is projected "within himself" ("au-dedans de lui-même"). Hugo's favorite method, in this regard, is allusive. Valjean, facing the abyss of his conscience and about to make a first sacrifice that will lead to resurrection, is compared to another condemned man, the Man of Sorrows (XI, 205).

Opening signals once again are revealing. The novel begins on a religious note, with a lengthy, almost hagiographic account of the saintly bishop of Digne. The ex-convict's confrontation with this "just man" produces a spiritual trauma. Bishop Bienvenu "hurt his soul," just as too bright a light can hurt the eyes. An invisible bond will henceforth tie him to the one who becomes his intercessor, and whom he venerates as a martyr. The suggestion is that of a spiritual family kinship. When news of the bishop's death reaches Valjean and he appears in mourning, gossip has it that he must be a relative of the bishop (XI, 127, 189, 167).

The polemical intentions underlying the philosophical preface are once again apparent, for Bishop Bienvenu has his limitations. He is a "just man," rather than a visionary or a true martyr. He lacks what might be called a radical dimension. Capable of love and charity, his soul cannot glimpse the apocalypse. He has nothing of the prophet, nothing of the seer ("rien du mage"—XI, 91). This lack of spiritual radicalism is specifically related to a political flaw, royalism—or rather to an undeveloped political consciousness. Hence the importance of the august, persecuted figure of the Conventionnel—the old member of the revolutionary Assembly that governed France in the period of greatest violence. When the bishop and the revolutionary meet, it appears that religion and revolution come into hopeless clash. Yet the confrontation leads to an illumination. The chapter is entitled "The Bishop in the Presence of an Unknown Light." It is the bishop, come to assist the dying political radical, who ends up kneeling in front of him, asking for his blessing.

This act, which so profoundly disturbed some of Hugo's Christian readers, is in reality not the most surprising feature of this scene in which bishop and revolutionary are at first locked in a verbal battle, each accusing the other of responsibility for violence in history. The real surprise is not that the bishop goes down on his knees in front of the old Conventionnel; it is that the Conventionnel speaks the language of religious mysticism. The moment has its peculiar beauty. The death of the outcast in the presence of the bishop and of a child (symbol of innocence and of faith in the future) is illumined by a setting sun and has an iconic quality. Serenity is the prevailing note, and this serenity has much to do with the witnessing of a solemn moment("Il est bon que ce moment-là ait des témoins"—XI, 78). But the real impact of the scene must be attributed to the unexpected religious rhetoric of the dying jacobin. Words such as *sacre, ciel, infini,* and *Dieu* come quite naturally to him. The articulation between the religious and political spheres is implicit in the comparison between the revolution of 1789 and the advent of Christ. Conversely, Christ is seen as far more radical than Christians such as Bienvenu. Would the bishop take a whip and purge the temple? Is he not afraid to face up to the brutal truths of history? The scene ends with a hint of apotheosis, as the dying man raises a finger toward heaven and refers to the "I of the infinite," whose name is God (XI, 82).

Yet somehow the ultimate message of belief seems no longer addressed to the good bishop. The real interlocutor—absent, but very present in the scene—is the atheistic socialist of the 1850s (Proudhon was very much on Hugo's mind, but so were a number of fervent Republicans who shared his exile), with whom Hugo felt he no longer had a common language. It is no doubt for the sake of this invisible adversary-ally that he has the old Conventionnel, the former representative of the people, adopt an anti-atheistic revolutionary stance: "Progress must believe in God. Goodness cannot have an impious servant. An atheist is a bad leader for mankind" (XI, 82). Matter exists and the belly exists, but the belly, as Hugo puts it later in the novel, must not be the "sole wisdom" (XI, 864). Nothing would be more intolerable than the death of the spirit. This resistance to a program for progress founded on a purely economic doctrine helps explain the novel's peculiar perspective on the proletariat, which is seen not as an honest working class but as a hotbed of misery, greed, and crime. Conversely, Hugo's brand of metaphysical socialism, which has its roots in the work of Ballanche, explains why Valjean, as Christ of the people, remains a fundamentally apolitical figure.[24]

"The Last Drop in the Chalice" ("La dernière gorgée du Calice") is the symbolic title of one of the final sections of the novel. Though the mystery of Valjean, the "homme précipice" (XI, 966), may strike obtuse inspector Javert as a simple police problem, it is of a profoundly religious nature. Valjean's self-sacrifice and self-abnegation begin with a clear image of separation from the self. This occurs as soon as the conversion following the encounter with the bishop becomes effective. Having, in a trance, stolen money from a little Savoyard boy and thus committed a crime of which he is in fact no longer capable, Valjean sees himself as "séparé de lui-même" (XI, 127). His hallucinatory experience amounts to an "ecstasy." His vision projects an immensely aggrandized image of the bishop while his own self seems to shrink and vanish ("Jean Valjean s'amoindrissait et s'effaçait"). This self-effacement is part of a system of transience and transcendence that allows Valjean, while still alive, to become a luminous mediatory figure. He continues to venerate the bishop, but it is he who acquires a halo. When the ex-convict, now a respected mayor, denounces himself to save a falsely accused vagabond, a "great light" dazzles the spectators in the courtroom (XI, 239).

Though Valjean modestly continues to look to the bishop as a model, there can be little doubt that it is he who becomes the chief intercessor. Fantine, on her deathbed, sees him "in a glory," surrounded by celestial forms. Cosette learns through him the joy of prayer. And prayer, for Hugo, is the supreme experience of contemplation and communion. Numerous passages stress Valjean's mediatory role. Little Cosette becomes less afraid in a world that has treated her cruelly, aware that "there was someone there." Walking hand in hand with Valjean, the little child feels "as though she were beside the good Lord." The text becomes more explicit still: "The entrance of that man into the destiny of that child had been the advent of God" (XI, 242, 331, 342).

Viewed in a broader thematic perspective, Valjean's spiritual adventure parallels the fall and rehabilitation of Satan in Hugo's mythology of universal pardon.[25] Even the compositional chronology is revealing. Hugo returned to the long neglected manuscript of *Les Misérables* in April 1860, only a few days after abandoning *La Fin de Satan*. The biographical and thematic links are obvious. Yet Valjean is neither a redeemed Satanic convict nor a modern apocalyptic visionary, though his name—originally Vlajean—evokes the author of the Book of Revelations.²⁶ His image quite specifically merges with that of Christ. Allusions and references abound: the Mount of Olives, Calvary, the carrying of the cross. "Lui aussi porte sa croix" ("He, Too, Carries His Cross") is the title of one of the chapters describing Valjean's agonizing progression through the sewers, with the unconscious Marius on his back. His ultimate struggle with his conscience leaves him, after a sleepless night, prostrate in a symbolic position, "his fists clenched, his arms extended at a right angle, like one taken from the cross" ("un crucifié décloué"). And when Marius comes to realize the extent of Valjean's sacrifice, he sees the convict (avatar of Satan) transfigured into the image of the Savior: "Le forçat se transfigurait en Christ" (XI, 953, 990).

The Self and the Text of God

The image of the proletarian Christ points to a conceptual difficulty at the core of Hugo's work. For how compatible is the drama of the human soul, always enacted in the singular, with the pressure of collective issues? The spiritual value bestowed on the individual's moral crisis carries politically heretical implications. Hugo himself raises the question just before recounting the heroic revolutionary struggle on the barricades. "What are the convulsions of a city compared with the mutinies of a soul?" And he adds this even more direct challenge to prevalent glorifications (his own included) of the Messianic People: "Man is a still deeper reality than the people" ("L'homme est une profondeur plus grande encore que le peuple"—XI, 807). No authorial statement could proclaim more clearly the precedence of spiritual needs over political commitments.

The priority of selfhood and the "insubmersible" nature of the *I* (as he was to put it in a later novel)²⁷ are for Hugo directly related to the principle of the Godhead, the supreme selfhood of God. The dying Conventionnel in fact defines divinity as the "moi de l'infini" (XI, 82). To be sure, the implicit divinization of the individual soul is not radically incompatible with collective political salvation as understood by post-Revolutionary doctrinaires. Neo-Catholic utopian ideologues, in the first half of the nineteenth century, having espoused the controversial idea of progress, worked out the dialectical complexities of their unorthodox stand. Lamennais, one of the most vigorous spokesmen of the new political-religious movement, stated the case with much clarity: "One must beware of thinking that individual salvation is the unique or chief aim of Jesus' teachings . . . It is mankind he wanted to save, and each individual salvation is only a means toward, and an element of, the salvation of all." And again: "Man by himself is but a fragment of being; true being is collective being."[28]

Yet there can be no doubt that for Hugo the priority of the individual soul remained unchallengeable. Politically oriented religions of humanity struck him as limiting and dangerous. The "convulsions of a city" were too closely allied to the violence of the rabble; they carried a permanent threat of *spiritual* death. For death itself should not be allowed to erase identity. Notions of reincarnation, popular with Saint-Simonian thinkers such as Prosper Enfantin and Pierre Leroux, met with Hugo's hostility. He needed to preserve the sense of personal identity.[29]

This concern for the integrity of selfhood logically extends to the realm of literature. It is hardly surprising that when, in *William Shakespeare*, Hugo surveys world literature and discusses the nature of genius, he shows a clear preference for authored texts ("oeuvres nommées") over anonymous, collective works, no matter how impressive. For certain exceptional beings—and this is perhaps the nature of genius—at once embody and transcend collectivities. They *represent* nations, as they represent the abstraction called "the people." Once again the *I* of the individual is valued as larger and deeper ("plus vaste et plus profond") than the *I* of the group (XII, 189–190).

What is involved is not merely a suprapolitical glorification of the institution of literature but an implicit correspondence between the selfhood of the genius as author and the selfhood of God as the supreme authority.[30] The fine line of demarcation between these identities affects Hugo's narrative technique. His particular type of omniscient perspective posits the essential mystery of fictional characters. Thus, Valjean is no more "explained" than is the nature of good and evil. It is as though Hugo the author believed in the inviolability of his own characters; he comments, observes, and judges—but he remains *outside* them. He may occasionally encroach on their privacy, but he never annexes them. The soul of the protagonist remains private property. As Georges Piroué astutely put it, with Hugo *I* never becomes *He*.[31]

This tendency to be at once on the side of his characters and on the side of God is further complicated as God himself is cast in the double role of witness and participant. The ubiquitous glance is thematized. "White Night," the section referring ironically both to the nuptial joys of the young couple and to the agony of Valjean, ends with rhetoric questioning itself about the impersonal pronoun *one*. The narrator, describing Valjean stretched out on his bed as though crucified, first observes that "one would have said he was dead"; then, as Valjean kisses Cosette's garments, that "one saw that he was alive." He asks: "What one?"—immediately providing the answer: "The One who is in the darkness" ("Le On qui est dans les ténèbres"—XI, 953).

Much earlier, during the Champmathieu crisis, the same impersonal pronoun already pointed to a supreme witness—but internalized and made to participate. The *on* is seen as Valjean's conscience, and this conscience is said to be synonymous with God ("Sa conscience, c'est-à-dire Dieu"—XI, 203). The impersonal pronoun thus serves as a bridge between supreme witness and supreme protagonist.

Preterition creates a further bridge, suggesting an implicit cosubstantiality or symbiosis between author and Auctor, between the authorial glance and the glance of God. When Valjean speaks in a whisper to the dead Fantine, Hugo strings together a succession of rhetorical questions about the nature of his words, and concludes on an ambiguous note: "They were heard by no one on earth." The supreme glance is not only the one that sees darkness ("Celui qui . . . voit toute l'ombre," but characterizes the ubiquitous narrator: "the eye of the drama should be everywhere present" (XI, 248, 180, 850).

If the narrative glance is ultimately never extraneous, this is precisely because at a certain level the narrative procedure locates an omniscient, immanent consciousness in the action. God is repeatedly made manifest as the "engaged" author. Or rather, he becomes a protagonist. When Valjean, at a critical juncture, attempts to flee from his conscience, he feels as though "someone" catches him in his flight and brings him back. This "someone" is obviously the same presence that always points its "mysterious indicating finger" at the more difficult road. Not everyone, of course, struggles with this absence-presence as relentlessly as Valjean. His case is, in this sense, tragically privileged. As he himself puts it to Marius toward the end of the novel, he belongs to no family; he remains "outside" ("je suis dehors"). But it is also this apparent exclusion from the human family that makes it impossible for him to silence that "someone" who speaks to him when he is alone (XI, 228, 951, 958). Valjean's secret—his mysterious status as a "tender Cain"—is the "secret of God." Conversely, the supreme author becomes, in the ex-convict's spiritual adventure, as visible as Valjean himself—chief protagonist alongside the modern redeemer figure: "Dieu était dans cette aventure aussi visible que Jean Valjean" (XI, 966–967).

The double status of the Supreme Being—author and protagonist—is far from contradictory for Hugo. God's personal intervention in history (He is the victor at Waterloo) must be read as the obverse of historical necessity—the "force des choses" (XI, 596). For this "force" of circumstances, this apparent historical determinism, is described in terms of a "hand" carrying away the "stage set" ("châssis de théâtre") of succeeding political regimes. The theatrical metaphor is appropriate. The stagehand turns out to be the director as well as the author of the scenario. "Scénario divin" is indeed the expression that Hugo uses as he writes of revolutionary turmoil. Ultimately, all of history is viewed as the text of God. In *Quatrevingt-Treize*, Hugo was to refer to God as the "rédacteur" of the grim but providential pages of the Terror. But already in *Les Misérables*, the Revolution is described as a "geste de Dieu" (XI, 862–863). And the word *geste*, with a mere variation of grammatical gender, can refer either to action or to text.

Over and above the implicit notion of writing as heroic action, Hugo problematizes the relation of text to ideology, and of ideology to text, by means of a central figure of decipherment. What asks to be *read* is indeed the divine text of history; but this very reading is a form of action as well as a form of writing. In a complex digression on the beginnings of the July Monarchy, Hugo offers the following:

> God makes visible to men his will in events, an obscure text written in a mysterious language. Men make translations of it forthwith; hasty translations, incorrect, full of mistakes, gaps, and misreadings. Very few minds understand the divine tongue. The most sagacious, the most serene, the most profound decipher slowly, and when they arrive with their text, the work has been done a while back; there are already twenty translations on the marketplace. From each translation a party is born, and from each misreading a faction; and each party believes it has the only true text, and each faction believes it possesses the light. (XI, 605–606)

In this crucial passage, translations (based on decipherments and misreadings) appear as new writings—texts on a text; and they represent renewed action in the form of ideological commitments. Thus, writing begets writing. But unless the reading-writing process is enacted by the "few minds" who comprehend the divine tongue, there is the steady danger of discrepancy between the authoritative text of origin (which is also the text of history) and the texts in history, its interpretations.

Hence the privileged status of the magus-poet, of the vatic decipherer. The poem "Les Mages" in *Les Contemplations* lists his virtues. The *mage*, actor-hero in a universal drama, carries from birth, inscribed in his skull, the text of God. Celebrant and revealer, he is fated to write the chapters of the "rituel universel," the Great Book. And this sacerdotal function, this "pontificat de l'infini," in turn leads to the ultimate breakdown of all barriers between transcendence and immanence, to the disturbing celestial fade-out ("évanouissement des cieux") of the final line of the poem. It would almost appear that, by a paradoxical reversal, the deciphering of the divine text implies the writing of it as well.[32]

Hence also the ambivalent readings called for by the key episodes: a historical reading, according to the rationale of progress and linear development; and a cyclical reading, by which the very idea of forward movement links up with a point of origin. Between the two, a complex system of exchange sets up elaborate binary structures.

The Two Readings

The major digressions again best illustrate the compositional principle of the novel. The parallel between the prison from which Valjean escapes and the Petit-Picpus convent in which he and Cosette hide from police pursuit (both are places of "expiation," albeit in a different spirit) provides the opportunity for a sustained thematization of binary opposites. For the concept of monasticism, as Hugo expounds it in a lengthy section entitled "Parenthesis," is filled with contradictions (error and innocence, devotion and ignorance, bliss and inhumanity) requiring the double answer *yes* and *no*: "Un couvent, c'est une contradiction" (XI, 396).

To account for some of the negative postures, there is Hugo's recurrent terror of being buried alive, the association of the convent-tomb with the black radiance of death (XI, 390). The yellow teeth of the nuns, as Hugo imagines them (no toothbrush, he claims, ever found its way into a convent), symbolize a spectral "death in life" that is the essence of conventual existence. But this personal revulsion in the face of self-denial and self-laceration must be replaced in a broader ideological context. It is in the name of history and progress that monastic life is here denounced. This abstract condemnation echoes the antimonastic prejudices of the eighteenth-century *philosophes*, as well as the themes of repressiveness and sterility associated with convents in Revolutionary literature.[33] It is the voice of history itself, insofar as history is conceived both as a force and a value, that condemns the convent as a ghost of the past.

The rationalistic perspective merges with personal revulsion. Hugo's terms for censuring monasticism belong revealingly to the realm of pathology. The moral and social noxiousness of conventual existence is seen as a threat to life. Monasteries are a "leprosy," a "consumption" ("phtisie"); monastic withdrawal is castration (Hugo puns: "Claustration, castration"); the world of cloisters is a world of "putrescence" whose infection spreads like a plague (XI, 391–392). Even worse, ignorance and superstition lead to self-destruction and to the sanctification of cruelty. The monastic excesses of Catholic Spain, exacerbated by fanatical asceticism, bring the world of convents (with their damp *in pace*, dungeons, iron collars, oozing walls) uncannily close to the most punitive forms of incarceration.

The parallel between convent and prison reaches beyond the register of horror into the area of political and moral concerns. The double denunciation operates at two levels. Progress calls for the disappearance of cloisters, as it demands the abolition of the death sentence—and eventually the eradication of all jails. More radical than most of his liberal contemporaries, who merely thought of controlling the carceral world through a more rational system of penology, Hugo had visions of a world in which prison would be as inconceivable as eternal damnation. Social and metaphysical dreams were ultimately to blend in a common utopia. Hell itself was to be effaced, and Satan saved. "Never a chain, never a cell," concludes Saint François de Paule in Hugo's late play *Torquemada*. God in person, as though to confirm this notion of progress transposed to the metaphysical realm, explains in the ultimate lines of *La Fin de Satan* that once prisons are destroyed, Gehenna too will be abolished: "la prison détruite abolit la géhenne" (X, 1762). This is, of course, the deep secret of the oracular *bouche d'ombre*, the voice from the dark: "No eternal hell."[34]

Yet there is a striking ambivalence in Hugo's digression on convents. If one of the chapters of this excursus is entitled "Precautions to Be Taken in Censure," this is not be be understood as mere lip service to a venerable institution. Hugo uses the word "respect" several times, but the word acquires a special resonance by contiguity with the word "infinite": "Whenever we meet with the infinite in man . . . we are seized with a feeling of respect." The convent may be a tomb, but it is also the place of luminous spirituality; it oppresses, but also liberates; it is a ghost of the past, yet it is a visionary outpost.[35] The convent, moreover, has all the ineffable charms of the secret garden of love, the *hortus conclusus.*

But this love, cultivated in solitude, is of a transcendental nature; its manifestation is prayer, which brings the infinite within (the "infini en nous") in contact with the infinite beyond (the "infini hors de nous"). Prayer, according to Hugo, is precisely the link between the two infinites: an act of mediation and communion. Valjean's first experience, after the redemptive fall into the convent garden, is to hear a hymn of prayer which brings him and Cosette to their knees. The scene rehearses an earlier one: the ex-convict's kneeling on the pavement, in the dark of night, in front of the bishop's house. The bishop, we are told, raises prayer to the point of "superhuman aspiration." Such praying before prayer suggests an endless spiritual chain which, in the Petit-Picpus convent is ritualistically enacted by the devotion of the Perpetual Adoration. This arduous twelve-hour prayer, which entails kneeling and prostration, is described by Hugo as "grand jusqu'au sublime" (XI, 394, 358, 91, 373).

It is difficult to overstate the significance of prayer for Hugo. "One can no more pray too much than love too much," he writes in a chapter devoted to the bishop (XI, 91). One of the chapters in the convent digression carries the terse title "Absolute Excellence of Prayer." More interesting still—especially in the context of a historical denunciation of the parasitic nature of monasticism—is the relation Hugo establishes between a life of prayer and "useful" contemplation. Hugo goes so far as to assert that there is perhaps no more sublime activity and no more "useful work" than that performed by these cloistered spirits (XI, 397).

Polemical and ideological reasons once again help explain apparent inconsistencies. In the philosophical preface to the novel, prayer is defined as the attempted "dialogue" with the unknown (XII, 71). This contact with mystery takes on full significance when measured against political and economic preoccupations. For Hugo, the self-styled "socialist," disavows solidarity with his fellow socialists, while claiming to praise a common ideal. A simple shift from the first person to the second person plural establishes the rift: "Your economic problems are one of the glorious preoccupations of the nineteenth century" (XII, 65). The manipulation of the possessive adjective from the expected *nos* to *vos* ("vos problèmes économiques") keeps atheistic socialism at a distance. The fact is that even before balancing *no* and *yes* with regard to the validity of monasticism, Hugo opted for the latter— in flagrant contradiction of all his strictures. "To *no*, there is but one reply: *yes.*" The words that follow make the polemical stance explicit: "Nihilism is powerless" ("Le nihilisme est sans portée"— XI, 395).

Beyond the polemical intention there lurks an argument *pro domo*. The notion of a "useful" contemplation is surely related to the poet's views of his own activities as prophetic poet, and more specifically as the visionary author of *Les Contemplations* (1856). "Contemplation leads to action" is the terse summation of the chapter on the excellence of prayer. The desire to reconcile prayer and revolution is paralleled by the urge to vindicate the contemplative mode—and poetic activity in general—as perfectly compatible with moral and political engagement. But such engagement requires separation, distance, abnegation. Exile, political and spiritual, becomes the convenient symbol. Hence the concluding aphorism: "Whoever goes into self-exile seems venerable to us" (XI, 397). The sentence, ostensibly referring to the nuns, has also a very personal ring, coming as it does from the one who chose voluntarily to remain on the island of Guernsey—away from the France of Napoleon III. It also confirms, beyond polemics and self-glorification, the deeply religious animus of *Les Misérables*.

Muck, but Soul

The other major digression thematizing a striking antithesis is the description of the Paris sewer system, which precedes Valjean's ultimate escape. The link between sewer and convent may not be immediately apparent; yet both are places of salvation, and both—

one literally, the other metaphorically—are places of putrescence ("Leur putrescibilité est évidente," Hugo writes of convents—XI, 392). But convents at least have gardens; and gardens, especially when protected by walls, are idyllic sites in Hugo's private mythology. In the bowels of the megalopolis, however, there is no visible reprieve from horror. "The Intestine of the Leviathan" is the title of the digression. The terms connote the monstrous as well as the excremental. The section heading points to the digestive system of the modern Babylon, filled with "caecums" (an anatomical detail) and infectious cesspools. Here too, as with convents, Hugo marshals the lexicon of pathology. The "evacuation crypt" (*crypte exutoire*) shows "herpetic ooze" (*suintement dartreux*) on its walls. Miasmas pollute the tract.

The other recurrent nightmare image, tightening the underlying link between the sewer and the convent episodes, is that of being buried alive. As Valjean moves deeper and deeper into the mire and is about to be swallowed by a gigantic mudhole, Hugo compares his ordeal to that of a fisherman on some deserted beach being sucked down by treacherous quicksand, condemned to a ghastly burial—"long, infallible, implacable"—in which the grave turns into a tide, reaching from the depths of the earth toward a living human being. Earth, having become as perfidious as water, is capable of drowning a man. This convertibility of solid into liquid is announced, at the very outset of the downward journey to the cloacal world, in a comparison between Paris and the sea (XI, 895, 885). So also the terror of being buried alive ("Inexpressible horror of dying this way!") is prefigured in the cemetery scene, after Valjean agrees to be carried out from the convent in a coffin and subjected to a mock burial.

The escape motif inevitably conjures up carceral metaphors, and those in turn lead to figurations of hell. A narrow passageway that ends in the form of a funnel is "logical in jail" but totally "illogical" in a sewer. Valjean, ironically, seems to have escaped into a prison. When release is finally glimpsed, Valjean—a reincarnation of the archetypal convict—is compared to a "condemned soul" who, from the midst of hell's furnace, suddenly perceives an exit (XI, 898). Revealingly, the "Intestin de Léviathan" section concludes with a most ambiguous image related to the disturbing figure of Marat, who fascinated Hugo both as the revolutionary *ami du peuple* and the embodiment of evil. The episode refers to the astonishing discovery, made during a survey of the sewer system, of a shredded sheet of fine batiste with an embroidered crown, a tattered and filthy remnant of what was once an elegant bedsheet that had served as Marat's shroud and that had been a souvenir of a youthful affair with an aristocratic lady (XI, 880). The antithetical elements (*ami du peuple* and aristocrat, horror and elegance, sex and death) are heightened by the realistic and symbolic setting juxtaposing excrement and salvation.

The association of sewer and revolution is ironic not only because Marat's rag is mixed with vestiges of natural cataclysms (the "shellfish of the deluge") but because violence and survival come into dialectical clash. The allusion to the deluge in the last line of the section has both destructive and redemptive connotations. The linear time of the revolution of men seems denied by the cyclical time of the "revolutions of the globe." Both do, however, function in a salvational scheme. The next section ("Muck, but Soul") in fact opens with a fall into the providential spring-trap of safety. The sewer turns out to be the place of "the most absolute security" (XI, 885).

Throughout the long digression, negative elements are in fact consistently translated into positive terms. The purgatorial features of the underworld mean purgation; the voiding crypt in the monstrous digestive apparatus signifies the cleansing of lesions; the burial alive foreshadows salvation; the apocalyptic horrors serve the vision of redemption. The value bestowed on the downward journey to the end of darkness is altogether consistent with the central vision of the novel. The ultimate metaphorical descent is prefigured in the section entitled "Marius Enters the Shadow"; the young man's journey to the barricades is compared to a "descente de marches noires." But it is in the subsequent literal descent to the sewer that the metaphor is most thoroughly worked out: "Jean Valjean had fallen from one circle of hell to another" (XI, 788, 886).

Contamination by diverse mythic elements signals, however,

the difficulty of a strictly theological reading. The branch of the sewer situated under Montmartre is described as a "dédaléen" network. Elsewhere, Valjean is compared to the prophet Jonah in the belly of the whale. Later still, the police patrol in the sewer network is compared to evil spirits ("larves"), to mastiffs that evoke images of Cerberus-like underworld creatures (XI, 887, 889). Such shifts and blendings of images relate the theological allegory to broader notions of a legendary quest. Valjean's entire career is indeed seen retrospectively as a combination of Christ-like sacrifice ("Voilà l'homme") and initiatory adventure: "il a tout traversé" (XI, 992).

But the sacrificial quest is also the poet's adventure. The downward voyage has visionary implications as early as in the poem "La Pente de la rêverie" (1830), not only because of Hugo's reverence for the work of Dante but because he believes that a vertiginal spiral leads to the ineffable "sphère invisible." Only a dangerous voyage into the night can bring one closer to the fateful enigma which it is the poet's mission to confront. In that sense, Valjean is also the *figura* of the visionary poet. During his daydreams in the Petit-Picpus convent (the echoes of "La Pente de la rêverie" are unmistakable), he slowly fathoms the "spirales sans fond de la rêverie" (XI, 425).

Valjean's visionary dispositions are at work in a strictly *moral* context. The darkness of the sewer is symbolic of the insight granted Valjean by a life of suffering. Just as the pupil dilates in darkness, so "the soul dilates in misfortune," until at last it finds God (XI, 886). Valjean's salvation, literally and metaphorically, depends on a fall. Hence the terse authorial comment: "Descendre, c'était en effet le salut possible." If Valjean is fated to be a martyr of the dark descent ("O première marche à descendre, que tu es sombre! O seconde marche, que tu es noire!"), it is because espousal of misery is what Hugo calls "sublimation" (XI, 893, 952). Unlike inflicted prison sufferings, which made Valjean morally worse, self-imposed sacrifices elevate and liberate him. Having shouldered the wounded body of Marius and reached the bottom of his underground Calvary, shivering, wet, and filthy, Valjean discovers that his soul is filled with "a strange light" (XI, 898). Once more he falls on his knees—this time, however, not before an intercessor. God is present to him in the dark. Valjean's foot, in the mire, has found the beginning of the upward slope. He can reascend toward life.

The ambivalences of the sewer episode and its religious symbolization are summed up in the ultimate collapse of the metaphor. Valjean himself, the man-precipice, is described as a human "cloaca" venerating innocence in the form of Cosette. And this metaphor is then telescoped into a larger trope comprising God himself. The figure of darkness, we are told, is "le secret de Dieu" (XI, 967).

The Death of Valjean

The logic of the story calls for an apotheosis. When Marius, having discovered the extent of Valjean's sacrifice, rushes with Cosette to his humble dwelling, they arrive in time to witness a scene of death and transfiguration. Hugo does more than compete with Balzac, whose père Goriot also dies as a "Christ de la paternité"[36] (though bitterly, and without the love of his daughters). It is as though Hugo had set out to rewrite this scene of pathos, and to give it an unironic twist. Hugo's chapter reveals the "majesty of the soul"; it confirms Marius' glimpse of a redeemer's destiny: "Le forçat se transformait en Christ." The scene marks a farewell to worldly ties. The little copper crucifix Valjean takes down from the wall is symbolically contrasted with the young couple's recently acquired fortune. Between him and them "there was already a wall" (XI, 990, 995).

Yet irony is reintroduced at a level which is not that of pathos. Two difficulties loom over the end of this novel whose preface denounces social damnation, the "hells" of modern society, and the degradation of the "proletariat": not a word is said about social conditions, while private property is justified, indeed sanctified. Is this closing a signal of the profoundly apolitical nature of a book that pretends to be committed to social and political change? What has become of the revolutionary revelation experienced earlier by

Marius, whose apprenticeship of historical realities is presented by the narrator as exemplary of the best minds of his time? Enjolras' heroic death as a revolutionary crusader, as well as the presentation of the barricades as a modern Golgotha, surely called for an ending that was not so squarely placed outside history.

Without concurring with Pierre Barbéris' denunciation of Hugo's deep-seated complicity with the bourgeois social order,[37] one must admit that Hugo's revolutionary rhetoric often camouflages the latent yearnings of an *homme d'ordre*. Or rather, revolution itself, in Hugo's private ideology, is made to serve the demands for stability and continuity. Thus, revolution is seen not only as radically different from and even opposed to rebellion and revolt; it is understood specifically as a "vaccination" for any form of *jacquerie* or popular uprising (XI, 708). This revealing unwillingness to understand revolution in terms of class warfare, at a time in Hugo's life when he claimed to have been converted long before to the redemptive virtues of socialism, must be read against his much earlier acceptance speech at the Académie Française (1841), in which he paradoxically invoked the great achievements of the French Revolution as a prophylactic defense against new revolutions—and this precisely in terms of the immunization metaphor: "une vaccine qui inocule le progrès et qui préserve des révolutions."[38]

As for the insistence on money and inheritance in the death scene, it may appear doubly surprising. Materialistic France was earlier criticized by Hugo for its genuflections before the all-powerful *écu* (XI, 864). The bishop, whose immaterial presence hovers over Valjean's death, loved specifically to recall the Church Father's admonition: "Place your expectation in Him to whom there is no succession" (XI, 61). Yet matters are not quite so simple. The money motif is from the outset linked to the figure of the bishop, whose accountings of diocesan administration, charities, and household expenses are described in elaborate detail. Bishop Myriel not only handles considerable sums, but it is he who provides the ex-convict with practical advice as to how to make money. It is this advice which is ultimately responsible for the fortune that Valjean accumulates and gives to Cosette. A direct link thus connects the spiritual message to the notion of a material legacy. The closing pages significantly juxtapose terms such as *commerce*, *argent*, *fortune*, and *léguer* with Valjean's expressed pride in being poor, his desire to have no name inscribed on his tombstone, and his conviction that it is a mistake to believe that one can *own* anything; for all is part of a larger inheritance. Symbolically, Valjean brought the 600,000-franc dowry in the form of banknotes wrapped in a package that looks like an "octavo volume" (XI, 926).

On the other hand, money is also associated, specifically through Valjean's rehabilitation process, with bourgeois virtues and values. In jail, Valjean learns how to save. He is quick with figures. Once settled in Montreuil-sur-Mer, he sees to it that his slender capital is "made fruitful by order and care." He helps Fantine to "live honestly by her own labor." It is through his eyes that the "evil poor," typified by Thénardier, are seen as more repulsive and more ferocious than the evil rich (XI, 161, 173, 619). To reduce poverty without reducing wealth seems to be the author's ideal! Valjean's advice to the young couple sounds like a trivial apologia of wealth: "Why not take advantage of being rich? Wealth adds to happiness" (XI, 709, 974). But how is this to be reconciled with Valjean's bitter knowledge of the limits of human happiness? Above all, what does this concern for money and legacies have to do with the solemn, transfiguring hour of his death?

Two answers are conceivable—besides the simplistic relegation of Valjean/Hugo to the limbo of petit-bourgeois utilitarianism. The first harks back to Hugo's polemical stance in his continuing debate with his fellow "socialists." The sacralization of property can be seen as a blow at atheistic materialism, as well as at Proudhon's denunciation of private property in *Qu'est-ce que la propriété?* (1840). The other interpretation derives from textual and metaphysical rather than polemical elements. *Les Misérables* is indeed predicated on the idea of redemption (from the Latin *redimere*: to buy back); and the French equivalent, *rachat*, is clearly proposed in dramatic as well as metaphorical terms. Not only is the silver piece Valjean steals from the little Savoyard boy (his last evil action) metaphorized into the staring eye of his own conscience (XI, 125), but the bishop, in offering Valjean a set of silver candlesticks, explicitly glosses this act of generosity: "Jean Valjean, my brother, you no longer belong to evil but to good. It is your soul that I am buying" (XI, 123). In the symbolic economy of a text that weaves individual redemptive efforts into the broader theme of collective redemption, it is striking that revolution itself, in its violence, is accounted for in terms of a terrible *price* to pay ("achats terribles") in order to achieve the future. "Une révolution est un péage" (XI, 835). But this ideal future, heavily paid for by history, also marks an exit from history.

Such a notion of an eventless ideal future reached through the tollgate of historical catastrophe, such a merger of individual and collective redemption, casts additional light on the special religious nature of Valjean's death. What is suggested—much as in the death scene of the Conventionnel, before whom the bishop kneels—is not a Christian regenerative meeting with the Maker but an effacement signifying a merger with infinity.[39] This obliteration-transcendence, this erasure of all traces, is a recurrent feature in the work of Hugo. The disappearance or absorption into the cosmic whole is repeated in the submersion-death endings of *Les Travailleurs de la mer* and *L'Homme qui rit*. The one-page epilogue of *Les Misérables* confirms this principle of death as effacement. Valjean's tomb in the Père-Lachaise cemetery is not only nameless, but even the little poem penciled on the stone by an anonymous hand has become illegible under the effacing action of the rain.

A fundamental Hugolian principle is at work, relating the prophecies of undoing and reconstruction to the dynamics of creation. The literary process itself is symbolized by the image of the dismantled book. In his philosophical preface to *Les Misérables*, Hugo writes of the relentless forces of transformation that depend on destruction, of disintegrations that are germinations (XII, 16, 35). These patterns of cyclical deconstruction are repeated in the later novels; they are related specifically to readings of history that problematize the ideological assumptions of the historical novel. But already in *Les Misérables*, there is the suggestion that Hugo's dynamic vision of history in progress ultimately leads not to a justification of history, but to the dream of an ahistorical point in time where history is denied and there will be "no more events" (XI, 835).

5

The Toilers
of the Sea

Le flot recommence . . .

After the large-scale evocation of Paris in *Les Misérables*—a Paris transfigured by memory and the perspective of his island exile—Hugo turned to confront the ocean. Writing his vast narrative of the sea, he hesitated about the title. He thought of calling it *L'Abîme*, a title that, hinting at sea perils, unfathomable depths, and the mystery of creation, corresponded to the mood of contemplation he associated with the deepest and loftiest poetry.[1] Only a year or so earlier, in *William Shakespeare* (1864), which had turned into a dithyramb in honor of genius (his own included), he had referred to the "hommes océans," the inexhaustible creative spirits of all time, the revelatory poets who had known the "intoxication of the high seas."[2]

He finally chose as the title for his new novel *Les Travailleurs de la mer*, thus stressing from the outset the notions of toil and unremitting effort. The plural—*les travailleurs*—set this toil in an epic perspective. Hugo's notes for the original preface make his intention clear. After dealing with "Misery" in his previous novel, he was now attempting "the glorification of Work." Why, he asked, should the epic be reserved for war? "Le travail peut être épique." The epic struggle against the *ananke* of the physical world had metaphysical implications. It signified even more than a struggle with an angel: it represented a direct confrontation with God (XII, 797).

At the level of realism, the novel describes daily activities on the island of Guernsey, with which Hugo had become thoroughly familiar. What interested him, however, was not the sailors' life of toil and hardship, which he had idealized in the poem "Les Pauvres Gens." Nor was it the technical mastery of the sea, though the novel incorporates an abundant nautical vocabulary—inventories of harsh-sounding words, which the reader is unlikely ever to have encountered and which Hugo doubtless gleaned from various dictionaries and specialized works. His deeper interest in toil had to do with the taming of natural forces, as illustrated in one of the novel's central episodes: the protagonist's daring retrieval of an engine from a wrecked boat. This lonely rescue on a savage reef is an allegory of salvation and rebirth. The engine is literally "delivered" from the belly of the shipwrecked *Durande* under the most trying circumstances, as the hero, Gilliatt, struggles against darkness, winds, fever, the tides, the fury of the storm, and finally a horrendous octopus. He is the epitome of the worker, summing up all human resourcefulness and labor. Capable of improvising as blacksmith, carpenter, mechanic, and engineer, this new Crusoe reinvents and reconstructs tools with odd pieces of wreckage.

But beyond the exploits of the protagonist, Hugo projects visions of cosmic labor. This universal work—"travail d'ensemble" (XII, 809)—goes on unbeknown to the individual participant in the larger, collective drama. The worker is but an atom in the universal perspective, much as the atom is the "worker" in the immeasurably vast work of the universe. Worker and work confront each other at every level of *Les Travailleurs de la mer*. All of nature is in steady labor. *Sex, procreation,* and *work* seem at times like interchangeable concepts. If clouds are described as lasciviously in pursuit of one another (XII, 789), this is not to be taken as a baroque effect. Everywhere Hugo deciphers divine fullness, mysterious pregnancy, the universal sap at work ("l'effort panique et sacré de la sève en travail"—XII, 790). All nature is engaged in nuptials. But this pervasive sexual drive (*rut*) and fearful coitus also mean destruction. In "Philosophie. Commencement d'un livre," Hugo points out the fundamental link connecting sexuality, inexhaustible transformation, and ruthless devastation.

The revels of nature are seasoned with disasters. The mighty encounter of forces leading up to the "festival" of the storm is described as a feast marked by extermination. Hugo's metaphorical verve rises to the occasion. In anticipation of the great clash of elements, the sea itself is "in heat" (XII, 722). One of the principal "toilers" suggested by the plural title of the novel is, in fact, the endlessly active sea: "La mer travaille" (XII, 26). The dynamics of the ocean shape weird, even artistic sea constructs; but they also wreak havoc, subjecting the hardest granite to their erosive power. In "L'Archipel de la Manche," a long preliminary chapter that he finally decided to publish separately, Hugo speaks of the "prodigieux travail" steadily eroding and reshaping the Atlantic coastline (XII, 515).[3] Creative effacement is one of the telling oxymoronic images in this poetic fiction about sea change.

Opening Signals

Les Travailleurs de la mer begins with haunting suggestions of effacement and dissolution: footprints and handwriting in the snow. The overture imposes determining images: it is Christmas on the island of Guernsey; three figures—a child, a young woman, a man—walk in the same direction but at a distance of a hundred feet from each other; silence reigns. Among these figures there is no visible link. At one point, the young woman in this dream landscape turns around to look back, stops, and with her finger traces some letters in the snow. When the man reaches the place where she halted, he reads his own name—Gilliatt—inscribed in the snow. He gazes for quite a while at his own name next to the tiny footprints in the snow, then continues his way, absorbed in thought.

The snow blanketing this island landscape is clearly an ambiguous element, neither solid nor liquid, neither earth nor water, related to death but also to survival: the word *Christmas* appears in English in the first sentence. The footprints and the inscribed name are, however, bound to disappear: the snow will melt. What is remarkable about the opening paragraphs—Hugo himself uses the word *remarquable*—is that they serve as prefiguration and also project, as it were, the memory of the text. Gilliatt, stopping at exactly the same spot in the last chapter, will recall how Déruchette had written his name in the snow. But where is that snow now? "Il y avait longtemps que cette neige était fondue" (XII, 789). Conversely, oblivion is metaphorized into melted snow. The girl's memory of the event vanishes as snow melts: "Chez Déruchette le souvenir s'évanouissait comme la neige fond" (XII, 595).

The memory of the text is, of course, different from the memory of the fickle protagonist. Textual retrospection implies prefigurative structures, as well as an order of simultaneity. The novel ends as it begins: with an effacement. As Gilliatt watches the boat that carries away Déruchette and his unfulfilled dream, he allows himself to be gradually overtaken by the rising tide. The verbs glide into each other tellingly: *s'évanouir, mêler, pâlir, s'amoindrir, se dissiper*, and, at the point of suicide, *s'effacer*. "At the moment when the vessel vanished on the horizon, the head disappeared under water." The instant of self-effacement by suicide corresponds to the indefinite pronoun *rien* in the last sentence of the text.

The symbolic instabilities on this eerie Christmas morning, as the narrative gets under way, cannot escape notice. Earth and water are shown to be in more than close proximity; they have blended, merged in the inconstant form of snow. And snow is treacherous. It is related to death, in ways that also suggest, in Hugo's fiction, the disturbing discovery of sexual identity. At the beginning of Hugo's next novel, *L'Homme qui rit*, an abandoned boy encounters a hanged man on a blizzard-swept plateau, then is led by footprints in the snow to a dead woman, whose infant daughter—his future love—he heroically saves.[4]

Les Travailleurs de la mer begins, moreover, with deliberate references to the writing process. The footprints, the finger tracings, and the whiteness of the snow all point to a textual reality. The title of the first chapter is "A Word Written on a Blank Page." But the whiteness of this *page blanche* is ambiguous: it relates to the virginal sheet on which the word is inscribed, but also to the snow which condemns the written word to obliteration. Unavoidably, the question arises: Why would a novel that opens with an explicit reference to textuality also imply from the outset the disintegration of the text?

What is written on the road by the sea is not just any word but a name, and this stresses the numenic nature of the act of writing. The written name (Gilliatt's own) falls into the unexplored depths ("profondeur inconnue"—XII, 597) of his consciousness, thus locating in the act of writing the point of intersection between horizontal and vertical images. Two axes are delineated: the horizontal axis, represented by surface snow and surface water, as well as by numerous references to landmarks that have vanished; and the vertical axis of immersion, which corresponds to the descent into reverie—the submersion into the awesome, metaphorizing realm of dreams. Gilliatt carries in him an abyss. The word *abîme*, which was to be the original title, recurs in the text. Gilliatt is not only chronically "pensif," but he explicitly experiences the "immersion sans fond de la rêverie" (XII, 604). Immersion and submersion—with their connotation of plunging and sinking— become the metaphor of metaphorical inversion. The posthumous *Promontorium somnii*, Hugo's pre-Freudian meditation on dreams which he wrote at the time he conceived *Les Travailleurs de la mer*, presents a vertical shuttle as the condition of poetic fabrication: Jacob the poet, the open-eyed sleeper, watches his own creations climb his dream ladder. But this ascent toward the light is possible only because consciousness has surrendered to the vertiginous downward spiral. "La rêverie est un creusement," Hugo writes, echoing his early poem "La Pente de la rêverie," in which images of descent and submersion lead to a vision of the "double sea of time and space" (XII, 456, 465; IV, 429).

This association of water imagery with poetic reverie and the subconscious explains why the sea—as J.-B. Barrère so aptly put it—literally has "the last word."[5] The double vanishing of the departing ship and the hero's life in the penultimate sentence leads to the final statement: "There was nothing left but the sea." But this *nothing* is all-embracing. The sea is mother and nurse (*mer* and *mère* are conveniently homonymous in French). In the sea's vast laboratory of metaphors, the appeasement of death becomes indistinct from the appeasement of the womb, the cradle, and the nursery. At one point, after the storm, the now tranquil and tranquilizing sea is "murmuring like a nurse beside her child" (XII, 753).

"What an Artist Is the Abyss!"

The violence and treachery of life-giving forces, the soothing yet mysterious presence of the vast expanse, the disquieting awareness of depth—all these are encompassed by Hugo's sea poetry in *Les Travailleurs de la mer*. Some of the most astonishing prose Hugo ever wrote describes the conflict of water and reefs, the haunting monologue of the waves, the sculpting power of tides, currents, and winds. Shortly before the shipwreck, as the *Durande* plunges into the fog, it is as if the reader, too, has crossed a line of demarcation, penetrating into a world that is drenched in the strange light of visionary poetry. A diffuse whiteness enshrouds the death-bound vessel, and all becomes wan and pallid. One of Hugo's favorite adjectives, *blême* ("Tout était blafard et blême"— XII, 643), suggests the frightful and revelatory "white obscurity" of an apocalypse. The circumscribed opaqueness of the shipwreck scene allows glimpses of cosmic images. As the *Durande* glides through the ominous quiet, its long trail of smoke becomes "a black comet in a white sky." The fog obviously provides more than just a setting for catastrophe. The experience of otherworldly luminosity, of the whiteness of the night, has been for some time—

as Jean Gaudon so convincingly demonstrated—the prime condition of Hugo's "contemplative" poetry. It is what makes *Les Contemplations* essentially "un livre blême."[6]

The sea itself is viewed as a shaping artist, a tireless carver of stone. Hugo's seascape is the archetype of all contrasts. Next to the fog, the rock. Hewer, carver, lapidary, and architect, the sea exercises its willful fantasies even on granite: it constructs pilasters and lays beams; works out bas-reliefs, delicate carvings, and arabesques; builds vast underground monuments. "What an artist is the abyss!" (XII, 693). But this convergence of savage force and artful design results in more than "architectures of chance"; it provides the analogue for poetic creation, and, more specifically, projects the patterns of Hugo's own poetic imagination. In making the sea the architect of an underwater city, Hugo converts the cliché "Paris as ocean" into a vision of the ocean as Paris. The inversion-conversion cannot be explained merely in terms of the exile's nostalgia for the capital. The spectacular reflection seems related to a mythopoetic fascination with selfhood and identity. It is surely not a coincidence that the towers of Notre-Dame de Paris, as well as the column-like rocks of the Douvres reef, present themselves in the form of an immense capital H. (See Illustration 12.)

The imaginary sea constructs do indeed have personal aesthetic implications for Hugo. The novel projects a vision of fluid architectures (the reef is "tempest petrified"—XII, 690), a fluctuating solidity consisting of a "battle of lines," a dynamic process that allows for no finished product. This transformational submarine edifice, with its illogical equilibrium and apparently senseless *babélisme*, involves an aesthetic that is diametrically opposed to the Parnassian ideal of statuesque fixity. In a somewhat later text, referring again to intimate contact with the ocean, Hugo speaks of the "terrifying pleasure" caused by its unceasing movement, its lack of sobriety, its chaotic harmonies and extravagances—in other words, all the characteristics he proudly recognizes in his own writings. Much as he claims to have appreciated Flaubert's recently published *Salammbô*, he was surely not in deep sympathy with such an epic of immobility.[7] His own notion of the epic is never monumental but rather teratological. It is animated by monsters. The same epic savagery is associated with the sea. The ocean, in *La Légende des siècles*, undergoes avatars of animal fierceness: it is a *fauve*, a wild beast, a reptile, a hydra, a triple Cerberus, a dragon.[8] In *Les Travailleurs de la mer* such epic and mythical fantasy culminates in flourishes of Pan's "fanfare prométhéenne," which seems to announce some of Rimbaud's exuberant imagery (XII, 721). It is hardly surprising that the word *blême* finds its way into Rimbaud's most Hugolian lines in "Le Bateau ivre": "où, flottaison blême / Et ravie, un noyé pensif parfois descend." All the key terms of this stanza about the "Poem of the Sea" can be traced back to Hugo's oceanic lexicon.

The Ambiguity of Progress

The recommencing sea, though indifferent to historical time, does not cancel history. The peripheral Channel islands may seem located outside the currents of events, yet the word *Christmas*—the seasonal opening signal of the narrative—is immediately followed by the temporal indication *182–*, a reference to an entire decade that clearly places the narrative in a historical perspective. A later chapter stresses the fact that this period of the Bourbon Restoration is a time of political reaction. Topical allusions to the imminent fall of Villèle and the death of Pope Leo XII, referred to in snatches of conversation at the captains' table in the St.-Malo inn, situate the action of the novel more precisely in the late 1820s, immediately preceding new insurrections in France. Numerous other passing references to exiles and fugitives, and to arms sales to the tsar for the repression of Poland, conjure up the larger background of revolutionary and counterrevolutionary tides.

Precise references to the French Revolution occur throughout the text. Lethierry, the owner of the *Durande*, is not only a "revolutionist" in navigation (his is the first steamship to link Guernsey to the French mainland), but his devotion to progress is explicitly inspired by the Revolution. This anticlerical, freethinking reader of Voltaire and of the *Encyclopédie* is proud, as he puts it, to have been "suckled" by '89 ("J'ai tété 89"). If his *Durande* is launched on a fourteenth of July, this is not a coincidence. Lethierry cries out to the sea: "The Parisians took the Bastille; now we take thee!" (XII, 584). The reader is even given to understand that the old skipper, known on Guernsey as "the Frenchman" and later defined by a double-substantive metaphor as "l'homme révolution," had happened to be in Paris in 1789 and had probably been involved in one way or another in the assault on the king's fortress.[9]

Gilliatt's own background seems linked to revolutionary events. His mother (she is known as the "Frenchwoman," partly because she does not go to church) had settled on the island with her small child "toward the end of the Revolution" (XII, 559). Gilliatt himself is looked upon with suspicion by the tradition-bound islanders, who resent and envy his daring and resourcefulness. His rescue of the engine is hailed by Lethierry as a great feat, as an act of almost superhuman heroism, with the exclamation "Quelle révolution!" (XII, 771). Even the fearless little leader of the children's gang, the "déniquoiseaux," brings to mind motifs and attitudes associated by Hugo with revolutionary street fighting in *Les Misérables*. This carefree orphan, this son of chance also "born in France," this cousin of Gavroche, would have felt perfectly at home on the Parisian barricades.

The bond between revolution and progress in the form of the steamship is obvious. In the struggle of human intelligence against the brutal forces of nature, in man's insurgence against what Hugo calls the "*ananké* of things," the skills of the toilers of the sea become emblematic of heroic revolutionary achievement. Ulysses the traveler is, we are told, greater than Achilles the fighter (XII, 816). But more important than this glorification of the navigator (Columbus in the poem "Océan"—IX, 677) is the metaphor that links Fulton, the steamship designer, to Danton, the fiery revolutionary leader. Pierre Albouy put it well: in the struggle that situates technical progress in the broad revolutionary perspective, "Fulton complète Danton."[10]

But progress, which in the larger epic of human endeavor is to substitute freedom for necessity, has an ambiguous status in the novel. The steam engine is saved not by modern means but by primitive skills; it is retrieved by the old-fashioned *panse*, Gilliatt's small sailboat. Progress is in fact repeatedly seen as moving in a problematic, if not nefarious direction. The revolver bought by the villain Clubin is ironically referred to as a "useful invention" recently imported from America.[11] Even more telling than these incidental ironies is the narrator's attachment to a past that is being obliterated by so-called progress. He bewails the disappearance of the old Guernsey. Landmarks are gone, and the spirit of the old place is dead. But in the same paragraph, and without any transition, Hugo states that "thanks to progress" everything on the Channel Islands has been transformed—that where there was "darkness" now there is "light" (XII, 610).

Remarks such as these become less incongruous if one recalls that Gilliatt is essentially a nocturnal figure, accomplishing, so the rumor has it, an "oeuvre de nuit." They must also be set against the many ironic references to local superstitions—references that fill, in a seemingly digressive manner, the early chapters of the book. Repeated mention of such superstitions—the islanders' belief in witchcraft and a haunted house, the *Durande*'s reputation as a "devil-boat"—doubtless contribute to local color and realism. But these superstitions also possess a poetic power that inspires Hugo's graphic imagination. On a page of the manuscript of the novel, he drew a picture of the demonic king of the Auxcriniers, whose slimy belly, warty skull, and sinister grin at the sight of ships in distress are described in the same chapter in which Gilliatt is said to be suspected of witchcraft (XII, 562–563; see Illustrations 11, 15, and 16).

The paradox is striking. Ironic rationalism and enlightened thought denounce intolerance, yet they do not cancel an underlying yearning for darkness; they even feed this yearning. Thus, the superstitions of the islanders help establish from the outset a climate of poetic unreality and mystery, as the text glides from the reassuring world of facts to that of fantasy and even terror. The haunted house is simply a smugglers' meeting place; but it is also a nest of darkness and specters. The children out hunting for birds' nests function symbolically: in their active imagination, the ordinary hunting expedition becomes an adventure that transgresses the tenuous borderline separating the visible world from the invisible. "From prey to prey, one reaches the demon. After sparrows, hobgoblins" (XII, 616). The local legends gradually transport the reader to a supernatural reality ruled by forces that are propitious to mythical enlargement. In the popular imagination, the *Durande* is a devil-boat from the start—"a monstrous silhouette that whistled and spat, a horrible thing that breathed hoarsely like a beast and smoked like a volcano, a sort of hydra slavering into the foam" (XII, 578).

The Hero and His Monsters

The hydra belongs to the realm of myth. The tales of long voyages told by the old skipper to his niece—tales of terrible bat people in virgin forests and of fierce spiders in Paraguay—set the scene for the mythopoetic developments. In the poem "Océan," Hugo had already associated the names of Hercules and Theseus with epic victories of man over the supposedly untamable (IX, 676). Ever since writing his early essay on Walter Scott, which called for "epic" works of fiction, Hugo's ambition had been to write novels that would project epic dramas that no theatrical stage could encompass.[12] The epic intentions in *Les Travailleurs de la mer* reveal themselves not only in the gigantic forces at work, in a cosmic animism (the thunder rolls in a "chambre de géants," the storm is the mighty blowing of the "poumon de l'infini"), but in the traits and destiny of the hero, Gilliatt. Alone against the concentrated anger of the elements, naked in the face of the immensity of the sea, he puts up a "titanic" struggle in a "one-man Iliad" ("Iliade à un"—XII, 752).

Allusions to Homer are explicit as well as stylistic. After the battle with the storm, Gilliatt feels the "immemorial desire to insult his enemy that goes back to Homer's heroes" (XII, 735). But it is the rhetoric of the text that more than anything conveys the tone of the epic: paratactic structures, one-line paragraphs alternating with ample developments, heavy concentrations of substantives, epic enumerations such as the one describing the Legion of Winds in the chapter titled "Turba, Turma." Allusions and references are at the same time humorous and self-serving. About to list the staggering variety of winds that the storm mobilizes for the battle, the narrator wryly observes: "Homer would have shrunk from this enumeration" (XII, 723–724).

The epic traditionally sings of war. Hugo provides a full order of battle. The chapter entitled "Le Combat" is one of the longest in the book. During the duel between the lonely individual and the "legion" of the elements (the word *armée* also appears), the overwhelming metaphor is military. The encounter is told in terms of tactics, strategy, roaring cannons, sieges, assaults, sallies, and skirmishes. Archaic and modern war images are blended. Gilliatt dons his pilot's coat "like a knight putting on his armor." Having completed his "toilette de guerre," he takes up his command post like a "general." Hugo sustains the epic tone to the very end of the chapter, endowing the encounter between man and nature with the conventional poetry of war. The storm abates as the "immense machinery of the clouds" collapses and the rear guard of the thunder retreats like "a horde of terrible chariots" (XII, 725–726, 735).

Yet the shift away from the traditional poetry of war is noteworthy. What interests Hugo is the greatness and misery of solitary work ("misère du travail solitaire"), which allows man to achieve full moral and spiritual growth. Gilliatt's prodigious vigor is not due to unusual muscles. His real strength—his energy—is seen as a "moral force" (XII, 704, 681). Hugo doubtless had his own lonely struggle with words and ideas in mind, as he has Gilliatt experience the full difficulty, but also the exhilaration and inebriation, of what he revealingly calls his "oeuvre." The image of this inebriation with one's work is not without humor: "Son oeuvre lui montait à la tête." Yet it leads to grandiose literary references. Gilliatt on his rock (could Hugo on his island ever forget that he was the Defiant Poet?) is transformed into a Promethean Job. In a similar vein, an earlier chapter devoted to Gilliatt's "labor" is entitled "How Shakespeare and Aeschylus Can Meet," followed by a chapter whose title refers to Gilliatt's "masterpiece" (XII, 704, 698).

Gilliatt, a new Crusoe, uses nature against herself. He reinvents the crafts and reorders the world out of the accumulated chaos— the wreckage—in his improvised workshop. He is the archetypal *faber*, the maker and shaper of forms. But there is another archetypal dimension to Gilliatt. His are the traits of the mythical hero engaged in a quest. Richard B. Grant, in what is perhaps the best chapter of his book *The Perilous Quest*, has persuasively shown that Gilliatt's destiny conforms to the basic patterns of mythical narrative as outlined by Joseph Campbell in *The Hero with a Thousand Faces*: penetration into a region of "supernatural wonder," encounters with "fabulous forces," and a victorious return of the hero, now capable of bestowing "boons on his fellow men." Gilliatt, according to Grant's excellent analysis, must undergo initiatory tests, experience a "typical process of human isolation," confront the unknown as well as his inner terrors, and ultimately, like all mythical figures who are "too great for any accommodation to this world," he must disappear.[13]

Such a pattern of myth points to spiritual rather than strictly epic values. Hugo's deliberate references to the structures of quest narrative stress the fable and the symbolic trial. Gilliatt has a mission that must be accomplished alone. His departure is secretive, almost a form of escape. Along his "perilous route" (XII, 669) he must cross thresholds, overcome obstacles. He must find his way to the inside of "the place." Chapter headings, once again, provide key signals. The central section of the novel begins with the suggestive title "The Place That Is Hard to Reach and Difficult to Leave." Like some of the great heroes of antiquity, Gilliatt is said to have visited hell itself ("Tu es donc allé jusqu'en enfer"— XII, 772). A sense of ultimate destination confers on his quest a religious and salvational value. The savior-hero is not only to marry the daughter of the "sick king," but he actually cures him of his sickness. As though to confirm the spiritual and visionary nature of the quest, the expression *en quête* occurs precisely in the chapter carrying the Latin title "Sub Umbra" ("Under the Shadow")—the chapter in which Gilliatt, with his eyes open on blackness, glimpses things hidden and forbidden, and experiences under the roof of shadows the "sacred terror" ("effroi sacré") that leads him to mystic insight and soon after to prayer (XII, 705–706).

Terror in myth takes the form of monsters. If mention of weather conditions brings up the Etruscans and the Chaldeans (XII, 602); if the winds evoke Pan, and clouds the Gorgon masks or the Danaides; if the Atlantic archipelago recalls the Aegean with its sunken labyrinths (XII, 602, 635)—this is no doubt to provide the flavor of ancient legends. But the world of myth is fraught with dangers. The Cyclopean architraves of the ocean may allow glimpses of a Venus, an Amphitrite, or a Tethys; they also reveal the bestial and the horrible. The reef is compared to a dragon with gaping jaws; the movement of the wind resembles the undulations of a wild beast; the rocks seem to bear cataclysmic wounds. Similes grow into metaphors. The sea foam becomes the "saliva of a leviathan." And the pillars of the Douvres mark the entrance to the underworld from which the hero must wrest a secret (XII, 694, 703, 730, 680).

That secret is both beyond and within. Intimacy with the monsters of the physical world reflects an inescapable intimacy with the monsters of the psyche. Sexual fantasies transmute the seascape. At the entrance to the underworld stand "erect and upright" two black columns still dripping from the previous day's tempest and bearded with seaweed ("velues de varech"). The narrow entrance to the grotto is lined with blood-colored stones covered with hairy, sticky seaweed ("conferves poilues et gluantes") and leads to still narrower passages, to gradually contracting "fissures" filled with "oozing darkness" (XII, 670, 690).

Gilliatt's most dramatic intimacy with the monsters occurs during his struggle with the giant octopus known as the devilfish— the horrendous *pieuvre*. (See Illustration 13.) Also known as the bloodsucker, this sea vampire, this Medusa with its eight snake-like arms and hundreds of suction cups, enlaces and paralyzes its victim, before consuming it alive. Gelatinous and flabby, endowed with an obscene sucking apparatus, the *pieuvre* is defined by Hugo as a glutinous mass filled with hatred (XII, 741). Malicious intent, lethal power, and unspeakable repulsiveness all combine in the *pieuvre*, whose horror outdoes that of the dragon in ancient myth and the kraken in sea legends.

This horror is obsessional in a manner that integrates the monster in a complex personal mythology. The *pieuvre*, whose orifice functions as both mouth and anus, empties its victim of its living substance. Its embrace is an evacuation. Roger Caillois, in a fascinating study of fabulous and zoological accounts of the *octopus vulgaris*, has traced the genesis of a mythology and has indicated the privileged place of Hugo's *pieuvre* in the bestiary. Since ancient times, the octopus has been a focus of oneiric fantasy. But it was Hugo, in *Les Travailleurs de la mer*, who became the mythographer of the *pieuvre* as a symbol of libidinous threat and absolute evil. [14]

Chaos at Work

The central issue in the novel is the relation between violence and creation. *Chaos*, with its multiple denotations of space, formlessness, and disorder, is a key term. The sea is the protagonist and the setting of a primal war. *Mer* and *guerre* echo each other in an early passage that speaks of "ambush" and of an "invisible clarion" sounding the alarm of war. [15] After the shipwreck, Hugo compares the confusion of the elements known as chaos—the great "mêlées d'éléments"—to the *mêlées* known as battles (XII, 673). The ocean's music is cacophony. Chaos is its reality and its language. The ocean disturbs lines, undoes all symmetries, indulges in colossal disproportions. [16] Yet in these dissonances there is harmony. In the multiplicity of "confusion" there is the principle of unity. Diversity melts ("se fond") into identity. *Chaos* is defined as the great reservoir, the "universal recipient." "Il a tant d'éléments qu'il est l'identité" (XII, 677).

In this crucible of chaos, "monstrous masterpieces," gigantic and exquisitely delicate forms, are wrought (XIV, 400). An oxymoronic master design seems to stress the "exquisiteness of the terrible." Hugo compares this design to that of a titanic goldsmith. The encounter between savage forces and subtle sea changes produces evil jewels—"bijouteries sinistres" (XII, 694, 746).

The predominant metaphor is, however, architectural. Piranesean formations suggest both ruin and incompleteness. Pediments, entablatures, and colonnades stand side by side with broken bridges, truncated columns, and barricaded entrances. Other forms introduce the maximum structural heterogeneity: pyramids, pagodas, dungeons, alhambras, and sepulchres coexist with gothic cathedrals and massive citadels. Underwater urban images (sections of streets and walls) appear next to Babel-like constructs. To the glory of the "immense architect" (XII, 690), a rock formation on a huge pedestal towers in the shape of an enormous H: the signature of the masterbuilder.

The author's personal signature is, of course, stylistic and thematic. The horror and the beauty of the sea are clearly related to Hugo's notion of the grotesque. The most bizarre shapes are here situated precisely in a grotto. When the giant octopus is first glimpsed as something "indescribable"—a floating strip of rag—moving in the transparency of the water, it seems to have the shape of a jester's bauble ("marotte de bouffon"—XII, 695). All of creation seems to indulge in weird fantasies. Dizzying structures are held together in senseless suspension. At the level of rhetoric, Hugo's representation of nature is one vast oxymoron. But the system of antitheses is far from immobilizing. A figure of speech that opposes seemingly contradictory terms functions as the linguistic analogue of a structure in motion. The language of creation animates the stone. Describing ominous cloud effects, Hugo speaks of "immobilité en mouvement" (XII, 725). The beginning of the storm is signaled by the arrival of a huge, perpendicular cloud bank moving forward like a wall of granite. Elsewhere, Hugo refers to the extraordinary *dynamics* that constantly deny the stasis of achieved forms. This restless and illogical equilibrium, this system of enmeshed contraries, he calls a "combat of lines" (XII, 690).

These self-negating transformational constructs, these dynamic processes that allow for no finished product, explain the exceptional importance of the winds, whose power is both disruptive and generative. What complicates the underwater disintegrating constructionism is the above-surface despotism of the winds. "La Mer et le Vent" became so long a chapter that Hugo was forced to consider publishing it separately. The wind's disintegrating function has a long history in Hugo's work. As far back as "La Pente de la rêverie," the phrase *souffle du vent* opens up visionary perspectives. This *souffle*, in the early poem as well as in the sea novel, is of course the divine anima, the very breath of God. Throughout Hugo's work, tempestuous winds mark the encounter in history of physical and metaphysical forces. The Terror in *Quatrevingt-Treize* is a "vent de prodige," and, more specifically, the "souffle de Dieu" (XV, 379–380). Yet the principles of disruption and effacement operate even at this lofty level. The despotic winds reign over chaos ("Ils ont la dictature du chaos"—XII, 720): they compose, distort, disintegrate, germinate.

The sexual metaphor, too, remains ambiguous, projecting the oxymoron of fertile destructiveness. Wind and water meet in a "terrifying coition" (XII, 721). The love-hate struggle of the elements during the storm foreshadows the encounter with the *pieuvre*. The words *succion*, *ventouse*, and *tumeur* announce the sea monster. The bestial avidity of the wind declares monstrosity on a cosmic scale. The metaphor of copulation applied to natural forces takes on the widest range. It extends from playful lasciviousness (there are gentle carresses and quivers; the waters mount the rocks, penetrate fissures, are sucked up by "inexhaustible mouths"— XII, 729), to procreative energy (the sea is a vast laboratory of fecundation and transformation), to sheer violence, rapacity, and wanton lust. Hugo describes the "rape" committed by the storm (XII, 672). But the word *viol* is not to be read in a moralistic sense; for only through violation can forms be born. The "dictatorship of chaos" means that acts of nature resemble crimes, that creation depends on deeds of darkness and violence. Gilliatt learns that a vision of the dynamics of creation means not only exposure to the horrible glance of the monster but the courage to stare into the face of evil.

The Vision

The seeing and seen eye is the symbol of visionary consciousness. The "Eye of the Tempest" at the heart of darkness prefigures the eyes of the *pieuvre* at the center of its slimy mass (XII, 734, 739). The suggestive chapter describing Gilliatt as a "seer of nature" ("voyant de la nature") is entitled "Ce qu'on y voit et ce qu'on y entrevoit" ("What One Sees There and What One Gets a Glimpse Of"). Even prayer is understood as a form of seeing: it means looking at the mystery of life with "the very eyes of the shadow" (XII, 759).

The eye remains for Hugo a source of pleasure, as well as a symbol of guilt and fear. His own powerful visual imagination caused him, throughout his life, both delight and apprehension. The eye of conscience, in the famous poem of *La Légende des siècles*, pursues Cain into the tomb.[17] The generative value of Hugo's drawings deserves special attention in the case of *Les Travailleurs de la mer*. On the manuscript of this novel Hugo drew a good number of illustrations, and it would seem that in many instances the image drawn preceded and determined the narration.[18] It is as though the words were at times a second stage, as the vision was translated into a poem about strange forms, lighted shadows, and phosphorescent irradiations of the sea.

Hugo's visionary poetry is intimately associated with the sea. It is near Jersey's dolmen of Rozel, which Hugo called the Rock of the Proscribed, that he set the revelatory scene of the great poem "Ce que dit la Bouche d'Ombre," imagining that the local promontory was a new Patmos for a new vision of the apocalypse. The "visionary diffusion" of the grotto light that so overwhelms Gilliatt is precisely a "lumière d'apocalypse" (XII, 694). Gilliatt, the man of the sea, has a visionary disposition from the start. He is the "man of dreams," the mediator who glimpses the invisible text. If his glance penetrates through any rent in the surface fabric, it is because he has the insight of blindness that comes with being *pensif*, because he experiences the visionary occultation of the true seer and prophet (XII, 745). His "other" eyes open onto prodigious metamorphoses. Agent of a mediated vision, Gilliatt the somnambulist stares into the "aquarium of the night" (XII, 570). He scrutinizes darkness, and what he reads in the darkness of his dream, together with the enigma of evil, is the ceaseless process of construction and effacement.

From the outset, the *songeur-penseur* Gilliatt is presented as a man of the night. The islanders suspect him of nocturnal deeds. His nickname, Gilliatt le Malin, suggests craftiness as well as dark intents. An early chapter heading ("A Maison visionnée habitant visionnaire") attributes to the inhabitant of the haunted house a disposition to have hallucinations and visions. He is the *voyant* (also the *voyeur*) of nature, and his real vocation is to contemplate darkness. The words *contempler* and *contemplation* are loaded terms in Hugo's lexicon; so is the word *mage*, used in an early description of Gilliatt (XII, 562, 695, 567). They signal his ability to decipher invisible reality, and they announce his poetic function.

The characteristics of Gilliatt's vision cannot be defined simply in terms of a dream-world enlargement and distortion of familiar forms. His is a determined vertical movement down the axis of immersion and submersion. The risks of such a descent are made very clear. Gilliatt, surrounded by his own hallucinations, plunges into the realm of the "impossible." For ordinary mortals, this would be the descent to madness. One must not measure the depth too far ("Ne jetons pas la sonde trop avant"), warns Hugo (XII, 684, 814). It is impossible not to recall "La Pente de la rêverie," which opens with the warning not to spiral down the vortex of reverie, and concludes as the visionary poet confronts the unknown, aghast: "ébloui, haletant, stupide, épouvanté."[19]

The effect of this submersion is a metaphorical inversion. Hugo conceives of the emblem of two Towers of Babel constructed in opposite directions, one downward and the other upward. Once Gilliatt penetrates into this topsy-turvy world of sunken and inverted sea constructs, he discovers that the abyss is above ("le gouffre d'en haut") and that the light comes from below (XII, 813, 722). The sea cave has the shape of an enormous skull (the vault is the cranium; the arch is the mouth) but also of an underwater cathedral, with its porch, ogival arches, pillars, and altar. The metaphorical inversion is part of a disquieting revelatory process.

What is being revealed in these sunken hieratic architectures is a sense of almost sacred horror. (Hugo refers to an "émotion inouïe, presque sacrée"—XII, 694). The viscous transparencies of this cavern ultimately reveal a monstrous submarine spider— the *pieuvre*—seen in the full horror of its spectral irradiation. The chapter "Discovery" introduces a series of transformational images leading from Cyclopean monuments to fantastic vegetation, to chaotic stratification, to sexual fantasies (breasts, hips, naked deities emerging from chaos), and finally to the horror of the *pieuvre*, lying in wait to embrace her victims with her arms and mouths and suck them to death.

The association of the spider and the threat of sex is a recurrent feature in the work of Hugo. In *L'Homme qui rit*, the satanic Eve named Josiane will display her triumphant flesh behind the center of a semitransparent curtain, like a spider lying in wait at the center of its web. But the fear of sex is never so intense as in the case of Gilliatt, whose only physical contact with a female threat occurs precisely in his life and death struggle with the octopus. His other contacts are strictly visual. The voyeuristic impulse suggests the sense of a taboo. Gilliatt, we are told early in the novel, is in the habit of hiding behind the rocks of an inlet to watch the peasant girls bathe. But he experiences a sense of revulsion at the sight of naked women: "une femme nue lui faisait horreur" (XII, 597, 599).

Gilliatt's ultimate sacrifice, as he arranges for Déruchette's elopement with another man, thus cannot be attributed solely to selflessness and higher love. Marriage itself, at the end of the novel, is associated with death. Shroud and wedding gown become identical as Hugo comments that the tomb is also a betrothal (XII, 786). Gilliatt's withdrawal from life is not a simple matter of generosity; it is a refusal of the violence of passion, perceived as a threat and a fundamental evil. He allows himself to drown precisely as all of tumescent nature, filled with sap and moist with voluptuousness, is engaged in nuptials. But Gilliatt turns his back on the allurements of life. After his visionary descent into the underworld of the sea, he knows what the Bouche d'Ombre had taught the vatic poet: that evil itself is part of creation.

The Enigma

But evil wears a mask. The hidden efficacy of evil—its "hypocritical" patience and delayed violence—is made manifest in Gilliatt's encounter with the *pieuvre*. It is also illustrated earlier, in the figure of a human monster, Captain Clubin, who has laboriously constructed a life-long reputation of honesty in order to commit a perfect crime: the shipwreck of the *Durande* and his escape with Lethierry's fortune. The gleeful self-unmasking of Clubin, after the crew and the passengers have left the boat, is melodramatic, but its true import is symbolic. The theatrical gesture assumes an allegorical dimension: Clubin's transmutation of impeccability into the joy of crime proclaims the joy of Satan. The evil captain, when finally he shows his true face after the inebriating "arrachement du masque" has a menacing light in his eye and a sinister laugh (XII, 649–651).

It is both ironic and logical that the rapacious deceiver should fall victim to the giant octopus lying in wait for its prey. The deeper irony, however, has to do with the sea itself and—beyond the sea—with all of nature. For the sea is the great "hypocrite," and the hidden evil of all creation is the unexpected and disturbing message of the book. This message is prepared by a number of metaphors directly linked to Clubin. Hypocrisy is defined as a cavern; the obscenity of crime is said to exist at moral "depths" that are rarely "sounded." The message later becomes more explicit. The wave is called a "hypocrite"; it slays, devours, steals, conceals—yet continues to smile (XII, 650, 670). Like Clubin, the ocean wears a mask (Hugo calls it "le masque de l'abîme").

Early on, in the opening pages of the novel, the English Channel is declared capable of an "ambush," a "guet-apens" (XII, 719, 602).

The "crime" of the sea[20] is, of course, a metaphysical challenge. The threatening forces lurking in the darkness, behind the smiling mask of nature (earlier, in "L'Océan," Hugo had spoken of "blind creation"—IX, 675), might lead one indeed to question Providence. But Hugo steadfastly rejects the notion of blind forces. In his darkest pages, faced with the irrecusable evidence of horror and pain, he refuses to question the existence of God. The enigma of evil thus becomes even more disturbing, for it must be made to fit into the divine scheme. More disturbing still: it appears directly to involve the responsibility of God.

A profound anguish, worthy of Job, responds with unanswerable questions to the darkest revelation made by the Bouche d'Ombre: that evil itself is part of creation, that everything in the universe is devastation.[21] The "perfection of evil," in the chapter "Monster," seems to prove that a supreme will is at work. The *why* of this will, Hugo states, is the torment of the religious thinker. The absolute nature of horror provokes Hugo into a meditation on the nature of God.[22] But this meditation is far from reassuring. "When God wills it, He excels in the execrable" (XII, 743, 739). This astonishing statement explains not only why Hugo refers to the immense "sob of creation" but why he feels compelled to refer to "creation's blasphemies against itself" (XII, 806, 742).[23]

The direct linking of God with the forces of evil is in itself a theological concept. It is in this crucial chapter that Hugo mentions the formidable double-headed (*bi-frons*) divinity of the Manichaeans. Such duplicity signifies an immanent involvement in the dynamics of a cosmic moral struggle. In this agon, masked evil may itself be a mask. The divinely enacted antithesis of good and evil affirms the dynamic principle of all creation. The very dissatisfaction with the order of reality ("Why not another order?"), and the aspiration to brighter worlds are signs pointing to process and progress. Death itself is a kind of threshold ("que la mort nous soit progrès"—XII, 743). Creation remains a project. And the supreme author, coexistent with this (his) project, is responsibly involved—as is the artist-author—in an apparently ceaseless activity of productive rewriting.

A Poem of Effacement

The novel opens, as we have seen, under the sign of effacement and dissolution. Associated from the start with the activity of writing, effacement remains an obsessive motif, most notably in the dramatic episode dealing with the disintegrating function of wind and water ("Tout s'effaça dans de l'écume"—XII, 729). The unstable nature of reality, its constant shifts and metamorphoses seen as the analogue of creative decomposition, held a fascination for Hugo even in his earliest compositions. The poem "Soleils couchants," written almost forty years before Les Travailleurs de la mer, not only evokes "archipelagoes of clouds" but delights in changing shapes and in the "destruction" of the clouds' edifice. "La Pente de la rêverie," written during the same early period, indulges even more systematically in the decomposition of several levels of reality. The image of the great continents devoured by oceans ("par les grands océans sans cesse dévorés") clearly prefigures one of the obsessive motifs of Les Travailleurs de la mer (IV, 440, 427).

After an interval of more than thirty years, creative decomposition remains a central theme. The Paris of "La Pente de la rêverie" dissolves and evaporates into mist, giving way to other levels of reality, which in turn "efface" one another, gradually leading to a vision of the invisible world. The original beginning of L'Homme qui rit, Hugo's penultimate novel, still relates creative power to oceanic forces in terms of mighty processes of disintegration ("L'océan trouble toutes les lignes, désagrège toutes les symétries"—XIV, 401). In Les Travailleurs de la mer, poetic reverie is from the outset specifically associated with the verb désagréger. Gilliatt, who in his trance-like states glimpses other worlds, is struck by the stupendous "decompositions" of the realm of twilight. The following is a significant passage: "The darkness of night is vertiginous. Whosoever sounds its depths is submerged and struggles. No fatigue can be compared to this scrutiny of the shadows. It is the study of an effacement" ("C'est l'étude d'un effacement"—XII, 706).

Nature's work of effacement and construction, a labor of love, projects the basic life principle of violence and death. A typical metaphor, in the early pages of the novel, refers to the "cimetière océan." The sea is cruel; the reef is a "charnel house." The sea cave displays the bloody oozings of a butcher's cellar or a slaughterhouse (XII, 563, 675, 690). This is the kingdom of endless devastation. The wave itself takes on the form of huge jaws ("le flot dévore; la vague est une mâchoire"—XII, 673). But this devouring is lifegiving: the ocean destroys and creates ("il dévore puis crée"). Hugo puts it more tersely still: all of nature is devouring and devoured ("mangeante et mangée"—XII, 743). The forced rhymed parallelisms of puns further stress the paradox: "Pourriture, c'est nourriture" (XII, 673, 677, 743).

The reader is warned, however, that nature always remains "suspect" (XII, 811). What we do not see is what counts. The mask conceals not only destructive but procreative forces. The ceaseless toil of nature may seem devastating, or at least utterly futile. Echoing his title, Hugo speaks of the "prodigieux travail inutile de la mer" (XII, 689), yet in the long chapter on the sea and the wind, this negativity is denied. The useless is converted into the useful through a rhetoric of negation: "L'inutile n'existe pas" (XII, 808). The mystery of toil remains the mystery of evil. The giant octopus is first perceived as a murky evanescence, an effacement rather than a presence. But evil itself is part of the form-giving process. The word *décompose* almost automatically calls for the word *recompose*: "Les moires du flot . . . s'y décomposaient et s'y recomposaient sans fin." The sea becomes the theater of a cosmic choreography—"un mouvement de danse mystérieuse" (XII, 692).

This double movement, or dialectic of constructive effacement, is nowhere more sharply outlined than in the pages entitled "L'Archipel de la Manche," which were originally to serve as a preliminary chapter. Hugo draws attention to the ocean's prodigious work of erosion. Yet this unending destruction of the Atlantic coastline involves a game of illusion and mirages, a vanishing of stone ("la pierre a de ces évanouissements") that brings about metamorphosis. The shape of the rocks shifts, as does the shape of the clouds. The spectacle is kaleidoscopic: forms are "disintegrated" and again "recomposed" (XII, 519). No line remains fixed in this permanent process of mutation and creativity.

The constructive dynamics of destruction are surprisingly confirmed in a political address in which one would not normally expect to find such a pattern. In "Consolidation et Défense du Littoral," a speech that Hugo had delivered to the House of Peers some twenty years earlier, he denounced the destructive effects of the sea, which erodes the coast and clogs harbors. He called for emergency measures to protect the coastline. But although the ocean, in this speech, is described as the enemy (attacking, invading, degrading, destroying), the imagery, in obvious contradiction to the professed political and technical intentions, veers toward spontaneously reconstructive processes. The obstruction of the ports is described in terms of "invisible construction," "immense edifices," "gigantic arenas"; the ocean appears as a tireless, mythical "worker"; the destructive forces are presented as repairing and creative principles.[24]

Poetic vision clearly takes precedence over immediate political efficacy. In *Les Travailleurs de la mer*, chaos is seen as endlessly supplying life; it is a "réservoir pour les fécondations." The eternally recommencing sea is part of a vast cyclical genesis described as a permanent transformation.[25] Creation is defined as a "decomposition immediately recomposed" (XII, 677, 807). Nothing is lost, nothing is aimless. Progress itself—and revolutionary progress most of all—feeds on ruin. And what is true of progress and revolution is true also of literary creation: text feeds on text.

The dismemberment of the text is a recurrent image in the work of Hugo. Some thirty years earlier, in *Notre-Dame de Paris*, Hugo had described the advent of printing as the undoing of one text by another. But the new textual edifice, which replaced the old monuments of stone, was itself metaphorized into a new Tower of Babel, ominously suggesting a construct destined for ruin. Later, in *Quatrevingt–Treize*, Hugo would provide another paradigmatic image of the dismemberment of the book: a "massacre" of a rare *in quarto* by a group of children—an act of infantile violence ambiguously described as a "vanishing" into the blue. It is a disturbing scene, if one considers that this youthful aggression against the past occurs in Hugo's last novel. Again, an intertextual reading proves illuminating. The deck of the shipwrecked boat in *Les Travailleurs de la mer* is compared to a book that has been pried open; the word *démembrement* follows immediately, leading to a surgical and then more specifically obstetrical image, as the salvation operation is implicitly compared to childbirth (XII, 733).

These problematics of the text raise a fundamental question: If writing itself is destined for effacement, if the book is doomed to deconstruction, what then is the text's relationship to the "reality" it supposedly represents? What, in other words, is the mimetic or poetic link between a system of vanishing traces and a referential "nature" which is itself viewed as a process of disintegration, a vast laboratory of undoing? It is here that one might be tempted to situate Hugo's greatest textual complexity. Since "reality" itself seems to be a continuous project (all realizations are merely sketches),[26] since it is subject to the same universal law of dissolution, then this double negativity—this constant thematic effacement of the literary text, as well as of the "text" of the world—not only turns out to be positive but provides the illusion that poetic language has an essentially mimetic function. What Hugo has done, and done deliberately, is to provide himself with a contextual system that comprises all his own texts (already written, or to be conceived), as well as the hypothetical text of the supreme author in whose name he speaks without appearing to do so.

Ego Hugo

The self-referential presence of the author calls into question the auctorial status in the novel. The "magisterial fantasy" (XII, 670) prevalent in the work of nature is a constant reminder of the problematic relation between the two "creations": How does God the artist relate to the artist as God? Hugo's book on Shakespeare, a panegyric on the nature of genius, presents the revelatory poets— the *hommes océans*—as reflections of the divine principle. They are "All in One" in their inexhaustibly varied monotony. Revealingly, Hugo's list of the world's fourteen great men (the fifteenth remains modestly unnamed) includes as many as five prophets or Biblical figures: Job, who achieved greatness at the bottom of his spiritual pit; Isaiah, the "mouthpiece of the desert"; Ezekiel, the wild "demagogue of the Bible"; Saint John, the man of Patmos with a tongue of fire and the "profound smile of madness"; and Saint Paul, who, on the road to Damascus, "fell into" the truth.[27]

The poet, it would seem, is a celebratory participant in divine creativity. He is both *sacerdos magnus* and an instrument of creation: "Dieu crée l'art par l'homme" (XII, 170). Yet almost in the same breath, Hugo declares that works of genius are superhuman creations created by man ("des oeuvres de l'homme").[28] Matters are further complicated, since all creation is viewed as a text. In "Philosophie. Commencement d'un livre," Hugo refers to rock formations as pages of an undecipherable palimpsest (XII, 15). In *Les Travailleurs de la mer*, God himself is presented as a literary artist, a master rhetorician: figures of speech, antitheses, identity, synonomy, analogues—these are God's devices, his *procédés*.[29] Even his redundancies are put in terms of writing: "omnipotence copying itself" (XII, 811). This divine text—whether self-effacing or repetitive palimpsest—allows for no gap. All is "coefficient" (XII, 810); all contraries unite. Nature is held together by design, even though the "mask" suggests that contingency rules.

The disturbing association or interchangeability of artistic and divine purpose finds its humorous illustration when Gilliatt is referred to as author and as demiurge. Hugo clearly plays on the word "author"; Lethierry presents Gilliatt as the hero of the rescue operation: "Et voici l'auteur." The author image is further exploited when Gilliatt's name, like that of a successful playwright, is said to be on everyone's lips (XII, 774, 790). There is self-directed irony in Hugo's description of Gilliatt's creative high spirits on the reef. Revealingly, it is just before and after this high point of creative exaltation that Hugo refers to Prometheus, Aeschylus, and Shakespeare. Humor and irony only underscore the equivocal God-artist analogue, as Gilliatt the demiurge, in his almost superhuman struggle, seems to be associated with the forces of darkness (his is truly an *oeuvre de nuit*), thus justifying the nickname *le Malin*. For beyond the struggle with the material world, he does seem to be engaged in an extraordinary confrontation, which Hugo announced in his unpublished prefatory note: "He struggles with God" (XII, 797).

Gilliatt thus mediates between the author of the literary text and the author of the palimpsest of nature, between competing authorities that blend in an overwhelming principle of authorial individuation. This latent identity is repeatedly affirmed in *Les Travailleurs de la mer*. The supreme selfhood of the poet is in the image of the selfhood of God: the "moi énorme," the "perpétuité du moi," the "opiniâtreté insubmersible du moi"—the indestructible obstinacy of the self (XII, 707, 807, 809).

Yet this glorification of selfhood is far from reassuring. Like the ocean itself, God as well as the *hommes océans* are caught in the dynamics of excess. They know no moderation and no respite. "Dieu exagère," writes Hugo in the crucial chapter on the sea and the winds (XII, 813). Excess—or *démesure*—is in fact the true sign of creativity. Genius—defined in *William Shakespeare* as a promontory jutting out into infinity—cannot ever be measured in terms of an aesthetic of sobriety, or by the norms of "good taste." Great art, for Hugo, is orgiastic; it has profound affinities with the carnival, the Mardi Gras. The mysterious, ferocious laughter of art is the manifestation of an excess of vitality.

Even the underlying unity is disquieting. To be sure, cosmic harmony means that all apparent contradictions merge and vanish, that there is no real discontinuity, that gaps are illusory, that there can be no lapses or hiatus. But this solidarity of creation also means that it is an unending process, that all work, including the poem, is a flux of becoming, a fluid and live project rather than a well-wrought urn. The obsessive water images, as Jean Gaudon has persuasively argued in *Le Temps de la contemplation*, suggest a notion of creative flow that leads Hugo to prefer the absolute and unrealizable demands of poetry over the satisfactions of the self-contained poem.[30]

This dynamic and exhilarating participation of authorial will in the flow of creation has its tragic side. Vertical images are constant reminders that the vatic descent may lead to madness and self-destruction. The inverted Babel and the inverted cathedral are directly associated with the "crepuscular majesty" of the immense capital *H* looming on the novel's horizon (XII, 670). Throughout, there is the suspicion that all creation is dark, that it is—as the original title was to remind us—an abyss. "Noir génie" is an expression Hugo had associated a few years earlier with divinely assisted genius:[31] it points to the bond between the creative artist and the forces of darkness. Increasingly, Hugo seemed haunted by the belief that poetic vision depends on the dangerous intimacy with evil, that God and the artist join in a theology of shadows.

This notion of the "dark poet" is even more pervasive in Hugo's next novel, *L'Homme qui rit*, where it is related to the obsessive motif of laughter.

— 6 —

L'Homme qui rit:
From Laughter
to Vision

Ce monstre, la matière . . .

If Hugo, in *Les Travailleurs de la mer*, strove toward a poetic and mythic construct that would sing the puzzling solidarity of all creation, his ambitions in *L'Homme qui rit* (1869) had even greater scope. In a projected preface, he referred to this novel as a "drama beyond ordinary proportions."[1] Only a few years earlier, in *Promontorium somnii* and in *William Shakespeare*, he had praised excess, even extravagance, as indispensable elements of great art. The normal criteria of balance, measure, economy, and verisimilitude simply do not apply to this transgressive narrative.

Literal-minded readers could have a field day pointing out the implausible situations and downright absurdities in the book. An abandoned ten-year-old boy saves an infant lying next to its dead mother in the snow, and then carries it, barefoot, across miles of deserted countryside back to civilization and life; a mutilated buffoon, beloved by a blind girl, discovers that he is a nobleman and becomes a revolutionary orator in the House of Lords; a decadent duchess makes lascivious advances to a monstrously ugly histrion; a ventriloquist mountebank, who lives misanthropically in the company of a humane wolf, writes Spanish dialogues for English crowds at a fairground; sudden reversals of fortune lead to a double-death scene after repeated rituals of degradation and elevation. The list could go on. The very names of the characters are bizarre: Ursus, the garrulous charlatan given to interminable monologues; Gwynplaine, the mutilated "man who laughs"; Hardquanonne, the outlaw who disfigured the child Gwynplaine long ago; Barkilphedro, the ingratiating villain. Pathos, sentimentality, grandiloquence, and melodramatic effects are indulged in without reticence. Hugo seems to have been determined to set up as many obstacles as possible to the "serious" reader in search of conventional literary entertainment.

Hugo in fact sends clear signals from the outset that the code of nineteenth-century "realistic" narrative is here disregarded and undermined. The lengthy double prologue (one chapter on the mountebank's ménage with the wolf, the other on a group of child-buying *comprachicos*) functions as an initiatory textual threshold. It suggests that what follows must be read not as a mimetic account of "real" life but as a fable. The ironic opening signals concerning the friendship between the bear-like man Ursus and the civilized wolf Homo, and later the style itself (with its frequent recourse to one-line paragraphs and the illusion of parataxis), convey the impression of a fairy tale within the context of a historically situated action. The names present a striking combination of the extraordinary and the commonplace. All seems to hint at archaic, archetypal patterns. The hero faces the hostile elements; he brings back innocence and beauty from the realm of death; he is instructed by a wise old man who comes close to being a magician. Symbolic and allegorical elements abound. A circus wagon is described as a small universe containing the human, the animal, and the divine; it is a rolling temple, complete with enigmatic inscriptions. The Blind Maiden in love with the Soul behind the Ugly Mask illustrates insight into true beauty. The presiding myth is the ideal coupling of the imperfect parts; what is involved is the figuration of the total psyche. Last but not least, the castle in which Gwynplaine, oblivious for a short while to his moral duties, is trapped by the carnal lady obviously belongs to the tradition of high romance.

As one becomes acquainted with the mixtures in modes and styles, one realizes that the most stunning descriptive and dramatic passages are never intended to be merely picturesque but are in all cases thematically and symbolically functional. A blinding snowstorm at sea, the silent violence of an endless shipwreck, fading glimpses of a tragic lighthouse, a child's encounter with a hanged man and his struggle across a bleak landscape, his dream-like nocturnal arrival in a lifeless town—such early scenes prepare us to read the other great dramatic moments of the novel as elements of a larger symbolic structure.

A Double Destiny

The plot itself is provokingly preposterous. The king of England (James II), out of vindictiveness toward a self-exiled nobleman faithful to Cromwell's republic, has the nobleman's little boy sold to the infamous *comprachicos*, who cruelly mutilate him, transforming his face into a permanent grimace. Forced to flee the country, the *comprachicos* abandon the child in a snowstorm on the craggy coast, intending to have him perish. The child, however, courageously makes his way through the blizzard, and even manages to save a baby girl about to die of exposure. They are both adopted by a traveling mountebank. As Gwynplaine, the disfigured boy, and Dea, the blind girl, grow up (she is blind as a result of her exposure in the snowdrifts), they fall in love. They live together chastely, like brother and sister. In the meantime, a measure of prosperity has come to the small family in the circus wagon. Gwynplaine, the "man who laughs," draws large crowds at the provincial fairgrounds. The group, seeking still larger fame, ultimately reaches London. But the arrival in the big city, with its attendant dangers, marks the beginning of a rift. Various events transform their lives. Gwynplaine is doubly "tempted": by the flesh, in the form of a lustful duchess, Josiane; by vanity and ambition, when he discovers that he is the son of a nobleman, and is made a member of the House of Lords. But he has also learned, by contact with the common people, to become their spokesman. His powerful political speech in the House of Lords is denunciatory and prophetic. To his dismay, it is met with jeers and laughter. "The man who laughs" finds himself condemned to provoke horror and derision. His own grimace, as well as the laughter he causes, are politically ominous; but they are ineffectual in the immediate context. Disheartened, Gwynplaine gives up all worldly hopes, and joins up again with his by now outlawed circus "family." The novel ends with the love-death of Gwynplaine and Dea, as their boat glides eerily down the Thames in the night fog.

The nocturnal navigation toward death, which completes the thwarted embarkation of the hero at the beginning of the novel, suggests that Hugo conceived the delayed voyage structurally as a symbol of personal destiny. At one level, *L'Homme qui rit* describes the adventure of the soul. Hugo himself, in his notes for a preface, refers to Gwynplaine's story as "Le Drame de l'Ame."[2] Before reaching his destination, Gwynplaine must take the painful road, the *via dolorosa* mentioned in the title of an early chapter. The salvational motif is further stressed by the oceanic imagery of the beginning, as the repentent *comprachicos* go down to their sea death in prayer, leaving afloat a corked and tarred gourd containing their collective confession—a symbol of survival through the written word.

Collective issues are, at another level, one of the concerns of the novel. The transition from singular to plural comes easily to Hugo who, in *Les Misérables* in particular, had already confirmed Ballanche's dictum "The story of a man is the story of man."[3] Gwynplaine, as he grows up, takes stock of the suffering of the common people. His is a grim vision of the shipwreck (*naufrage*) of the downtrodden and disinherited, as oppression inflicts on them misery, hatred, ignorance, war, unemployment, humiliation, and hunger—a bestial existence. He sees the horrors of legal "justice" and of feudal abuses, the inequities of unshared wealth. Gradually this vision leads to a political consciousness which transcends his own experience, as well as that of his period. The perspective becomes prerevolutionary and even reaches into the nineteenth century, as topical allusions set up parallels, first with the Restoration under Charles X, then with the "corrupt" Second Empire and the rule of Napoleon III (Hugo's archenemy) over a society of "Babylonian" luxury and festivities.

The problem for Hugo—a life-long problem—was how to articulate the political on the spiritual, how to relate the clown's grimace to his political discourse. The link, as well as the historical model, is hinted at in the chapter describing Gwynplaine's confrontation speech in the House of Lords: it is the figure of Mirabeau, the prestigious revolutionary orator, known also for his remarkable ugliness. The comparison is explicit, and hinges on the the image of disfigurement: "Ainsi en France Mirabeau, difforme lui aussi" (XIV, 348). Interestingly, the link between the private and the collective had been established by Hugo some thirty-five years earlier, and this precisely in his revealing essay "Sur Mirabeau" (1834). Mirabeau, we are told, was able to blend his personal passion with the collective passion of France: "il . . . amalgamait . . . sa passion personnelle et la passion de tous" (V, 199).

The Mirabeau essay, an intensely personal text, affirms the "predestined" nature of great men, the necessary evolution of the exceptional child into the exceptional adult. But beyond the wishful projection of Hugo's own destiny, this early essay also foreshadows the silhouette of Gwynplaine. Mirabeau, like the hero of *L'Homme qui rit*, is a "monster"—not only because he happens to be unusually turbulent, proud, and insubordinate (his family nicknamed him the Hurricane), but quite literally because of his impressive ugliness. Repeatedly Hugo refers to his deformity, to his misshapen body, to his face scarred by smallpox. The adjective "monstrous" stands out in italics. Mirabeau's ugliness, like that of Gwynplaine, is "grandiose" and "terrifying." This "monster," a force of nature, is endowed with fierce energy and a supreme talent for passionate oratory. His laughter is spellbinding—a powerful sound and sight, a "chose formidable." And like Gwynplaine thirty-five years later, the Mirabeau of the essay provokes the anger and derision of the assembly. His oratory is a function of the hatred he encounters. For Hugo, this demonic figure becomes the symbol of 1789, the human emblem of the Revolution. The bond between the monster-orator and the historic moment finds its figural corollary in *William Shakespeare*, where the spirit of the Revolution is indeed defined as "le monstre sublime."[4]

A Prophetic Voice

More sharply than any of Hugo's other texts, with the exception of the poem "La Révolution," *L'Homme qui rit* thematizes a pre-revolutionary situation. Strong hints appear early, in the cryptic inscriptions on the walls of the wagon, as well as in Ursus' ironic approval of arbitrary power. The theme of revolution is implicit in the revealed horrors of the legal system, in the penal cruelties that make up the "ferocious Mass" of the law. This suggests a connivance between the hangman and the king. Even more threatening than the descent to the hell of legal torture is the image of the petrification of a legal system serving royal authority and feudal privileges. The mute *wapentake* who comes to arrest Gwynplaine is another of Hugo's walking statues, a symbol of oppression and death. Gwynplaine's cry "All of mankind is in jail!" may have a Pascalian resonance,[5] but it must be understood in a political context. The metaphysical dimension of the prison image does, however, add religious pathos to the suffering inflicted by the social order. The gallows are repeatedly associated with the Cross—the "tree of human invention."[6]

The stress on master-slave relations functions even more powerfully as a prerevolutionary theme. This theme also accounts for the interminable list of privileges, properties, and immunities inscribed on the wagon, as well as for the insistent references to royal caprice and to the affinities between the throne and the gibbet.[7] All expresses indignation and announces upheaval. The impertinent elegance of hands that have never worked, the allusions to the power of the king's buffoon, and the memory of Louis

XV's debauchery must all be understood in the same light as the comparison between London's Newgate prison and the Bastille.

Gwynplaine the monster, an aristocrat by accident of birth, a republican by affinity with the exiled father, a revolutionary by contact with suffering, becomes the spokesman for the still silent people. "Le peuple est un silence" (XIV, 364). He chooses to be the voice of that silence. But once again, Hugo's attitude toward *le peuple* is ambivalent. Lively and robust, yet blind and mute, the lower classes are literally infantile (from *infans*, meaning speechless); they require a spokesman as well as a guiding conscience. Left to their own devices, they are unaware of their strength and even admire the power that crushes them. Thus, a form of contempt feeds Gwynplaine's solidarity and compassion. The populace is not only blind and mute; it is thoughtless. Ursus, a caricature of the social philosopher, is even more contemptuous: the people are but a crowd of fools, a "multitude d'insensés"—even worse, the dregs of the city, the *fex urbis* (XIV, 124, 292).

The political mission of love is thus inseparable from a hostile stance. The recurrent theatrical metaphor clearly implies an antagonism between actor and public. But if the populace can be shaped into an audience, this means that it can also be shaped into a positive political force. It is in this sense that Gwynplaine, first as histrion, then as political orator, comes to feel that he is destined to be a master of crowds, a "souverain des populaces" (XIV, 202). Only such mastery is capable of transforming a lost cause into a future victory. In its own way, Gwynplaine's political speech is also a message tossed into the sea. In the meantime, the heard voice, though unheeded and mocked, is already the prophetic "Word of the People" (XIV, 364). Out of the "bleeding mouth" from which the gag has been torn comes a Promethean utterance of human pride and collective salvation. The prophecy is blatantly revolutionary, denouncing the parasitism of kings and announcing the dawn when finally the true master of the house will knock at the door. Gwynplaine understands his own rhetorical fervor, his *cri*, as serving the noblest cause. Yet his destiny as prophet of a kingless society and of a higher justice is doubly bound up with his status as buffoon. If Lord Clown, as he is tauntingly called during his great speech, announces the doom of all kings, it is also because he cannot forget that it is none other than the king—*jussu regis*—who has inscribed that threatening laughter on his face.

Histrio! Mima!

Gwynplaine's speechmaking, no less than Ursus' feats of ventriloquism, have their origin in the fairground. Whether he faces the heckling peers in the House of Lords or the gaping crowd amid the tumblers' booths, Gwynplaine is a *monster* made "to be shown" (*montré*) at the fair (XIV, 191). The novel begins under the sign of the traveling carnival: a mountebank, a tamed beast, and a child with the skills of a rope walker occupy the foreground of the scene. The earliest references to London evoke the bitter winter of 1690, when a fair, with spectacles in tents and with bear and bull baiting, was held on the frozen Thames. There seems to be, the text suggests, a permanent need for monstrous display, for voyeuristic merriment at the sight of deformity. On the other hand, the carnival atmosphere also implies mobility, evanescence, rootlessness. The booths can disappear from one hour to the next. It is a world that caters to the world; it is also a world apart.

But the fairground laughter (Hugo made the point long before Bakhtin) has a liberating potential. The Mardi Gras expresses an alienated popular vitality; it is by nature ebullient, boisterous, even seditious. "Le mardi gras vous rit au nez," Hugo had written many years earlier in his polemical preface to *Le Dernier Jour d'un condamné*.[8] The insurrectional potential of the carnival is, moreover, well known to those in power, who have learned to control and degrade it for counterrevolutionary purposes. "The carnival is part of politics," Hugo observed in a curious chapter of *Les Misérables* describing the "official" encouragement and even orchestration of popular festivities.[9] Bakhtin later developed in critical and ideological terms what Hugo had intuited and put into fictional practice: the grotesque as a positive force, laughter and popular comic rituals negating hierarchical distance, unmasking the lies of law and order, generating the dynamics of becoming. *L'Homme qui rit*, with its fairground, its laughter-producing performances, its circus-booth theatricals, its monster-hero whose mouth has been slit from ear to ear—*usque ad aures*—seems made to order to illustrate Bakhtin's notion of the *carnavalesque*.[10]

Hugo marshals a lavish terminology to conjure up the world of jugglers, tumblers, acrobats, sword swallowers, and contortionists. Words such as *bateleur, saltimbanque, baladin, escamoteur, équilibriste*, and *sauteur* stud the text. Colorful names of archaic instruments and allusions to trumpet flourishes provide the background for the Tarrinzeau field, a large bowling green, now a fairground, on which stands out Ursus' colorful wagon, the "Green Box." But Hugo departs from a simple message of *carnavalesque* vitality. For Lord David and Duchess Josiane, the kermesse corresponds to the aristocrat's depraved taste for slumming (*s'encanailler*); it offers temporary relief from what Baudelaire called the "delicate monster" of boredom. Lord David, *magister elegantiarum*, passionately fond of street shows, circus freaks, and low haunts, regularly appears at the fairground under the name of Tom-Jim-Jack, dressed as a sailor, and plays the role of blackguard with zest. Conversely, the world of the performer and the clown is seen in a grim and even pejorative perspective. Characterized by the grotesque slave mask of the *mascaron*, a word previously associated with the gruesome lighthouse glimpsed in the storm (XIV, 93), the mummer's world is also described in pathological terms as a pariah community, a colony of lepers. Such images reflect more specifically upper-class revulsion, and contempt for the rabble come to "stare at the devil"—emotions summed up by the jeers of *Histrio! Mima!* with which one of the lords tries to shout down Gwynplaine.

Revealingly, Shakespeare's name appears in just this context of insults hurled at actors. Between the world of the fair and the world of the theater the text establishes a solid metaphorical and thematic bond. These analogies confirm the political significance of the theater for Hugo. It is worth recalling (certainly Hugo could not forget it, even after all those years) that it was precisely a play about the hatred of a buffoon for his king, *Le Roi s'amuse* (1832), which had been prohibited by the censor for its political-cultural impact and "subversive" nature. The intentions of that play, as well as its repression, were thus part of a personal political history. No theatrical detail in Hugo's fictional world is ever politically innocent. This is particularly true in *L'Homme qui rit*, where the many theatrical references at first seem in excess of the dramatic requirements of the plot. Ursus, playwright and director, who has been denounced to the authorities, is highly suspect to the inquisitional tribunal. Ultimately, he and his little theatrical group are banned. In the meantime, his frequent soliloquies are not merely an old actor's idiosyncrasy or a symbol of theatrical illusionism. They are the camouflage idiom of a continuing subversive discourse that occasionally erupts into unequivocal indictments.

The references to the theater are certainly not in excess of the symbolic and ideological dimensions of the novel. Not only is the specular play at the center of the novel more of a dream (*songe*) than a piece of dramaturgy, but the setting of the performances, in the courtyard of an inn, is clearly designed to recall the circumstances of Shakespeare's own performances.[11] Beyond the pleasure Hugo may have taken during his exile in evoking his former intimacy with the theater, there is the deeper satisfaction of creating a world in which illusion, fantasy, and "divine laughter"[12] serve a political purpose. The word *songe* unavoidably brings to mind the French title for *A Midsummer Night's Dream* (*Songe d'une nuit d'été*), a parallel that is confirmed in Hugo's contemporaneous fantasy play *Mangeront-ils?* by references to Puck, puckish laughter, and imps and clowns in the woods. What makes the double parallel (between Ursus and Shakespeare, between *L'Homme qui rit* and *Mangeront-ils?*) more interesting still is that the *Théâtre en Liberté*, to which Hugo's fantasy piece belongs, not only translates the freedom of laughter into the laughter of freedom but conveys unmistakable revolutionary motifs: a denunciation of both throne and church, an ironic treatment of the powerlessness of the king, the themes of forced abdication and regicide.

The full potential of the theatrical image in *L'Homme qui rit* depends, however, on our reading laughter as a polyvalent sign, thereby grasping the dialectical link between laughter and the tragic experience. The larger *commedia*, of which Gwynplaine's grimace and the Green Box performances are a part, represents an "univers complet" (XIV, 184), a total stage. It is in the light of such a totalizing spectacle, merging the grotesque and the highest pathos, that we must understand the reference to the theater as a pillory ("ce pilori qu'on appelle un théâtre"—XIV, 315), which metaphorically inverts the famous description in *Notre-Dame de Paris* of the pillory as a public spectacle. Hilarity becomes ominous, even tragic. The mask of laughter carved on Gwynplaine's face, the petrified *rictus* of his distorted features, conjures up in Hugo's mind the ancient face of Comedy affixed to the pediments of Greek theaters. The laugh acquires mythic grandeur. The "sepulchral immobility" of the sneering face becomes an emblem of eternal punishment (XIV, 182).

The laughing and laughter-producing monster brings out the essential link among fantasy, the comic spirit, and the tragic experience. But Gwynplaine's laughter, so violently inscribed on his face, also contains the potential of hatred and further violence. It is the "eternal laughter" of suffering calling for redress, the "incurable laughter" of victimhood demanding to be healed. Thus, in the very horror of the petrified spasm, there is rebellious hope. In an image that once again invokes the *mascarons* of the Pont Neuf, Hugo sees the Laughing Man as the "Caryatid of the weeping world" (XIV, 365)—an image which, together with that of the grinning stone figures supporting the heavy bridge, is at the very center of the political poem "La Révolution" written in 1857, only a few years before *L'Homme qui rit*.

The Politics of Laughter

The political thrust of the novel is written into Gwynplaine's disfigurement, which was ordered for political reasons by the king. "Par Ordre du Roi," the title of part 2, was the title originally planned for the entire novel. The historical and political connotations of laughter, so clearly suggested by this shift of titles, go back more than thirty years to the time when, in *Le Roi s'amuse*, the court jester Triboulet assessed his relation to François I: "I am the man who laughs; he is the man who kills."[13] But though laughter is doubly murderous—the laughter of oppression and the laughter of revenge—the issues involved cannot be reduced to this simple antagonistic scheme. The dramatic and symbolic range of laughter encompasses almost every aspect of Hugo's work, including unpleasant memories of the collective hilarity that often interrupted his own political speeches. Years earlier, in *Notre-Dame de Paris*, laughter had already proved protean—joyful, subversive, and sinister. By the time of *L'Homme qui rit*, it had assumed a "universal" significance: Gwynplaine's face wears the imprint of a "grimace totale" (XIV, 365). It sums up the dreams, fears, and potential of all mankind—including the potential for cruelty.

Even the traditional polarization of negative and positive values is blurred. At times, pejorative connotations seem to dominate. The world's inhumanity makes it impossible for Ursus ever to smile; but even his laughter is bitter, a "petit rire sec." Typically, laughter in the novel denotes the opposite of joy. The mimicry of fun resembles a communicable and hopeless disease: the crowd experiences a "contagion du rire," an "épilepsie d'hilarité"; Gwynplaine's laughter is seen as "incurable" (XIV, 289, 229, 347). The grimace of joy is essentially the expression of nonlaughter. "His face laughed, his thought did not." Suffering, punishment, and degradation are inherent in the physical manifestation of laughter. Hardquanonne dies laughing under the instruments of torture. Death and laughter seem, in fact, to be coupled from the early pages of the novel, as the child glimpses the skeletal grin of the hanged man. And Gwynplaine, we are told, wears on his face the death mask of ancient comedy (XIV, 182).

But in this comedy there is vitality: the denial of death. Just as Josiane knows the spontaneous laughter of earthly appetites, so the crowd at the fairground experiences a "sunburst of laughter" when the full monstrosity of Gwynplaine's face is revealed. Comic convulsions extend to nature itself. Hugo refers to a "cosmic" manifestation of hilarity, in the conflictual and rebellious context of the "immense rire prométhéen" (XIV, 199–200). Ursus glimpses, beyond Gwynplaine's mask of flesh, the great "grimace" at the bottom of infinity (XIV, 204). He dimly suspects that laughter corresponds to a deeper truth. Did Democritus not answer with a laugh when asked why he knew? Ursus inverts Democritus' answer: if asked why he laughed he would say, "Because I know" (XIV, 213).

And what Ursus knows or intuits is precisely what the narrator recognizes in Gwynplaine's laughter, which, like the force of events, is "as irrisistible as the tide" (*reflux*—XIV, 183). *Flux* and *reflux*, ever since the time of *Notre-Dame de Paris*, were associated in Hugo's mind with revolutionary thrust and with the counterthrust of political reaction. In one of the political poems of *Les Feuilles d'automne* dated May 1830, just a few weeks before the July Revolution, Hugo warned all kings that the high tide of popular forces would sweep them away, that past and present were bound to disappear "sous ce flot qui n'a pas de reflux."[14] Vital forces, in these endless fluctuations, are thus repeatedly characterized by violence and destruction.

It is in the thematic context of vital violence that we must interpret the irresponsible "Babylonian gaieties" of monarchs and the antagonistic complicities that bind the mob to the tyrant, as well as the formula with which Hugo sums up one of the preliminary chapters of his novel about the laughing man: *"The Exploitation of the Unhappy by the Happy."* The judgment is harsh. Significantly, it follows close upon the earliest reference to the king's and the people's ambiguous need for laughter: "Le peuple a besoin de rire; les rois aussi" (XIV, 139, 45). But a judgment, as Hugo himself indicates toward the end of the novel, is an act of defiance: "Qui juge, confronte." Far more than merely grotesque horror is involved in Gwynplaine's standing up to the lords: "I came to strike terror . . . I am the frightful Laughing Man" (XIV, 368, 353). The hour of laughter is the hour of fear. It is also the hour of history.

Two important texts, or intertexts, may help us understand better the politics of laughter in *L'Homme qui rit*. "La Révolution" (1857) and "Le Satyre" (1859) precede and prepare the story of Gwynplaine. "La Révolution,"[15] which, as we shall see, Hugo chose not to publish, is a narrative, visionary, and political poem describing how the bronze statue of Henry IV came down from its pedestal on the Pont Neuf, sought out the statues of Louis XIII and Louis XIV on their respective sites, and proceeded with them through the nocturnal, windswept, nightmarish cityscape toward an ominous assignation with history. On the large square near the Champs-Elysées, where they expect to find the statue of their descendant, Louis XV, the so-called Bien-Aimé, they meet instead with the full horror of the guillotine and the free-floating, decapitated, bleeding head of Louis XVI. And as the royal procession of equestrian statues moves along the somber quais, there can be heard, coming from other statues—the slave statues supporting the Pont Neuf—an explosion of vengeful laughter.

The interest of this ghostly parade of statues is multiple. On one level, it is a fine example of Hugo's ability to give an apocalyptic cast to a familiar setting. The funereal voice of the wind and the lament of the Seine provide the accompaniment to a grim vision of suffering in history: carceral oppression, torture, frightful executions—the stark rehearsal of all the crimes against human dignity that justified the excesses of the Revolution.

Yet the voice of the wind calling for an encounter with history leads to a confrontation with what is most abhorrent to Hugo: the guillotine. No matter how genuine his declared sympathies for the cause of revolution may be, the imaginary encounter with the instrument of political murder is, as always with Hugo, articulated around the difficult—if not impossible—justification of violence. The guillotine is a vision of horror, a nightmare silhouetted against the surrealistic background of the city, tragically encoding for all time the fateful number *93*, while oozing blood seems to be spelling on the paving blocks the ironic word *Justice*. The loud peals of laughter heard coming from the sneering stone masks that support the Pont Neuf add further irony to this episode. Filled with the vengeful memory of the common people's long martyrdom, these specters of a "sinister Mardi Gras" laugh as though theirs were the laughter of history itself. Indeed, in a fragment originally destined to take its place in *La Légende des siècles*, Hugo begins a section entitled "Histoire" with the warning: "Et fais attention. On rit."[16] The explosion of laughter directed at the royal statues on their way to meet the guillotine is ideologically charged. The hour of laughter is the hour of revolution:[17] "voici l'heure d'en rire."

It is to a sixteenth-century sculptor, Germain Pilon, that Hugo attributes the creation of the grimacing and threatening *mascarons* of the Pont Neuf. Twenty-five years earlier, in describing Quasimodo's election as Pope of Fools, he had already alluded to the *mascarons* as the "petrified nightmares" sculpted by Germain Pilon (IV, 51). The laughter of these statues is explicitly *carnavalesque*. Hugo, in "La Révolution," has them participate in a political-metaphysical "carnaval de l'infini." Behind Pantagruel looms Ugolino—"Masque de Rabelais sur la face de Dante." The tragic grotesqueness of the stone mask, challenging the order of things, hides a deeper defiance. And this spasmodic laughter of the slave statues is made more threatening still by the sulfurous flash ("lueur de soufre"—X, 233) illuminating their spokesman's grin. The negatory, destructive, and infernal quality of this rebellious laughter is brought out by the perpetual grin ("rictus sans fin") which the *mascarons* are condemned to wear. (X, 228–229, 233).

The ambiguity of this mutinous laughter, at once a liberation and a form of damnation, casts renewed light on Hugo's equivocal view of the revolutionary and prerevolutionary *peuple*. For *le peuple*, which the *mascarons* both announce and represent, is at the same time a work of art and a still shapeless mass ("difforme" is the poet's own word). Shape and shapelessness are oxymoronically wedded, as Hugo describes the "populace horrible des statues," the "visage informe et profond de la masse." If the flaming eye and the volcanic anger of long suffering bestow dignity on Germain Pilon's stone effigies of the proletariat, a number of derogatory terms, as well as images of a teeming subhumanity ("le fourmillement des cloportes humains"), recall the sordid criminal underworld of the Cour des Miracles in *Notre-Dame de Paris* (X, 230, 226).

What is really at stake, as happens so often in the work of Hugo, is the difficult relation of the poet to revolution. For it is an artist, more specifically an image maker, a "pétrisseur des formes ténébreuses," who is the prophet of the hour of laughter and revolution, the true creator or pro-creator of the future: "tu fis le peuple, toi!" But if that laughter is dark indeed, the artist himself is a prince of darkness, a "noir génie" (X, 226, 232). For there can be no doubt; the prophet of the revolutionary apocalypse haunts the darker regions. "Je suis un oiseau de nuit"—"j'habite l'azur noir," Hugo writes about himself.[18] He is, like Germain Pilon, the nocturnal genius forever attentive to the darkest side of the mystery (the "côté le plus noir du mystère"—X, 228), almost an accomplice of blackness.

The relation of laughter to revolution is a recurrent and complex feature in Hugo's writings. The dwarf clown Habibrah in *Bug–Jargal*, whose face condemns him to "perpetual laughter," dreams of inflicting atrocious punishment on his master. In *Le Roi s'amuse*, Triboulet—who was to become Verdi's Rigoletto—defines himself, anticipating the title of the future novel, as a vengeful "homme qui rit." An extraordinary pen drawing by Hugo, almost contemporaneous with *Le Roi s'amuse*, is entitled "Le Dernier Bouffon songeant au dernier roi" and depicts the vengeful grimace of the King's fool.[19] (See Illustration 19.) In *Le Rhin*, the wooden statue of the buffoonish dwarf speaks to Hugo the tourist of the jester's age-old yearning: his snicker announces the vengeance of one who knows he will outlive the king he slavishly entertained.[20] Laughter and revolution, with time, become increasingly bound to each other, transcending the specific dialectic of king and buffoon which Anne Ubersfeld masterfully analyzed in her study of Hugo's theater. In *Les Misérables* the lower classes are seen, in their historical development, as increasingly given to laughter ("Les voilà presque gaies"). But theirs is, as Hugo puts it, a "diabolical and enigmatic mirth."[21] In a chapter whose title juxtaposes laughter and power

("Railler, régner"), Hugo posits a link between the laughter of the *gamin* Gavroche, the guffaws of the Parisian populace, and the sharp teeth of the revolutionary city: "Paris always bares its teeth; when it does not snarl, it laughs."[22] In *L'Homme qui rit* the equation between revolutionary thrust and laughter is even more explicit. The statement "Je suis l'effrayant Homme qui Rit" follows close upon the self-proclamation: "Je suis le peuple" (XIV, 353). The laughter in question, inflicted by order of the king, clearly signifies hatred, revenge, and power; it announces the violent twilight and death of all kings.

The poem "La Révolution" works out the dialectical relation between the laughter from above and the laughter from below, the subtle interdependence of tyrant and jester. The grotesque stone masks carry symbolically far more than the weight of the bridge. They are the laughing and grimacing bearers (*portefaix*) of all mankind. But coming from above, another laughter can be heard: the laughter of the kings. For just as laughter defines the revolutionary spirit, so too does it define the institution of royalty. "You laugh; you reign" (X, 228, 241). Henri IV, we are told, spent his entire life in laughter—he even laughed while praying. But not far from this throne of joy, peasants who refused to pay taxes were condemned to be hung. Louis XIII found entertainment in executions, tortures, and charnel houses. Louis XIV sought in the holocaust of war a cure for boredom. Under his reign, triumphant and repressive orthodoxy became a "tigre qui rit" (X, 233, 238). As for the debauched laughter of Louis XV, it sums up the insolence and inequities of all royal power. This power laughter, or "rire de force," still rings in Hugo's ears. A scorching title of *Les Châtiments* refers to his archenemy Napoléon-le-petit: "L'Homme a ri." Other titles of the same collection ("Joyeuse vie," "L'Empereur s'amuse") similarly characterize the Second Empire by the cruel laughter of tyranny.[23]

That is the laughter from above. But coming from below, from "under," another laughter can be heard. The preposition *sous* ("sous le tyran," "sous Valois," "sous Bourbon," "sous l'olympe royal," "sous les monstres d'en haut") literally invades the space of the text (X, 229). This laughter from below is, however, also monstrous; to the "monsters above" correspond the "monsters below." This shapeless, anonymous populace binds the victim and the criminal in a common laughter. Gwynplaine's somber conclusion in *L'Homme qui rit* is that all of human agony finds its expression in a frightening grimace of joy. The verb *rire* speaks of the infinitely repetitive nature of suffering. "Le meurt-de-faim rit, le mendiant rit, le forçat rit, la prostituée rit, l'orphelin, pour gagner sa vie, rit, l'esclave rit, le soldat rit, le peuple rit."[24]

By the time he wrote *L'Homme qui rit*, Hugo came to view the dialectics of laughter as part of a universal master-slave relationship. In some remarkable pages entitled "Sur les Bouffons et la société," he opposes sneering and laughing: "jamais l'esclave ne rit. Il ricane. Ce qui rit, c'est le maître." The verb *confront* appears in this context: "confrontez son rire avec le vôtre."[25] But master and slave need each other: "You are his puppet, but he is yours." And around this double notion and interdependence of royal and buffoonish laughter, Hugo develops a psychological theory of revolution, involving a dramatic and so to speak historical progression: from regal boredom requiring distraction, to sadism (playing with the weak, transforming torture into laughter), to a complicity in self-humiliation (the "misère consentante" of the underdog), to the vengeful sneer (the laughter of rebellion), to the laughter that makes the mighty tremble, to the *Peuple* emerging as a universal force. The link with the poem "Le Satyre" is obvious. In a key chapter of *L'Homme qui rit*, the desperate laughter ("rire de force") associated with the word *Republic* is indeed personified as a symbolic figure of all-powerful humanity quite reminiscent of the Promethean Satyr: "Je suis un symbole . . . j'incarne Tout."[26]

The myth-making process binding laughter and revolution is in fact most powerfully at work in the poem "Le Satyre," as the visionary faun stands up to the assembled gods on Olympus. If, in *L'Homme qui rit*, the kings' laughter is compared to the laughter of the gods, the gods in "Le Satyre" appear as oppressive tyrants. In the poem "Le Titan," these same gods will even more explicitly be treated as *parvenu* despots, as heartless criminals thriving on the "altar of fear."[27] Needless to say, all these despots laugh. In the poem "Le Satyre" they split their sides laughing, treating the Satyr as a court entertainer ("Allons, chante"), unaware that these spasms of laughter announce their downfall. The mythopoetic construct thus opposes the Satyr's laughter from below (his *rictus*) to the merry-making explosion of the gods having tempestuous fun at the expense of the peasant faun. But the poem leads to an upheaval. The clumsy Satyr assumes Promethean dimensions, then cosmic dimensions. And once the word *liberté* is pronounced, the poem logically concludes with Jupiter on his knees: "Place à Tout! Je suis Pan; Jupiter! à genoux." The hour of laughter is the "heure énorme" when the Olympian kings will be dethroned—the hour of revolution.

The intertextual importance of "Le Satyre" becomes even more obvious if one recalls that in "La Révolution" the institution of royalty is referred to as "l'olympe royal," that Germain Pilon is called the artist who lit up the faun's eye with the bright light of revolutionary fervor, and that the lackey's laughter makes him a brother to the Orphic faun: "Le valet rit, surpris d'être aussi le satyre" (X, 228). But the symbolism of the poem extends beyond politics. If the Satyr is there to remind us that enslaved humanity, once engaged in "holy rebellion," is destined to be enthroned, he is also the emblem of all visionary poetry. His is the "eye of the cavern," staring at the world's enigma, at nature's violent nuptials. He sees the tree from the perspective of its roots; he penetrates into the shadowy underside of creation. On the Orphic lyre, he sings the mysteries of fruitful decomposition. He is the delirious rhapsodist, the poet of excess, ultimately growing into a dark figure occupying all space. The revolutionary myth thus leads to a cosmic myth that dehistoricizes revolution.

It is, however, in *L'Homme qui rit* that Hugo's dialectics of king and jester attain their greatest complexity. The subject becomes so pervasive that it overflows into the contemporaneous fantasy play *Mangeront-ils?* which interlocks the figure of the king with that of the Ariel-like robber Aïrolo, the "man from below." This playlet stresses the dependence of the king on the buffoonish challenger of his authority, as well as the basic complicity between the throne and the world of criminality ("In his gibbet, I recognize my throne").[28] Hugo's diagnosis of this complicity is harsh indeed. He defines the king as a living scaffold assisted by two figures: the hangman and the buffoon.

The novel casts an even gloomier light. Gwynplaine's laughter is but the expression of a sob. "I laugh; which means: I cry" (XIV, 353). The master-slave complicity blurs any clearcut antagonism between them. In an obvious reference to *Le Roi s'amuse*, the narrator explains that one pole requires the other: François I needs Triboulet. The court jester participates in the exercise of power. "Whoever makes the king laugh makes all the others tremble" (XIV, 163–164). Gwynplaine, like the *mascarons* of "La Révolution," carries the weight of all suffering. But there is more than pathos in his mask of hilarity. This mask is a living denunciation of the laughter it represents. Humanity has been defaced, degraded: the image of man has been transformed into a bestial mask of flesh. Laughter, the instrument of denunciation and revelation, is thus also the signal of a profound dehumanization, a fall from grace.

It is the essence of laughter which thus appears deeply troubling—a stigma on the image of man. Gwynplaine's comic mask is, in fact, called a "rictus stigmate." The marks of this wound have a distinctly evil connotation. Gwynplaine, scarred by the stigmata of hilarity, is condemned to an incurable, eternal laughter: "*Masca eris, et ridebis semper*" (XIV, 347, 182, 128). The notion of eternity carries here the darkest possible undertones. The petrified death mask of hilarity is seen as an "infernal head," condemning the monstrous hero to a perpetual state of looking "hellishly buffoonish." One is reminded of Baudelaire's spiritual derelicts "au rire éternel condamnés"; they can no longer smile. Laughter, for Baudelaire as for many Romantics, is a sign of satanism: the Word Incarnate never laughed.[29] Laughter is thus more threatening than the death announced by the grin of the hanged man. Gwynplaine's stigmata have made him into a demonic oxymoron: "Il était le maudit élu" (XIV, 182, 187). If the carnal Josiane is drawn to what she defines as his "grand rire infernal," this might be attributed to her perversity. But what is one to say of the narrative voice that refers to the "chaos des rires noirs" as hell itself? And how is one to read the surprising statement that if Satan had Gwynplaine's laughter, "that laughter would condemn God" (XIV, 368, 354)?

One can only suspect that the principle of authority itself is in question, that the dialectics of laughter stretch, beyond the theme of revolution, to the auctorial complicity with darkness. Much like nature, which, in one of Hugo's great lines of poetry, couples maximal suffering ("l'immense deuil") with the loudest laughter ("rire énorme"),[30] so art expresses its terror of itself through what Hugo calls the "inquiétant rire de l'art."[31] In *Promontorium somnii*, Hugo refers to the disturbing hilarity of dreams, the nocturnal laughter of the subconscious, the "hilarité des ténèbres," which seems so closely allied to the sources of artistic creation.[32] But it is in *William Shakespeare* that he develops this notion of the great laughter of art, explicitly linking *le rire* to the abyss of poetic creativity.[33] The great artists themselves—like Germain Pilon, the dark genius—are the high priests of laughter, "prêtres du rire," as Hugo puts it in "Les Mages."[34]

This perspective on genius takes on an even more ominous quality if one remembers that already in *Le Dernier Jour d'un condamné* laughter was specifically associated with criminality— namely, with the bloodthirsty mob and the demonic convicts whose strident laughter continued to echo in *Les Misérables*. In *L'Homme qui rit*, Hugo extends the sense of anxiety and guilt. Not only is Gwynplaine explicitly referred to as Lucifer, both a sinister figure and a carrier of light (XIV, 365), but all of creation seems to indulge in grim merrymaking. "L'océan s'amuse" is the self-parodying formula Hugo applies to the cruel sea in the shipwreck episode. The whirlwind at the center of the storm is a menacing sneer: "le rictus de la trombe." Behind these unleashed mocking forces, the mysterious evil laughter of nature's animating spirit can be perceived: "le ricanement du combattant inaccessible" (XIV, 100, 103, 99).

The rhetoric of metaphysical anguish casts light on Gwynplaine's withdrawal from political action. His ultimate choice of Dea and death in preference to ideological commitment is symptomatic of underlying retractile tendencies. It is one of Hugo's many variations on the themes of effacement and initiatory thresholds, for it is hard not to read this disappearance as a decision not to pursue the political path so clearly designated by laughter. The same page that proclaims the tragic buffoon as a *total* symbol ("Je suis l'Homme . . . J'incarne Tout") also declares that even the best revolutionary action is the "dawn of catastrophe" (XIV, 354). The politics of laughter, it would seem, have brought Gwynplaine to the edge of a larger issue. Once again, Hugo's narrative leads to a transcendence that signifies the denial of politics and of the imperatives of history. Like Germain Pilon and the Satyr, like all the high priests of laughter, Gwynplaine is an Orphic visionary.

This ahistorical transcendence is itself, however, articulated on the problematics of laughter, that is, on the displacement of laughter by the smile. For in choosing to follow Dea to a love-death by water, Gwynplaine can smile for the first time. The word *smile* appears three times on the last page, always in proximity to words denoting *vision*. And as Gwynplaine enters through the river fog into the luminous night of a smiling death, this turning away from politics and laughter is made more intelligible by the memory of a sentence earlier in the novel—a sentence that also helps explain why Hugo chose not to publish his poem "La Révolution": "There is acceptance in the smile, whereas a laugh is often a refusal."[35]

The Flesh

To attain the serenity and wisdom of the smile, the monster Gwynplaine must first confront greater monsters. He is, in fact, surrounded by monstrosity. The giant Irish boxer Phelem-ghe-madone and his Scottish opponent Helmsgail beat each other into a bloody pulp, until the former is transfigured into a one-eyed creature, a Cyclops (XIV, 178). This crippling, murderous bout, which Gwynplaine does not witness (it has been arranged for the exclusive delight of an aristocratic public), is indicative of all human relations that are characterized by mutilation.[36] It would, however, be untrue to the spirit of Hugo to view monstrosity as essentially man-made. Society, because of its hierarchized structures of power and prerogatives, is a moral monster. As he prepares to begin his novel, Hugo remarks: "A certain deformity occurs in old societies. Everything ends up by being monstrous." He adds: "The king is a case of teratology, the lord is an excrescence."[37] Yet the more pervasive monsters in Hugo's world involve his vision of the deeper mystery of life.

For nature itself, indeed all of creation, is presented as monstrous. "Portentosum mare" is the title of one of several chapters that deal specifically with the horror of the sea, described as a beast undergoing metamorphoses: it has scales; it looks like a dragon; it becomes a crocodile, then a boa. The bubbles of the swell are pustules; the sea foam is a leprous surface. The storm, accompanied by the "immense bestial voice" of the ocean, is likened to a mythological bull (XIV, 87). And above the waters, a great turbid cloud appears, like the livid belly of a hydra whose pouch-like adherences pump the sea with deadly suctions. The seascape evokes the full hideousness of the giant octopus, God's masterpiece of horror. Even the coastline (Hugo plays on the word *côte*, meaning both coast and rib) has the "hideous anatomy" of some prehistoric monster (XIV, 110). All of nature, not only the hostile landscape and the windswept fury of the water, participates in the monstrous "premeditation of creation" (XIV, 237). Hugo's Satyr, it must be recalled, sings "la terre monstrueuse."[38]

The monstrous premeditations of nature are most flagrant in the sexual drive. The flesh, like matter, remains a threatening reality for Hugo. Matter is evil ("la matière, c'est le démon");[39] and the flesh is synonymous with matter, synonymous indeed with the word *monster*. In the notes for *L'Homme qui rit*, the three terms are bound to one another: "ce monstre, la matière, la chair."[40] No other novel of Hugo's is so sensuous and at the same time so suffused with the terror of lust. Faced with the opulent physique and provocative sexuality of Duchess Josiane ("Josiane, c'était la chair"—XIV, 144), Gwynplaine experiences the frightful mystery of sex; he glimpses the turbulent surface of the unknown. The allurements of the temptress are thus situated at a point of intersection between evil and visionary insight.

The danger of sex looms strongest in the hothouse atmosphere of Corleone castle, the luxurious palace of evil. At the center of this labyrinthine construction, in the heavily scented grotto of mirrors surrounding her bed, Josiane assails Gwynplaine. The symbolism of the episode is multiple. The daedalian nature of the bewitched palace suggests both initiation and perdition. The frenzy of the aristocratic bacchant has mythical dimensions. The monster motif is heightened by the avatars of the "wild woman" in her den: now Messalina, then an undulating serpent, then again a tigress provoking the brutal triumph of instinct. The chapter entitled "Eve," followed by the longer chapter "Satan," betray an almost theological fear of woman. Eve is, in fact, declared "worse than Satan." In the chapter "Abyssus abyssum vocat," Hugo goes one step further: it is Eve who tempted Lucifer (XIV, 311, 237). This surprising twist takes on added meaning if one recalls that after his revolutionary speech in the House of Lords, Gwynplaine is described as none other than the ominous torch bearer Lucifer (XIV, 365).

The real monster is thus Eve-Josiane, the blue-and-black-eyed amazon whose perverse heart contains the world's corruption. Depravity is her pride. "Je suis donc un monstre," she says with delight as she links her destiny with that of Amphitrite giving herself to the Cyclops, Penthesilea lusting for the Centaur, and Queen Rhodope in love with Pteh, the man with the crocodile's head (XIV, 316). Animal images repeatedly signal the threatening nature of perverse woman. Hugo stresses the "bestial aspect" of the Olympian prostitute (XIV, 242). He compares the embrace of her arms to the twinings of a viper (XIV, 316, 242, 367). More significantly still, in terms of the monster motif, is the underlying link with the dreadful sea creature (Venus, too, is born of the sea): the naked body of Josiane, glimpsed by Gwynplaine through the double web of the transparent curtain and shirt, is compared to a spider—and this spider unavoidably brings to mind the giant *pieuvre* in *Les Travailleurs de la mer*, the vile octopus known both as the devilfish and the bloodsucker.

Josiane is sexually attracted to the misshapen Gwynplaine. Her delight at seeing him stumble into her chamber is overwhelming. He is, as she puts it, the monster of her dreams. With him she expects to experience "one of those great nocturnal adventures" (XIV, 314–315). But her case clearly transcends aristocratic depravity. Though Hugo invokes the popular belief that ladies of high society have a taste for dwarfs and hunchbacks, and though this British Venus yearns to be raped by a faun (a clear political note, in view of the Satyr's revolutionary challenge to the gods), the monster motif points to a larger theme of transgression. Josiane, a "lascivious dreamer," conceives of an unbridled betrothal ("fiançailles effrénées") outside all laws. Hers is a lust for the impossible, the expectation of a supremely lascivious *ideal* (XIV, 168, 314, 145).

But transgression in the form of sex is precisely what terrifies Gwynplaine. He has an innate fear of the "extase bestiale," of the brutal triumph of instinct, and he perceives Josiane's nudity as a fundamental threat: "La femme nue, c'est la femme armée" (XIV, 316, 310–311). Gilliatt in *Les Travailleurs de la mer*, as we have seen, similarly discovers that the sight of a naked woman fills him with horror (XII, 599). In fact, almost all of Hugo's heroes tend to be exceedingly chaste, even virginal: Valjean, Gilliatt, Gauvain—all of them are celibate. Their abstinence, as one French critic remarked, betrays a deep uneasiness about sex, a latent and largely unconscious rebellion against "the erotic origin of life."[41]

There is little doubt that despite Hugo's celebration of the great nuptials of nature, despite his dithyrambs to the rising sap and heady irradiations of nature, he perceived the inexorable call of sex as an alienation from the self, a threat to the integrity of being. There is more than a hint that the temptations of the flesh experienced by Gwynplaine correspond in Hugo to a deeply felt personal anxiety. "La Tentation de saint Gwynplaine" is the title of a key chapter. "The spinal column has its reveries," Hugo comments, as Gwynplaine experiences the dictates of physical desire (XIV, 237).

The obsessional nature of sexuality in Hugo's writings remains a subject largely unexplored. Though Hugo, even in his personal notes, rarely provides intimate details, he has left a few highly revealing documents. One such, dated 14 April 1861, couched in a private jargon of French expressions melded with a very peculiar Spanish, transcribes a dream in which his nocturnal self, together with a group of voyeurs, watches the humiliating public exhibition of the woman he has loved. The woman, known to him as refined and chaste, is slowly rotated on a wheel, naked and with her legs spread apart, while all eyes converge on her lower belly and dark pubic hair. With every turn of the wheel, all is brutally revealed: "todos ven todo."[42]

The abyss of degradation and raw sexuality is fully perceived by Gwynplaine. His fear of the flesh is part of a deeper fear of the fall. The trap of sexuality is more dangerous still than the trap of ambition: behind it loom chaotic forces. Gwynplaine's destiny is in fact a psychodrama whose stakes are victory or defeat in the face of chaos. What complicates this drama, however, is that chaos, in Hugo's perspective, is also synonymous with the life-giving forces of nature. In a projected preface to the novel, Hugo tersely remarks: "Matter oppresses. The soul struggles. Hence chaos." The answer to this oppression is equally terse. It sums up Gwynplaine's experience of true love: "Over chaos hovers the spirit."[43]

Chaos Conquered

The psychodrama of rehabilitation is not only acted out but structurally inscribed as a play within the narrative. The rehabilitation of the monster is thus intimately bound up with the self-conscious poetic process. It is worth recalling that Hugo, in discussing Shakespeare's dramatic art, was particularly interested in the technique of the play within the play, commenting on the efficacy of the "doubles actions" through which motifs echo themselves.[44] Did André Gide—as Lucien Dällenbach suggested—have Hugo in mind when he coined the expression *mise en abyme*?[45] Clearly, the inverted abyss is a recurrent figure in the work of Hugo: *gouffre en haut* and *l'océan d'en haut* are privileged metaphors for the space of infinity.[46]

The inversion, however, also functions in an artistic perspective: it is related to the notion of the grotesque, as well as to that of divine creativity. Josiane explains: "To mingle the high and the low, that is chaos" (XIV, 316). But chaos and the commingling of extremes also signal the beginning of all creation and of every poetic process. God-like, the poet is creator of chaos, at the same time as he engages in a struggle against the shapeless. Like Gwynplaine the child, confronting the hanged man on the desolate plateau, he finds himself between being and nonbeing. Poetry is chaos before it can be music, but the music continues to sing the chaos it has vanquished. The prodigious figure of the Satyr once again embodies Hugo's Orphism: "Le satyre chanta la terre monstrueuse." More explicitly—and this precisely in a description of the bay of Portland, originally intended for *L'Homme qui rit*— Hugo compares the energies of the ocean to the wild exuberance of genius, which dislocates all symmetries and introduces a harmony "made up of chaos."[47]

It is in this context that we must read Ursus' allegorical interlude *Chaos vaincu*, which dramatizes the second creation of man against the brutal forces of darkness. The brief scenario is made up mostly of pantomime, interspersed with initiatory songs based on a few lines of Hugo's peculiar brand of Spanish. In the narrative account of this nightly performance, dramatic effects of darkness and of light provide the visual background. The choreographic drama that unfolds describes a human figure (Gwynplaine) assailed by the forces of instinct (a bear and a wolf, played by Ursus and Homo) and struggling from under a winding sheet. The agonistic birth of the human spirit and its emergence from chaos occur to the accompaniment of Orphic music, performed by the celestial voice of the blind Dea. The saved one—for it is she whom Gwynplaine had found half-buried in the snow—here becomes the savior. The man-monster, guided and encouraged by the luminous voice of poetry, vanquishes the animals and rises up to a spiritual life, surrounded by what Hugo, in a striking image, describes as a "soleil de rire" (XIV, 199).

At the plot level, the encased allegory reenacts the love story of Gwynplaine and Dea. At the level of melodrama, the "sunburst of laughter" cruelly illumines the face of Gwynplaine as he is turned into a fairground spectacle. But it is the symbolic range of the scene that matters most. The allegorical interlude represents an initiatory mystery. The circus wagon becomes the theatrical sanctuary of a nightly ritual. The foreignness of the language used in this ceremonial performance only accentuates its liturgical and hieratic nature. *Chaos vaincu* is a sacramental celebration.[48]

The larger mystery of Ursus' play mirrors one of Hugo's most basic themes: the struggle and interplay between darkness and light. Dea's blindness is not just an accident, the grim result of her exposure in the snowstorm. Blindness, in *L'Homme qui rit*, is of the essence: it is the condition of insight and vision. If Dea illustrates "seeing blindness" ("cécité voyante"), it is because, blind to Gwynplaine's disfigurement, she can see the beauty of his soul. According to Ursus, the blind can see the invisible: "Conscience is vision" (XIV, 209, 186). Blind Dea stands for pure love. Innocence, the narrator explains, is made of "sacred darkness." To the extent that Dea can see the invisible light ("Je vois" are her last words), she is, in her blindness, perceived as a "mysterious priestess" (XIV, 126, 383, 215).

We are touching here on Hugo's fundamental belief that the loftiest poetry—the poetry of contemplation—requires the eclipse of the visible world. The poet-*regardeur* must learn not to see in order to attain the vision of the poet-*voyant*. To become "le grand oeil fixe" staring at infinity, the visionary poet must cease looking at the surface of things. To contemplate the world is to occult it: "contempler les choses, / C'est finir par ne plus les voir."[49] The theme of blindness is a steady reminder that the novel strikes close to Hugo's deepest poetic concerns. *Chaos vaincu*, which allegorizes the victory of light from within "sacred darkness," tells of the redemptive thrust of all creative efforts.

The symbolic meaning of *L'Homme qui rit* thus reaches far beyond the rehabilitation of the monster. To be sure, "saint" Gwynplaine is the savior saved; and the word "redemption" appears in the paragraph which expressly states that the hero's destiny is to live under a stigma. On the same page, this destiny is summed up by the oxymoron "maudit élu," which hints once more at the Lucifer motif (XIV, 187). But the anathema associated with this tragic light-carrying function clearly extends beyond the figure of Gwynplaine. It suffuses the text, and in particular all references to the poetic message. The sealed bottle entrusted to the sea by the sinister spiritual leader of the *comprachicos*, the bottle that contains their collective confession of crimes, is the conventional symbol of the surviving literary text. As he goes down to his death by water, Doctor Gernardus Geestemunde, the grim redactor of the text, holds up the tarred gourd as if showing it to the Infinite (XIV, 108).

The posthumous message—the manuscript—is here obviously associated with evil. The surviving text is literally the story of a crime. Doctor Gernardus, a baleful visionary, writes his ultimate text, to the sound of the chaotic ocean, on the verso of an old parchment. The self-parody is unmistakable, for Hugo himself had recently written a long and disturbing poem entitled "Le Verso de la page." But the author of the second verso—the one who dies in the shipwreck, leaving behind him the tarred gourd—is explicitly a dark genius, a poet of the abyss.

The latent association of vision with evil seems confirmed in the passage that presents blind Dea as a "mysterious priestess," for blindness is dignified as a metaphysical principle. Ursus hypothesizes that God himself is blind, that he did not notice—or chose not to notice—that the devil was implicated in the Creation (XIV, 215). This participation of evil in divine authorship, this connivance of God with the forces of darkness, casts a revealing light on the deep-seated links, in *L'Homme qui rit*, between chaos and writing, between salvation and the forces of destruction. It is as though evil remained a necessary and assimilable element in Hugo's metaphysics, much as chaos is for him the indispensable material of aesthetic form. The writer's vocation and quest imply a fundamental complicity with the very forces he sets out to tame.

Abyss and Creation

The writer's quest, though powerfully suggested, remains mostly implicit. It is hinted at early in the charcoaled inscription URSUS, PHILOSOPHE on the ceiling of Ursus' hut, and in his perpetual wanderings. The broader notion of a quest is systematically projected through archetypal episodes, as Gwynplaine confronts human laws and temptations.[50] His is an exemplary destiny. As a child hero, he undergoes a second birth when he brings a fellow creature back to life under the shadow of a hanged man. As a young boy struggling with fate and death, he is compared to Hercules. Mythological quest-images abound: Gwynplaine follows a trail of footprints in the snow as though guided by a thread in a labyrinth; he loses and finds himself in the forest of his dreams (XIV, 284, 112). As an adult, he pursues his vocation of *errance*: he penetrates into the dark entrails of a prison, and later into the maze of Josiane's pleasure castle, which Hugo compares to yet another dark forest. The entanglements of the castle's passageways, corridors, cells, and hidden doors are likened to the inextricable branchings in the mysterious dwellings of antiquity, and more specifically to those of Egyptian tombs. The quest motif is repeatedly signaled. On the same page that evokes the crypt of King Psammetichus, discovered by Passalacqua, the word *errer* is featured—with the additional stress of a Latin quotation referring to circular wanderings: "Error circumflexus. Locus implicitus gyris" (XIV, 307).

The initiatory nature of the quest is made perfectly obvious in the final chapter, as Gwynplaine moves toward a willed death, reassessing his life: "I have just passed through a whole life in a few hours" (XIV, 382). As the spectral ship glides slowly down the river to the ocean, Gwynplaine deliberately walks with a phantom's stride toward the watery abyss. His eyes fixed on a point of heaven at the very heart of darkness, he is as though drawn by a vision. His suicide is indeed not a death, but a reunion. Dea expects him. And for the first time, the Man Who Laughs can smile a mysterious smile of bliss, as he rejects worldly commitments for what must be understood as a better life.

But the smile is far from reassuring. The exit from the prison of existence suggests an escape from a world in which chaos cannot be vanquished. "Evil exists," says Ursus (XIV, 294). What is at stake is something more disturbing than the mere coexistence of good and evil. In "Le Verso de la page," Hugo had written of the awesome intermingling ("triste et difforme mélange") of good and evil, explicitly stating that one is born of the other: "Ils naissent l'un de l'autre."[51] In *L'Homme qui rit*, evil exists as gratuitous energy. Barkilphedro enjoys hatred for hatred's sake; he is an artist of evil. The narrator ironically concludes that art for art's sake exists in nature.

The gratuitousness of evil underscores its essential mystery. The dark side of the human soul remains inscrutable. To the question of the *why* of evil ("Pourquoi les malfaisants?"), Hugo replies that there is something in the great unknown that seems to be in the service of evil ("aux ordres du mal"). Biblical images—the serpent, Cain, Job—are invoked.[52] Satan, both as subtle logician and brutal antagonist, is here something more than a figure of speech. At one point, the narrator asks whether evil must be taken as an integral part of creation. The answer is suggested in the form of another question (XIV, 318): Might it not be that the devil himself is a *necessity*?

Discernible behind such speculations is the awareness of a mystery more directly disturbing to the author; for the comparison of consummate villainy to an *ars poetica* is reversible: the act of poetic creation itself can be suspected of complicity with the forces of darkness. The deepest anxiety in *L'Homme qui rit* may thus well be centered on poetic vision. The words *vision* and *visionary* are consistently associated with a terrifying reality. The spectacle of the cruel sea is broadened into the "visionary turbulence of the horizon" (XIV, 64). The sea metaphor is, in fact, expanded into a more generalized trope for human misery: Gwynplaine has a total "vision" of what Hugo, evoking the angry sea foam, describes as the "écume du malheur." But the word *visionary* ultimately also signals a very personal confrontation with tragedy. As Gwynplaine stares at unmasked destiny, yielding to the death wish, he appears as the "visionnaire éperdu" facing the inexorable (XIV, 203, 361).

More specifically, the all-seeing "vision" is related to gloom and obscurity. Dea is called a *voyante* precisely to the extent that, behind the black wall of blindness, she is a captive of the dark (XIV, 184). Partial or total occultation characterizes the visionary episodes. The elaborate pages on the shipwreck stress the interplay of darkness and light. What can be seen at a distance beneath the sinister lighthouse of the Casquets is like an extinction of light ("écrasement de lumière") at the center of nocturnal horror. (See Illustration 22.) Elsewhere black and white come into uncanny metaphorical association, as Hugo draws on the recently invented technique of photography. To the pariah-child moving forward in the snowstorm, the town of Weymouth appears as though drawn in white on a black horizon, "something like what today would be called a negative proof" (XIV, 96, 115). Interestingly enough, in "La Pente de la rêverie," many years earlier, Hugo had already referred to the "chambre noire" of his mind as the visionary locus.[53]

Twilight effects, forlorn nocturnal landscapes, the "black yawn" of infinity, the invading tide of darkness—these are among the familiar images of *L'Homme qui rit* (XIV, 103, 56). They are most often projected in a vertical perspective. Hugo's expression "l'abîme en perspective," defining the heart of the storm, also defines his visionary mode. Verticality, beginning with "La Pente de la rêverie," has ever characterized the vatic poet's exploration of his dreamworld. "Mon esprit plongea donc sous ce flot inconnu . . ."[54] Gwynplaine's affinity with the visionary poet-explorer is made perfectly clear in his great speech before the House of Lords: "I am he who comes from the depths"; "I was cast into the abyss"; "I am a diver, and I bring back the pearl, Truth" (XIV, 349).

Such a descent to the bottom of the well, the pit, or the abyss is of course fraught with danger. Appropriately, "La Pente de la rêverie" begins with a warning: the incline of reverie is perilous. This warning reverberates throughout Hugo's work. The terminology of "La Pente de la rêverie" is echoed in *L'Homme qui rit*. In the episode of the penal vault, Gwynplaine finds himself on a "pente douce," one of those "pentes insensibles" that pull one down to the terrible unknown (XIV, 256). There can be no doubt that this downward movement to the world of crime and suffering is conceived as an awesome visionary descent. Gwynplaine, we are told, is moving downward along the "sepulchral spirals" of meditation. But equally obvious, beyond the threat of estrangement and madness, is the association of reverie with age-old images of sin and evil. In the same context of the vertical spiral, Hugo states: "Hell, the Serpent, and reverie all coil around themselves" (XIV, 368).

The sinister implications of reverie are ironically confirmed by a figure intimately associated with evil. More disquieting than Gwynplaine's affinity with the visionary poet is that of Doctor Gernardus, the aged scholar-outlaw whom Hugo calls the "pédant de l'abîme" (XIV, 80). The authorial self-parody is flagrant, given the frequency of the word *abyss* in Hugo's lexicon. The somber philosopher-bandit is a disturbing textual presence, for this accomplice in the most horrible of crimes—a crime against a child, hence against God—is also a decipherer of the occult, a deep interpreter of the voices of the storm. He is of the visionary company, sinking into his thought "like a miner into his shaft." This "pensive" transgressor is a tragic dreamer, a "songeur tragique." He assumes a "pontifical attitude" and stands alone, in the midst of the unleashed elements, as the ominous "speaking statue" of darkness (XIV, 85, 77, 107).

The parody, including that of the otherworldly Commendatore, is at once strange and familiar. Gernardus' appearance is intertextually determined. His baldness, likened to a priest's tonsure, inevitably recalls the tormented physiognomy of Frollo. The swollen and senile veins on his head, his livid complexion, his fossil-like face, and his gestures of concentrated anguish indeed make him a brother to all the other Hugolian figures whose inner pathology condemns them without recourse to the foretaste and aftertaste of evil. Gernardus suffers from "spiritual chaos," but he is also called an oracular voice and an "augur" (XIV, 76, 80). All suggests the deep link between visionary power and the forces of the night.

An attentive reading of the novel thus reveals a latent sense of anxiety and even guilt associated with the seer's gifts and, beyond him, with the creative act itself. What is involved is more radical than the vague statement Hugo makes in *William Shakespeare* to the effect that every genius in also an *abyss*; or the inverted corollary, in *Les Travailleurs de la mer*, about the abyss as great artist.[55] What Hugo proposes is nothing less than the sinister textual presence of the vatic artist, the accomplice of the unnameable dark, the *poète noir*.

This textualized presence is fiction and metaphor, rather than strict autobiography. True, Hugo saw himself as a watcher of the nightlife ("vie nocturne") of his own mind. In *Le Tas de pierres*, he refers to himself as a "night bird" inhabiting dark space.[56] But the imagery of darkness has less to do with the man and his spiritual habitat than with the act of writing. In *Les Misérables*, and quite tellingly in the pages on the criminal lower depths where the hoped-for future is being worked out, Hugo speaks of the "sublime blackness" of the inkstand, the "noirceur sublime de l'écritoire."[57]

These problematics of the creative act must be read against a wider unease. The questioning of the authorial voice involves a questioning of the principle of authority. In the end, the complicity of visionary genius with the forces of chaos blurs and blends with the complicity of supreme authority. Laughter, we have seen, implicates not only Satan but God. It is not at all clear whose is the sneer of the "inaccessible foe." One must recall Gwynplaine's troubled remark: "If Satan had this laughter, it would condemn God" (XIV, 99, 354). God's responsibility for evil is more than hinted at in Gwynplaine's bitter and blasphemous hypothesis that if Dea were to die, this would prove that God is a "traitor" and man a dupe (XIV, 382). Dea dies within the hour.

Ursus' facetious manner of denying that he places his trust in Satan has far-reaching metaphysical implications concerning the relation of God to the devil. Accused of heresy by the inquisitional tribunal, the mountebank, philosopher, and playwright replies that faith in the devil is the obverse of faith in God (XIV, 225). The logician's clever rebuttal does more than help him out of a dangerous situation. It points to the unavoidable intermingling of night and day, lending heretical significance and theological validity to the omnipresent universal antithesis so dear to Hugo. Ursus dares to go beyond the bold hypothesis of the narrator, who asks: "Is there a demon's providence, as there is a providence of God?" (XIV, 181). Ursus puts it affirmatively, positing evil as an essence, an absolute: "Evil exists." God, in this perspective, is himself a victim of the devil. "Dieu se gratte à l'endroit du diable." Even worse, "God is blind" (XIV, 294, 215). In creating the world (impotence or connivance?) he let the devil be.

We are perhaps getting as close here as Hugo will ever allow us to come to that intimate zone of anxiety where his fiction making responds to the writer's haunting questions and doubts about himself as creator of a poetic universe. The poet-prophet may be a torch bearer; but when Gwynplaine begins to shoulder the responsibility of seer and political prophet, Hugo reminds himself that the torch bearer is none other than Lucifer. What Hugo calls the "enigma of evil" is at the heart of *L'Homme qui rit*. It has much to do with the notion of a *Deus duplex*, the Manichaean *bifrons* mentioned in *Les Travailleurs de la mer* (XII, 743). But more important perhaps is the writer's complex identification with the authority of the supreme author. God alone, we have read in *Les Travailleurs de la mer*, can shape creatures as horrible as the monstrous octopus. Such creatures are feats of the creative imagination, but they are also defined as "creation's blasphemies against itself." And Hugo makes a point of explaining that the English sailors call the octopus the devilfish (XII, 741–742).

The mystery of evil, as projected through the reality of the monsters in Hugo's fiction, is thus more than a subject to be probed and represented; it is constitutive of the literary act itself. It is telling that in so many of his books, the destructive and recreative violence of the ocean ("il dévore, puis crée"—XII, 677) plays such a heavy symbolic role; for the love of the ocean corresponds to Hugo's relentless fascination with chaos. It is no accident that *L'Homme qui rit* begins with a gloomy vision of the murderous sea ("l'océan s'amuse"—XIV, 100) and that it ends as the death-flow of the river enters the ocean. Gwynplaine's willful submersion in these waters is not merely a transhistorical escape from the violence of history. It is also an immersion in a recurrent and seemingly endless history of violence.

This in large part is the subject of Hugo's last novel.

The Violence of History:
Quatrevingt-Treize

L'Eté reste l'été.

Hugo's fascination with the violence and meaning of revolution has a long history. Even his early poetry—written long before his own political evolution led him from Napoleon to Mirabeau, from Mirabeau to Danton, and from Danton to the full horror of Marat—shows signs of intense concern. "Napoléon II" in *Les Chants du Crépuscule* is a case in point. Other texts come quickly to mind: "Ecrit en 1846," which stresses the monstrous therapy of revolution; "O soldats de l'an deux!" which exalts revolutionary deeds; the eighth section of "Nox" (also in *Les Châtiments*), with its titanic view of the Terror ("Titan quatre-vingt-treize") and its affirmation of the messianic myth of revolution. By the time Hugo wrote *William Shakespeare*, he considered the French Revolution as the single most life-changing and life-giving event in modern history. The opening of *Les Misérables*, which evokes Bishop Myriel's confronting the guillotine ("L'échafaud est vision"—XI, 64), furthermore suggests a religious perspective on the Revolution. Was not the storming of the Bastille to be a key episode in Hugo's unfinished metaphysical poem *La Fin de Satan*? Even Hugo's much earlier acceptance speech at the Académie Française (1841), at a time he hoped to play a role in the government of Louis-Philippe, included a surprising apologia for the "criminal" excesses of the Convention, which he attributed to the will of God (VI, 151). Ever since his conversion to Republican ideals after the coup of 1851, all through his exile years, Hugo's long-range effort had been to reconcile his political and metaphysical views. The spiritual adventure of Jean Valjean, victim and redeemer, is woven into a larger story that describes the providential role of the Revolution—a divine saga, a "geste de Dieu" accomplished with a flaming "archangel's sword" (XI, 862–863, 846). The convergence of the political and the metaphysical was, however, not easily brought about. This may explain why, in the late 1850s, Hugo turned again to the writing of fiction. It is remarkable indeed that *La Légende des siècles* (1859), a collection of poems conceived as an epic account of humanity's progress in history, failed to give the pivotal event of the French Revolution its due place. The climactic turning point was at best perceived as a vivid absence, a textual void. Many periods are conjured up in this series of epic frescoes: Biblical times, the Middle Ages, the Renaissance—even the utopian future, in the section entitled "Vingtième Siècle." But there is no direct treatment of the Revolution, despite its central importance. Similarly, *La Fin de Satan* remained incomplete, and what is missing is precisely the projected episode on the Bastille.

What happened is both complicated and revealing. Hugo had in fact composed for *La Légende des siècles* the poem "La Révolution"; but it had grown to be so important, so long, so complex, and above all so disturbing to the author that he decided not to publish it. And immediately, as though to exorcise his malaise, he set out to write another poem, significantly entitled "Le Verso de la page." It began by expressing Hugo's dismay concerning "La Révolution," proceeded to take an opposing view, and wound up disquieting him even more. He did not publish this poem either, and ultimately dismembered it, reallocating chunks of it to a variety of other works.[1]

This act of camouflage and cancellation, following an exercise in self-contradiction, must be taken as signs of Hugo's considerable uneasiness at the height of his preoccupation with revolution, and specifically with the events of 1793. The Terror, because of its violence, but even more because its violence did not appear vindicated by subsequent events, continued to challenge Hugo's faith in the providential thrust of history. It is as though Hugo could not come to terms with the mystery of a historical event that was to usher in a redemptive era of indefinite progress, but that instead, by some inexplicable irony, led to the farcical relapses of Louis Bonaparte's tyranny, then to the horrors of the Commune and its repression. The great revolution seemed forgotten, betrayed. The apocalypse had been made to appear meaningless, and tragedy had given way to parody. The reign of Napoleon III, in particular, had been a historical scandal for Hugo; for how was one to reconcile the notion of progress with such apparent success in setting back the clock?[2]

This disturbing tension between progress and recurrence, between concepts of linear and cyclical history, is manifestly at the center of Hugo's great novel on the Revolution, *Quatrevingt-Treize* (1874), written at a time when the problem was further complicated by the recent episode of the Commune, the events of the war, and the siege of Paris, starkly evoked in *L'Année terrible*. The apparent reversal of the historical process is a deeply troubling occurrence in the novel. Describing the period of riotous joy and permissiveness that followed the death of Robespierre, Hugo comments that this saturnalian atmosphere of the Directoire had forced the dread apocalypse of revolution to retreat (XV, 345). "L'effrayante apocalypse": the very choice of terms introduces an ominous question mark into the nature and meaning of the revolutionary moment.

Yet the seeming message of *Quatrevingt-Treize* is the justification of revolutionary violence. The time chosen by Hugo is the darkest hour, the period of the Convention and the Comité de Salut Public, a year of foreign invasions and counterrevolutionary revolts. Cruelty has become epidemic. The guillotine reigns. But it is the cumulative injustice of centuries that must be blamed, rather than the violence of the moment. The Revolution is the pivotal episode in a larger story that leads from oppression to hope and freedom—a story in which France has a heroic role to play. Hugo deliberately focuses on the inner conflicts of France, on those aspects of the civil strife that tore families apart, endangering, most crucially, the survival of children. The children's central role in this novel about the Revolution is not a simple matter of pathos; it has symbolic significance. It is the future that is at stake. Describing the street scenes in Revolutionary Paris, Hugo writes: "Ces petits enfants, c'était l'immense avenir" (XV, 344).

The immensely hopeful future can, however, come into being only after past crimes have been accounted for. The dread guillotine, whose wood recalls the "arbre sinistre" of the Cross, is the redeeming price to pay for the original sin of fratricidal violence and oppression. The guillotine thus engages the medieval tower in vengeful apostrophe: "I am your daughter" (XV, 506). In human terms, the violence of the Revolution is seen as radical and necessary surgery. But Hugo chooses to go far beyond a clinical perspective and to displace, as it were, the responsibility. The catastrophic present is viewed as part of a providential scheme. The climactic turning point in human history appears as a flaming sword. The tempestuous events reveal the "souffle de Dieu." The great actors of the Revolution—the Dantons, the Robespierres, the Marats—may think that they are writing history. They delude themselves. They are, in reality, carried by the flow, subject to the mystery of a text they neither write nor fully comprehend. This text may be grim, even sinister—but its authority is literally supreme: "Le rédacteur énorme et sinistre de ces grandes pages a un nom, Dieu" (XV, 380).

The word *sinistre*, connoting the mystery of evil, is thus associated not only with events (Hugo calls the link between dramatic dates an "équation sinistre"—VI, 413) but with God's participation in the unfolding of history. *Quatrevingt-Treize*, a title that implies far more than the four numerals composing the date 1793, imposes itself from the outset as a prophetic invocation. Hugo came to consider the four syllables of this title a supernaturally charged number, a "chiffre fatal," a "chiffre formidable" (VI, 369).

Even at an early stage, when he was still openly denouncing the brutalities committed in the name of the Revolution, Hugo's terminology betrayed a quasi-religious awe. In the political conclusion of *Le Rhin*, he referred to the four ominous numerals of the year of the Terror as a terrifying, otherworldly blaze—a "flamboiement hideux" (VI, 531).

Horror clung to the Revolution; but it was a kind of sacred horror. The revolutionary spirit, in *William Shakespeare*, is named a "monstre sublime" (XII, 307). Yet the specter of the guillotine was not to be reconciled easily with the inspired and revelatory nature of violence. The poem "La Révolution," we have seen, projects the nocturnal vision of the statues of four French kings moving toward an encounter with the guillotine and the head of Louis XVI. This description of a historic rendezvous with the Revolution weds the magic number ninety-three to the awesome geometric patterns of the guillotine: its frightening verticality, triangularity, circularity. What the stone horsemen see in this nightmarish scene is what Hugo projected into one of his most astonishing drawings, starkly entitled *Justitia*, which he kept in constant view on one of the walls of his Guernsey house:

> Deux poteaux noirs portant un triangle livide;
> Le triangle pendait, nu, dans la profondeur;
> Plus bas on distinguait une vague rondeur,
> Espèce de lucarne ouverte sur de l'ombre;
> Deux nuages traçaient au fond des cieux ce nombre:
> —Quatrevingt-treize—chiffre on ne sait d'où venu.
>
> (X, 243)

The horror remains nonetheless prophetic; the terrible year becomes providential. The number 93 is metaphorized into a ruthless voice ("bouche de bronze)" proclaiming a second *fiat lux*. Ezekiel, according to Hugo, is on the side of the Terror (XII, 306, 177).

Opening Signals

Quatrevingt-Treize, it would seem, sets out to justify the violence of the Revolution. The novel appropriately begins with a military operation, as the battalion of the Bonnet Rouge penetrates into the woods of La Saudraie, in Brittany, to flush out royalist guerillas. The first paragraph announces a time of "epic combats." Yet all the opening signals are double-edged: it is a military operation, but we are in the lovely month of May; the battalion searches for armed rebels, but discovers instead a defenseless peasant woman with her hungry children. Even Hugo's terminology is strikingly ambiguous. The lair (gîte) that the soldiers expect to find in this manhunt turns out to be a natural cavity formed by branches, a bower of foliage, half-open like an "alcove." At the center of this unexpectedly feminine setting is a woman breast-feeding an infant. The ambush has been converted into a trap of tenderness.

Even the word ambush (embuscade), repeated several times, is multilayered. We are literally in bosco, at the center of thick woods that foreshadow the seven dreaded "black" forests of Brittany evoked at the beginning of part 3. And forêt noire always meant for Hugo, even in childhood, a nocturnal world of horror and terror, the particular domain of a satanic hunt. His earlier travel book Le Rhin (1842) projected a number of visionary forest scenes. But the woods of La Saudraie, at the beginning of Quatrevingt-Treize, take on a special character. It is a place of violence (massacres have left branches splattered with blood), but it is also an Arcadian scene.[3] The soldiers' forceful penetration (s'y enfoncer and fouiller are suggestive of sexual aggressivity) occurs while the sunbeams themselves seek violent ingress, piercing the leafy canopy. The vocabulary of penetration and violation stands in sharp contrast to the delightful array of spring flowers, the exuberance of the vegetation, the freshness of the new season. Murderous action is set in the context of the wild narcissus and the wood daisy. Hugo sums up the deliberate contrast: "The birds twittered above the bayonets." In these sylvan surroundings, history and politics appear as obscene intrusions.

History and politics are deflated in other terms, too. The opening chapter stresses not the ideological awareness of the leaders but the common humanity and political innocence of very ordinary people. La Flécharde, the mother, much like Tellmarch the beggar in a later chapter, is politically ignorant to the point of "stupidity."

The lexical gap that separates her inherited notion of *pays* from the new political notion of *patrie* symbolizes her unawareness of political issues. But her instinctual perception, much like the beggar's, endows her with an insight that transcends the slogans of the day. What she knows, and knows for sure, is that guns kill and fire destroys. She knows what Tellmarch knows: "Les événements sont les événements" (XV, 329).

Equally telling, but more subtle, is the rapid shift from masculine to feminine values in the opening scene. It is a woman— the canteen woman, the *vivandière*—who cries out "Halt!" as the sergeant is about to command "Fire!" and who thus saves the mother engaged in the most maternal function. The word *vivandière* (from *vivenda*, that which feeds and sustains life) clearly points to the priority of human needs over and above ideological issues. The *vivandière*, though a hearty Republican, refuses to distinguish among the victims of the war. She offers drinks to all: wounded men are thirsty, and people die regardless of their political opinions. "How foolish to fight"—"Comme c'est godiche de se battre!" The conversion of militant (and military) values into feminine compassion implies an inversion. The *vivandière*, whose voice is at once "soldatesque" and "féminine," symbolically embodies a sexual ambivalence that she herself sums up at the end of her speech to the peasant woman: "je suis une bonne femme et un brave homme" (XV, 292). The gruffly reassuring statement broaches an important motif. Sexual ambivalence remains a significant feature in this political novel. Not only does Tellmarch the beggar look at La Flécharde's subsequent suffering with what is called "des pensées de femme," but the Republican soldier-hero Gauvain achieves a feminine kind of beauty that is not unrelated to his compassionate nature and need to reach beyond politics. "His fair neck reminded one of a woman's" (XV, 415, 508).

Even more revealing is the interplay of maternal and paternal principles. In the first chapter, the three Vendéen children are adopted by the battalion. Their conversion to the Republic is thus a weaning from the mother ("Il faudra me sevrer ça," declares the *vivandière*—XV, 290), a separation that is not without biographical relevance, since Hugo's own mother, a staunch royalist, was herself from the Vendée. In thematic terms, the conversion from natural mother to adoptive father would seem to imply a political commitment that, in some deep sense, is a turning away from nature.

The political message is indeed undermined by the first words of the first sentence, before mention is even made of the historic date: "Dans les derniers jours de mai . . ." The month of May seems to announce a program of hope and progress associated with the beginning of the year. But this annunciation of a fresh start and forward movement is largely canceled by what the month truly reveals: the yearly return of the same seasons—a cyclical process, rather than a linear history. Spring remains true to itself—that is what the woods are saying to the soldiers. *Quatrevingt-Treize* begins on this note of seasonal recurrence. It ends on the same note, as a radiant sun and sky witness the destructive work of the guillotine cutting short the life of the morally blameless hero. The spectacle of nature is a lesson in the depravity of man. While man in history murders and crushes in the name of progress, the lily and the star remain ever the same. "L'été reste l'été" (XV, 507).

The Denunciation of Ideology

The scandal of war is that the worst becomes the best. The success of a war depends on the amount of harm done. Violence escalates into savagery. In a civil war especially, the best leader is the most unrelenting, the most merciless—"hyena pitted against hyena" (XV, 321, 301). Killing the wounded, butchering prisoners, women, children—these are the ways of achieving distinction. Hugo's battle scenes are drawn with a surfeit of gory details. Nocturnal massacres, hand-to-hand combat in ravines, mutilations, disembowelments, broken jaws, eyes torn out of their sockets—Hugo spares the reader nothing. Even the natural elements and the settings (Hugo believes there are evil places, "lieux scélérats"— XV, 396) seem to echo this orgy of horror. The anger of the sea, the hidden cruelty of reefs, the irresistible pull of a shipwreck, the apparent ire of inanimate things—all participate in war's great choreography of destruction. Objects become accomplices and direct threats. Hugo comments on the wild movements of a cannon that breaks loose on a ship: "There is nothing so inexorable as the rage of the inanimate" (XV, 302). The supreme symbol of violence in the novel is, in fact, an object: the guillotine. Abstract and yet terrifyingly immanent, this modern instrument of death combines age-old ferocity with ideological dehumanization.

The shadow of history, the accomplice of this chilling fanaticism, is countered in the novel by the rhetoric of pathos. *Quatrevingt-Treize* is particularly rich in lachrymal episodes. Tears fall at the end, as they fall at the beginning. This structural articulation appears deliberate. The whole army's hyperbolic sob, as their leader is about to be executed, corresponds to the large tear rolling down the sergeant's cheek, at the end of the first chapter, when the three Vendéen children are adopted by the battalion. Hugo comments equivocally, as the blade of the guillotine is about to come down: "The tears of soldiers are terrible." The oxymoron reveals the link between terror and pity. When a little girl, Georgette, is saved from death by fire, the old grenadiers sob aloud; and even the stern Vendéen leader, Lantenac, when facing the radiant smile of Georgette, whom he has saved (a miracle not so much for the prowess involved as for Lantenac's mysterious, almost otherworldly motivation) begins to cry.

Were it not for the exceedingly brutal historical context, episodes such as these might flounder in sentimentality. Pathos is a dominant mode, but it never trivializes the plot. La Flécharde's anguish and her fixed idea of maternity express themselves in extreme moments in a cry like an animal's, but this cry is perceived in a mythical register. Mother sublime, this Breton *Mater Dolorosa* is explicitly linked with the image of Calvary, the "Voie Douloureuse"; and her maternal instinct, which Hugo qualifies as divine animalism, raises natural function and natural feeling to a supernatural level (XV, 452, 415).

The challenge is not only to the violence of war. The register of pathos also undermines the status of revolutionary ideology. For such ideology is viewed as a chief threat to justice and to clemency;

it inflicts the harsh rule of the abstract, the despotism of the inexorable. The guillotine is pitted against humanity; its inertness as object illustrates dehumanization by ideologies. If Hugo devotes a long section of the novel to the tumultuous meetings of the Convention, it is less a display of historical documentation than a way of encompassing the dimensions of political hatreds. The historical hall is a place of strident denunciations and verbal battles that reveal the deadliness of words. The language of ideology— and ultimately all political language—is viewed as aggression. The "vertigineuses paroles"—witticisms, aphorisms, threats, slogans—are words that kill. "No mercy" is the watchword of the Commune. Revolutionary language itself becomes power and destruction. Already in "Le Verso de la page," Danton's speeches, torrents of the "parole énorme," had been caught in the dialectic of utopian demolition (X, 263). In *Quatrevingt-Treize*, political language signals an even wider gap between the aims of the Revolution and its destructive reality.

The character who most sharply illustrates doctrinaire ideology is the ex-priest Cimourdain, an icily virtuous black eminence of the extreme left that came to be known as "l'Evêché." His incorruptible "commissar" mentality (he is, in fact, appointed Commissaire Délégué du Comité de Salut Public) thrives on intolerance of any deviationism, commitment to abstractions, ascetic self-repression, faith in logic and in his own infallibility, hatred for the present, and a chronic love of catastrophe. One of the ironies of the novel is that Cimourdain's beloved disciple Gauvain will say *no* to the merciless letter of Revolutionary law, having found a higher law in clemency. Forced by his abominable logic to condemn his spiritual son to death, Cimourdain commits suicide.[4] Love cannot be denied. The fierce political logician, whose sense of justice is utterly devoid of compassion, becomes the victim of a paternal passion for his disciple. In a daring image, Hugo makes of Cimourdain the "Pygmalion of a soul" (XV, 350). This almost carnal love for his spiritual son is Cimourdain's redeeming flaw. But it is highly significant that, as his love leads him to hitherto unsuspected emotion and suffering, there is also a revealing shift from the paternal to the maternal image. As he gazes on Gauvain asleep in a prison cell, a few hours before the execution, Cimourdain's facial expression is literally transfigured: "no mother gazing upon her sleeping infant could have had a look more unutterably tender" (XV, 501). The principle of maternal love, so intrusive in the first scene devoted to a political-military operation, ultimately appears to cancel out the political conversion symbolized by the "adoptive" father figures.

The Tower and the Book

Structure and imagery repeatedly remind us of the three children adopted by the Republican battalion in the opening chapter. By an ironic twist of events, they fall into the hands of their own countrymen, the Breton counterrevolutionary guerillas, who hold them as critical hostages in the besieged castle of La Tourgue. (See Illustration 23.) More ironic still is the fact that they are kept in the library of the feudal castle, in the very room where Gauvain, as a boy, was converted to revolutionary ideas through his readings. Yet this central episode deals with the destruction of books. The Tourgue library is about to be set on fire, while the children, unaware of the danger, continue to play. Their game, too, has a somber irony: they amuse themselves, while all around the revolutionary war rages, by tearing apart and utterly destroying a rare *in quarto* copy of *Saint-Barthélemy*—a title that refers to a Christian martyr but obliquely also to one of the darkest pages of French history, the massacre of Saint Bartholomew's Day in 1572. History, the existence of the text, and history as text are tightly interlocked in this symbolic scene.

It is a crucial scene, indeed: during the supreme battle everything converges on the castle, where Gauvain, the young Republican commandant, was raised. Homecoming, for the converted ex-aristocrat, is thus an act of violence. The native son returns as the liberating enemy. This inversion parallels the ambiguous status of the children who, though Vendéens, have been in a sense converted to the Republic by military adoption, and are now held captive by their own people. And even as the rare book is being destroyed, an escape ladder and a guillotine are converging on the ancient castle.

The bond between the children and the library has a privileged status in the genesis of the novel. Hugo's work notes refer as follows to the three towers of the medieval castle, originally named the Château de Mauvaise:

Trois tours: La tour Mauvaise
                La tour Poingdestre
                La tour de Fronpebent
(Corps de logis L. XIII, les reliant. Là est la
bibliothèque.)
                Les enfants.

                                        (XV, 279)

The episode itself is richly symbolic: the awakening of the children and their first impressions recapitulate the early stages in the development of mankind; their playful inventions repeat mankind's first discoveries. But there is something disturbing about their innocence and naïveté: the shredding of the book, a parody of a massacre, refers explicitly to the principle of violence: "The appetite for destruction exists" (XV, 441). The taste for violence is deeply embedded in human nature.

Yet the import of historical events (the French Revolution, the Saint Bartholomew's Day massacre) is somewhat deflated by the presence of the children. Violence appears minimized by the games they play. Humorous cultural allusions to Virgil and Dante, as well as parodic echoes of Boileau's Le Lutrin, further introduce reassuring elements, as though to say that the children's immediate experience is more significant than the sound and fury of history. This muting of the more strident sounds of political discord works specifically as a reduction in scale of war's inhumanity. For Georgette, the first cannon shot is but an amusing "boom," heard as she is about to fall asleep.

The long digression on the children trapped in the library allows Hugo to offer a double perspective on the historical moment. But that library in a besieged fortress has another, quite special meaning for Hugo. It is a sacred repository of the past, as well as a transmitter of a spiritual legacy affecting the future. Here too, the perspective is double. The legacy is a tribute to the past; but it has value only insofar as it can become an instrument of change and progress capable of challenging and even of denouncing the past. The library, symbolically the "côté civilisé" of La Tourgue, is also its most vulnerable side (XV, 430). In its conflicting temporal dimensions, the image of the library furthermore relates to the themes of paternity and continuity. There the family archives are kept, as well as the childhood crib and toys of the former aristocrat. It is there, too, that the future revolutionary's education took place, amid and through books. The destruction of the book by children thus unavoidably raises the specter of the self-destructive core of revolutionary ideology.

Yet even this self-destructive potential is problematized. To destroy a book is a serious matter; this dismemberment is viewed as an "extermination." But the book's real substance is always elsewhere. Little Georgette, as she watches the bits of torn pages carried away by the wind, cries out "Papillons!" Like butterflies, or rather like the petals of a flower, the destroyed pages seem to be carried off by the breath of a superior will.[5] The book's reality transcends its material status; this reality implies a disappearance, as well as a dissemination. That is no doubt the meaning of the final sentence of the episode: "Et le massacre se termina par un évanouissement dans l'azur." The association of images of physical destruction with a spiritual vanishing into blue space is further concretized in the oxymoronic metaphor transforming the guileless, mischievous children into smilingly ferocious "angels of prey" (XV, 441).

The Demise of the Epic

The presence of the children also serves to tarnish military prowess. Only a few years earlier, in *William Shakespeare*, Hugo had referred to the epic tradition as "bloodthirsty": "L'épopée est buveuse de sang" (XII, 379). *Quatrevingt-Treize* subverts the epic principle even more systematically than did *Les Misérables*. *Quatrevingt-Treize* begins on a seemingly positive epic note. The narrator announces a "time of epic combats." The opening signals, the repetition of the indefinite personal pronoun *on*, and the collective free indirect discourse set up a heroic mood made explicit later by the claim that these historical events have "epic stature." Epic devices crowd the text. The Convention, for instance, provides the occasion for what Hugo himself, alluding to the Homeric tradition, calls a titanic enumeration—a "dénombrement titanique" (XV, 346, 371). As the physical action intensifies, however, the epic context takes on an increasingly negative quality. The adjective "epic" is linked with the adjective "inhuman"; there is talk of "Homeric insults"; the "epic" moment in history is qualified as "cruel" (XV, 378, 390, 394). The terrifying Vendéen warrior known as Imânus—the name itself has a mythic resonance—is here the archetypal epic hero. He is a living archaism, a monstrous illustration of original violence, combining heroism and murder: "Il avait la férocité épique." He and his gang of Vendéens are placed in a setting reminiscent of a "Homeric cavern" (XV, 406, 454). The epic ritual itself is degraded, together with the idiom of the epic, when the besieged tower speaks to the besieging camp, and the feudal horn engages in an impossible duel-duet with the Republican clarion. The highflown reactionary idiom of Imânus, which here binds epic rhetoric to grandiose savagery, is directly challenged by the sobriety of Gauvain's response.

Gauvain's deeper response points, in fact, to a new kind of epic. For if epic notions have any merit at all in the eyes of this soldier-dreamer, it is in terms of the human conscience. "What a battlefield is the mind of man!" (XV, 484). As Gauvain nobly decides to free Lantenac by exchanging places with him in jail—a decision he well knows will cost him his life—one is reminded of Jean Valjean's sacrifice following the great struggle with his conscience in the epically titled chapter "Une Tempête sous un crâne." At stake is much more, however, than the conscience and salvation of an individual. Beyond the singular battlefield of a human conscious-ness, Gauvain glorifies humanity's epic quest for moral perfection.

Totus in Antithesi

The children who playfully destroy the book have yet another function. The striking expression "angels of prey" is part of a larger system of oxymorons to which Hugo resorts with revealing frequency when dealing with the double mystery of revolution and religion. The Revolution is monstrous, but it is also sacred; more precisely, it is a "monstre divin." The heavy concentration of oxymorons is a signal of ideological tension. The poem "Le Verso de la page," whose very title implies a program of contradictions, is particularly rich in oxymoronic constructs: the men of the Rev-olution are "demons of good"; theirs is a loving fury; they bring exterminatory salvation; they are destructive founders. Marat, Hu-go's *bête noire*, is the "auguste infâme," the "nain géant"— the gigantic dwarf. Oxymoron, a pointedly foolish and self-contra-dictory verbal juxtaposition, functions here as a condensed paradox, hinting at a deeper truth. It reveals, behind the co-existence of apparently irreducible opposites, the hidden bond between violence and love, between the infinitely small and the widest possible horizon. The oxymoron is thus a miniature rhe-torical affirmation of the essentially antithetical nature of the world.

Musing on the oscillations of history, the narrator of *Quatrevingt-Treize* invokes the eternal "antithèses de Dieu" (XV, 344). In striking pages of *William Shakespeare*, Hugo had already referred to "ubiquitous antinomy," as well as to genius's God-like ability to indulge in "réflexion double," to participate in the ceaseless ebb and flow of *yes* and *no* (XII, 236–237). *Totus in antithesi*— the formula refers to the cosmic spirit, and, analogically, to a literary strategy of universalization and reconciliation. Oxymoron and antithesis, ultimately blending and blurring all opposites, are here in the service of unity. Hence expressions such as "anges de proie"—much as "désaccord intime," "douceur colossale," "hideusement secourable," "sérénité terrible," "innocents vénérables," or "misérables formidables"—function to illumine what Horace called the *concordia discors rerum*, the jarring harmony of things.

Quatrevingt-Treize is deliberately structured around a series of antitheses ("hell in the very midst of dawn"—XV, 331), opposing the pathos of gentleness to the unleashing of destructive forces. One chapter ends with a dialogue between the Sword and the Axe; the title of the following chapter is, typically, the simple word *Dolorosa*. The language of catastrophe is pitted against the language of pity and piety. Yet opposition leads to resolution, to integration into a higher order. "The Two Poles of Truth" is the didactic title of another chapter, whose function is precisely to establish that antagonistic intentions can work toward the same aim (XV, 419, 416). The Hugolian antithesis thus poses its own problematics. Dramatically functional in a system of conflicts and ideological tensions, it also provides the signal for self-cancellation, transcendence, and harmony.[6]

The underlying premise is that violence itself is part of the divine scheme. God is the ominous author, the "rédacteur énorme et sinistre" of the brutal scenario of history (XV, 380). The coupling of messianic revolution with darkness, the dialectical coexistence of good and evil, were earlier confirmed in "La Révolution." This poem also stated the corollary of divine involvement in the somber text of events. If redemptive revolution is tainted with evil, then evil also invests the creative genius. If the sculptor Germain Pilon appears as a prophet of revolution, if he succeeds in creating the notion of *le peuple* (Hugo's own declared mission), it is because he is the visionary shaper of the threatening, buffoonish, and grimacing *mascarons* of the Pont Neuf—much as Hugo himself, in *L'Homme qui rit*, creates Gwynplaine's monstrous face and vengeful laughter, the laughter of revolution. For Germain Pilon, like Hugo, like all prophetic artists, can create only in cooperation with the darker side, the side of mystery. Their inspiration comes from "below," from darkness, death, destruction, and mourning.

Qui sait si ton poème inouï ne vient pas
De plus loin que la terre et de plus haut que l'homme,
Des profondeurs que nul ne connaît et ne nomme,
Du précipice ouvert au delà du cercueil?

(X, 231)

This mystery of occult forces and intentions is suggested early in *Quatrevingt-Treize*, in the suspenseful episode of the *caronade*. One of the cannons, which has broken loose from its fastenings, wreaks havoc on the gun deck and endangers the rolling ship. At one level of meaning, the twenty-four-pound gun, a beast-like battering ram, becomes the symbol of the rebelling slave and of irrational violence. But this obvious symbolism does not exhaust the possibilities of the episode. The struggle between the gunner and the runaway gun ultimately celebrates the victory of spirit over brute force. Yet even this interpretation fails to go to the heart of the episode. To do so, one would have to account for the all-powerful presence of the sea. Part 1, even though it begins in the woods, is entitled "En Mer." Caught in the mysterious movement of the sea, the destructive gun, which at one point appears as a supernatural monster, or as the living chariot of the apocalypse, turns out to be no more than a puny toy. The ocean is the real force, and that force is the spirit of God. Only an illusion can account for the apparent unrestraint or independence of the loosened gun. It is in fact moved by the ship, which is itself tossed by the sea, which in turn is kept in motion by the storm. And the storm is the breath and will of God commanding the blind waters.

The allegory takes on a historical and political implication when an extended metaphor later compares the Convention to a stormy ocean. The purpose is clear. The great actors of the Revolution may think that they shape events; they are in reality acted upon. The imagery harks back to the *caronade* episode at sea. To be a member of the Convention is like being a wave of the ocean. The leaders of the Revolution are mere playthings of the tempestuous waters; they are scattered like foam, dashed to pieces against the rocks. Hugo concludes tersely, "To impute the Revolution to men is like attributing the tides to the waves." Once again the real force of events is the divine breath, the "vent de prodige": it is right after the oceanic metaphor that Hugo asserts the ominous authorship of history-as-text: "Le rédacteur énorme et sinistre de ces grandes pages a un nom, Dieu" (XV, 379–380). By becoming a manifestation of the unknown, the historical event ultimately negates the priority of history. Hugo asks us to view it in a transcendental context.

Modes of Transcendence

What is involved is a system of conversion quite beyond the political scheme. Politically, the novel is predicated on the system of double allegiance, which stresses freedom of choice.[7] No socioeconomic necessity interferes with apparently "pure" ideological commitment. The Republican heroes in the book come from the royalist side; like Hugo himself, they are converts. Cimourdain is a former priest, and Gauvain was born a nobleman. But the case of Gauvain, who bears the name of the purest of medieval knights, also illustrates a nonpolitical, even antipolitical conversion. More sharply than anyone in the novel, he sees the gap between the means of revolution (upheaval, radical action) and its aims (hope, civilization, peace). This gap, or contradiction, cannot be wished away, for to deny violence and the reign of the scaffold is to risk the abortion of the revolutionary ideals. Yet that is what Gauvain chooses to do. He opts for clemency, and he must die for this antipolitical stance. This deeper faith, which fundamentally denies the claims of political action, is made manifest earlier when Gauvain counters the arguments of his political mentor, Cimourdain: "Mon maître, je ne suis pas un homme politique" (XV, 417).

The fundamental mystery of a spiritual conversion that negates political aims is dramatically illustrated by the marquis de Lantenac, the cold-blooded incarnation of the Ancien Régime, and leader of the Vendée counterrevolution. When Lantenac, in defiance of his character and battle plans, saves the children held as hostages by his troops, he inexplicably places himself in the service of a "higher truth." He becomes a witness to a stronger imperative. His conversion to the truth of love no longer belongs to the realm of political action; it is a transfiguration. For Hugo, this spiritual "metamorphosis" is the result of a redemptive illumination—a "coup de lumière." It is only fitting that this at first rather "faint ray," turning into a "higher light" and finally into a dazzling redemptive radiance, should penetrate a mind known to be thoroughly skeptical (XV, 485–486, 470). The full meaning of this conversion is soteriological: the one who saves is saved. Hugo goes so far as to transform the ruthless Lantenac, enlightened by divine compassion, into a symbolic carrier of light: "The infernal Satan had become once more the heavenly Lucifer" (XV, 488). The sentence echoes the key line of *La Fin de Satan*, Hugo's great poem of universal redemption: "Satan est mort; renais, ô Lucifer céleste!" (X, 1762).

The importance of the redemptive scheme is heightened by Hugo's choice of a prison cell as the setting for Gauvain's ultimate vision. This vision concerns a utopian future based on collective salvation. Beyond the spiritual battlefield of the individual human conscience, Gauvain glimpses the spiritual epic of all humanity. But if Gauvain thus peers into the future, it is because, unlike the cold and pragmatic Cimourdain, he is eager to retrieve poetry. The "lyre," he knows, stands higher than the scales. He thereby also retrieves past culture, and this precisely through a reference to the Homeric epic (XV, 502). His prison vision harmonizes future and past, thus canceling the temporal antagonism preached by Revolutionary doctrinaires. The lofty perspective, from within the quasi-monastic confinement, transcends all conflicts and all barriers; it becomes a cosmic glance: "through the dungeon vault, it seemed to him he could see the starry sky." The corollary of this transparency is the imaginary flight taking place within the enclosure of the poet's mind. Hugo speaks of the "voûte visionnaire de son cerveau" (XV, 504–505).

The metaphysical, apolitical nature of the prison scene has of course much to do with a long-standing carceral tradition—gnostic, Platonic, neo-Platonic, patristic—positing a dramatic relation of body to soul and of matter to spirit. The nineteenth century, for a variety of reasons (some of them obviously political), gave the prison metaphor a singularly inspiring status. The poetry of Hugo is particularly rich in symbolic prison images.[8] But nowhere in his work do dungeon walls harmonize so well with spiritual elation as in *Quatrevingt-Treize*. Clearly, the "awesome serenity" that pervades the prison space has to be understood in the light of a symbolic reversal of roles, which makes of the visionary disciple the teacher of his political master. Gauvain and Cimourdain share a last supper. And as Gauvain breaks the black bread and offers it to Cimourdain together with his message of clemency and harmony, the imagery of transcendence becomes increasingly vivid, until an entranced and speechless Gauvain, totally absorbed by his reverie, faces Cimourdain with an almost supernatural "light of dawn" shining in his eyes (XV, 505).

The sense of the ineffable explains the significance of speechlessness, even of silence. The fundamental mystery is not only "invisible"; it is unspeakable. Having reached a point of exaltation in his prophetic utterance, Gauvain breaks off in midsentence. His eyes shine, his lips continue to move, but he says no more. His vision has carried him beyond words. The discrediting of language is thus double in *Quatrevingt-Treize*: instruments of power and violence, words are powerless to account for the hidden reality, the "oeuvre invisible" (XV, 504, 501). "To describe terror is impossible," Hugo says about the catastrophe at sea. Hence the value of other languages: the mother's cry, the children's prattle, the poet's metaphors. Significantly, Lantenac says to Halmalo, the devout but uneducated sailor, "You do not understand the words, but you understand things." And when Tellmarch tries in vain to console la Flécharde, he takes full measure of the "impotence of speech" (XV, 303, 321–322, 415).

Such "speechlessness" is the price for intimations of harmony. These intimations pervade the novel, eventually canceling political oppositions as well as the dialectics of history. Antitheses dissolve into a hidden order. The children, in their innocence, hear the jarring battle sounds as a "sort of harmony." Tellmarch, the beggar hermit, also knows how to listen to the harmony that comes from the overwhelming tenderness in the world—a "douceur colossale" that excludes neither the violence of events nor that of nature (XV, 438, 442). For violence in history as well as in nature is part of the larger design; hence the importance of natural upheavals and cataclysms. "A storm always knows what it is about," Gauvain explains in the dungeon scene (XV, 504). Sound and fury always tell a meaningful tale.

Such a vision, in the last analysis, abolishes all contradictions. The network of antitheses serves a strategy of reconciliation. In Hugo's optics, everything tends toward fusion. Thus, Cimourdain and Gauvain, dying at the same instant in the last scene, are compared to twin souls, the shadow of the one blending with the radiance of the other. No literal language can account for such a union. But the inadequacy of individual words is in itself a metaphor. The limitations of the signifier do not exclude the signifying possibility of a text. One is reminded of the moving passage in which Saint Augustine, speaking of the death of each word in the temporal unfolding of the sentence, reads this death as the onward urge to reach the unity that no individual instant can by itself contain.[9]

An Exit from History

It is hardly surprising that ideologically oriented critics have found Hugo unsympathetic to the political thrust of revolutionary thinking and have accused him of "bourgeois" utopian idealism. Georg Lukács, though he appreciated the figuration of tragic political conflicts in *Quatrevingt-Treize*, commented negatively on Hugo's romantic poetization and on the limits of an abstract humanist conception of history. Pierre Barbéris, in an essay on *Les Châtiments*, was more severe still: Hugo, even though he denounced Napoleon III, never really understood the underlying socioeconomic problems—or rather did not wish to understand them; his "ideology of reconciliation" was essentially an attempt at justifying bourgeois liberalism—that is, "l'ordre bourgeois."[10]

These reproaches are not new. The socialist Proudhon repeatedly accused Hugo of intellectual parasitism, of being unable to grasp, and adhere to, the movement of history. Hugo, he felt, was a "disinherited poet," precisely because he did not face up to revolution. As for Marx, he tended to reduce Hugo's "bitter and witty invective" in *Napoléon-le-Petit* to a personal settling of accounts with an uninteresting tyrant. Hugo, according to Marx, was more concerned with individual moral conflicts, involving heroes and villains, than he was in understanding the realities of the class struggle.[11]

Unfair or even inappropriate as these reproaches may sound in view of Hugo's subsequent writings (including *Quatrevingt-Treize*), there is little doubt that beginning in the 1850s, when he ostensibly converted to the cause of militant Republicanism, Hugo felt a lasting political malaise, the depth of which is betrayed by the poems "La Révolution" and "Le Verso de la page." Hugo's discomfort with the theme of revolution is, in fact, double. The polemical discomfort is easiest to diagnose. All through the fifties, Hugo was perfectly aware that as a "Republican," as an apologist of the Revolution, he was considered a latecomer and was not taken seriously by Revolutionary thinkers. He was constantly being reminded that his current pronouncements were in contradiction with his past attitudes. "Ecrit en 1846," actually composed in 1854, was written, as we have seen, to refute such a view.

Hugo's polemical discomfort in the 1850s is, however, less interesting and less lasting than the inner contradictions that accompanied his justification of revolution. Two related problems continued to haunt him. The first was temporal. If the French Revolution was born from past experience as well as past culture, then how could the future mean a radical refusal of the past? Hence the centrality of the library in *Quatrevingt-Treize*, and the meaning of the destruction-survival of the book. The other problem was more personal: How could violence, especially political violence, ever be justified? It is in this context that the somber and misshapen figure of Marat becomes exemplary. For Marat, who makes a dramatic appearance in *Quatrevingt-Treize*, loomed large in Hugo's imagination, and probably in his subconscious. Hugo saw him as a monster; yet he was fascinated by this monster and almost irresistibly drawn to him. According to the diary of Hugo's daughter Adèle, it was none other than Marat's spirit who, in a séance of *les tables parlantes*, revealed to Hugo that in a previous incarnation the poet had been one of the men of the Revolution, and what is more, directly responsible for the beheading of the king.[12]

Marat's disturbing revelatory function suggests to what extent Hugo's apologia of revolution is fraught with guilt ("Qui n'a pas son remords secret?" he asks in "La Révolution"—X, 219). The justification of political violence, symbolized by the execution of the king, had far-reaching implications. For even though regicide (and regicide is nothing but an extreme form of parricide) was to be understood as a unique, never to be repeated event, and even though a long history of injustice inevitably brought about the infernal machine that beheaded the least evil of kings, it could not escape Hugo that the justification of even a unique expiatory act was a justification of murder, and more specifically a justification of capital punishment, against which, beginning in *Le Dernier Jour d'un condamné*, he had protested with genuine vehemence.

The figure of Marat, known as *l'ami du peuple*, further casts a problematic light on Hugo's attitude toward the idealized notion of the masses. For the *peuple* that Hugo claimed to love and to serve (believing all the while that it remained a noble reality to be created) was for him also the *foule*, the crowd, the ignorant and violent rabble. The poet's stance is often downright antagonistic: the thinker and the mob are bound to clash. "Le songeur et la foule ont des rencontres rudes," he says in "Le Verso de la page" (X, 271). There is a revealing lexicological degradation, as the text glides from the word *peuple*, to *foule*, to *masse*, to *populace*, to *cohue*, to *nombre*, to *esclave*. In the same poem, Hugo bluntly calls the crowd a bloodthirsty Messalina, a "lazzarone," a "cohue inepte, insensée et féroce," whose blind strength lies in sheer numbers (X, 273). In addition to a latent fear of mob psychology (he had seen angry crowds at close range), Hugo could not easily forgive or forget the submissive plebiscite of 1851, when the masses legitimized Louis-Napoléon's coup.

It would be narrow-minded, however, to limit Hugo's fear of violence to the specific issue of revolutionary action. A deeper love-hate relationship with history is involved. For Hugo's lasting fascination with the historical process is attended by misgivings and anxiety. In the total perspective, good and evil may be intermingled; but on the balance sheet of history, what appears is an excess of evil: "le mal est plus grand," Hugo says in "Le Verso de la page" (X, 268). He thus comes to question radically the ethics of a historical perspective, at the same time as he remains compelled to stare at the great scenario of events. The problematic nature of history is further underscored, at the beginning and at the end of Hugo's career as novelist, by the decision to explore the genre of the historical novel.

Hugo himself described how, facing the boundless and enigmatic horizons of history, he experienced metaphysical dizziness. In "Le Verso de la page," he refers to the "vertige" and "éblouissement" that accompany the confrontation with history—an awe-inspiring encounter that he likens to Moses' coming face to face with God (X, 266). Yet even the sense of terror is ambiguous. It seems to imply the acceptance of invisible laws ("Car c'est voir Dieu que voir les grandes lois du sort"—X, 266) but also the impulse to retreat from history, the yearning to escape from its laws. Another text of the 1850s, "La Pitié suprême," denounces "inexorable history" (X, 308). The brutality of historical events ultimately leads to the dream of moving outside history, of denying it, of closing history's final chapter. The exit from the forest of events which Enjolras prophesied from atop the barricades, the dream of putting an end to political adventure, of emerging from the sequential nightmare of crimes into the space of an ideal atemporality, must all be related to an almost metaphysical sense of the horror of history. History is darkness. The first page of man's adventure as recounted in *La Fin de Satan* is significantly entitled "L'Entrée dans l'ombre." The journey to the end of night turns out to be an endless catalogue of atrocities.

Hugo seems almost to espouse a Voltairean view of history as a succession of horrible acts. But he endows this horror with tragic grandeur and a sense of mystery. In "La Pitié suprême," he writes of the tragic sob of history, "le grand sanglot tragique de l'histoire." History is defined by the spilling of blood ("l'histoire où le sang reparaît"); it is the accomplice of crime. "L'histoire est l'affreux puits du forfait solidaire" (X, 300, 320, 308). *La Légende des siècles* was conceived as the epic of humanity across the centuries. But the word *siècle* also denounces the engagement in history, as opposed to the life of the spirit. "Le siècle ingrat, le siècle affreux, le siècle immonde" (X, 818). *Siècle* is indeed a pivotal term whose pessimistic connotations cannot be denied. The original poem-preface to *La Légende des siècles* leads up to the historic vision that informed the entire work: a terrifying Tower of Babel, the "lugubre Tour des Choses" (X, 822). But with it goes the vision of the tower's collapse, the vision of a disappearance, of a vanishing. History is hell. And Hugo's dream is the abolition of all gehennas. "Quand donc tous les enfers s'évanouiront-ils?" (X, 329).

History is, however, also the text of God; hence the gap between the reality of horror and its meaningful mystery. Hugo experiences concurrently the double temptation and double impossibility of dealing with the mystery of revolution and the mystery of God.[13] The long metaphysical poem *Dieu* was left unfinished, and so was *La Fin de Satan*. The poems on the Revolution, as we have seen, never found their place in *La Légende des siècles* and were moreover subjected to serious questioning and even dismantling. As for the historical novel *Quatrevingt-Treize*, Hugo's last work of fiction, culminating in Gauvain's speechless intimation of the future, it led to what Hugo himself, in his meditations on history, understood to be the prophet's blinding vision—the "éblouissement sombre" in the face of that which cannot be accounted for in political terms.

8

Epilogue:
Ego Hugo

*Pas d'autorité en dehors de
l'auteur.*

*C'est encore l'homme, mais
ce n'est plus le moi.*

There is a dramatic pen drawing by Victor Hugo, dated 1857, of a ship tossed by a cataclysmic wave. At first, one sees only the whirling mass of water. Almost submerged by the raging foam, the ship seems in danger of being pulled down by the vortex. Yet it pursues its course, with what appears to be a somber determination. The drawing is signed in dark letters against the dark void, and bears the caption MA DESTINÉE. (See Illustration 27.)

Hugo's obsession with his destiny is typically projected into onomastic inscriptions. His full name or his initials are spread out against the background of many a drawing. The letters of his name take on extraordinary shapes. Fragmented, interlaced, tumbling, monumental, they dominate landscape and seascape, encircle ruins, stretch over entire cities. They seem to reach beyond the horizon. *Ego Hugo* is the motto inscribed in the coat of arms he devised.

The personal signature—whether in the form of verbal allusions or constructs shaped as a capital *H*—appears repeatedly in his narratives. Even in his daily life, he could not refrain from imposing his signature. Hauteville House, which he decorated and furnished piece by piece in a highly personal manner, was aptly described by his son Charles as a "three-story autograph."[1]

From the outset, however, Hugo's determination to leave a mark is related to a posthumous perspective. His belief in the afterlife ("Qui mourra verra"—"He who dies will see"—are words that he jotted down in notes entitled "Post mortem") is the obverse of "When I shall cease to be, they will see who I was," recorded in an entry called "Moi."[2] Revealingly, the key verb is not *savoir* but *voir*. The visible trace was to be the written word. Immanent and transcendent all at once, the literary text meant spiritual power. In a deep sense, it could be said of Hugo that for him the letter was the spirit. Literature was a consecrating institution, and writing a sacred function. Discussing France's civilizing mission in *Le Rhin*, Hugo referred to the "formidable spiritual power" of the new "clergé littéraire."[3] Early in life, his highest ambition had been to sum himself up in a "livre complet."[4] But he also came to understand the immensity of such a project precisely because it was a never-to-be completed process. All great literature thus took on for him the form of the Unfinished Book. Like the figure of the Tower of Babel in the chapter on the printing press in *Notre-Dame de Paris*, it was a prodigious edifice, "toujours inachevé."[5]

The ambition to write a summa designed to be part of an endless process was a paradox that made special demands on the "contemplative" reader.[6] Such a "lecteur pensif," to whom Hugo at one point planned to dedicate all his works, would know how to read texts with multiple, and even contradictory, layers of meaning. For reading, like writing, was meant to be a creative decipherment. "Il faut savoir lire . . ." Hugo refers to great texts, especially in difficult historical times, as having hidden levels of significance: texts with a "double fond," a "triple fond"—perhaps even more.[7]

Despite this belief in secret levels, Hugo was at times tempted to assess the ultimate meaning of his novels. In a projected preface to *L'Homme qui rit*, he planned to state that all his works were "affirmations de l'Ame" ("affirmations of the human Soul").[8] Art in general he saw as committed to a struggle against matter. He liked to read his own narratives as adventures of the psyche, as allegories of salvation and rebirth. *Les Misérables*, whose genesis spans the years before and during Hugo's exile, is by his own account a religious text. But if Hugo was opposed to materialism and atheism, he was also hostile to the theological view of man. His quarrel with Joseph de Maistre went well beyond the question of the death penalty. In a remarkable passage in *William Shakespeare*, Hugo indicts the cold ferocity of de Maistre's theocratic faith.[9] He never ceased denouncing petrification, whatever the dogma. Life had priority over ideologies. In contrast to those who felt that religion and revolution were deadly enemies, he explicitly attempted to find a common ground for political and spiritual needs. This urge to reconcile religious aspirations and revolutionary ideals explains the importance of the Conventionnel in *Les Misérables*, whose ultimate message blends revolutionary and religious rhetoric, when he proclaims the advent of the French Revolution as the greatest event since the coming of Christ.[10]

But explicit intentions hardly account for the multiple truths Hugo liked to attribute to literary works. Can a writer ever properly read himself? Can the artist ever share his own secret? Interestingly, these questions are raised precisely around the themes of revolution, which appear to provoke in Hugo the greatest guilt and anxiety about the nature of the literary text. In "Le Verso de la page," Hugo refers to the mental torment of the creator as he faces his creation, the misgivings of the dreamer as he faces his dream.

Tourment de la pensée après l'oeuvre achevée!
Stupeur de l'aigle esprit en voyant sa couvée!
Scrupules du songeur sur ce qu'il a songé.[11]

More specifically, in "La Révolution," having conceived of the sculptor Germain Pilon as a prerevolutionary artist inspired by the "abyss," Hugo asks whether the prophetic voice can ever truly understand itself:

Ce prophète, était-il dans son propre secret?
Avait-il, âme vaste aux grands hasards poussée,
La révélation de toute sa pensée?[12]

These lines suggest that the glorification and interiorization of the mystery are linked. Masking and unmasking are essential to the revelatory process. In another poem about the artist's anguish, Hugo speaks of the vague sense of terror with which the author faces his dark inner world: "Je vivais tête-à-tête, ému d'un vague effroi, / Avec ce monde obscur qui se mouvait en moi."[13]

As reader and critic, Hugo liked to believe in the thematic coherence of structure and functional detail. It is not by chance, he points out, that Othello kills Desdemona with a pillow.[14] Rhetoric, much as dramatic devices, was to serve explicit themes. His own literary techniques, so dependent on figures of conflict and contrast, were part of a strategy of universalization and reconciliation. Ever since the preface to *Cromwell*, he had viewed all contraries as proof manifest of the world's solidarity with itself: "Tout se tient."[15] In all his works, the most jarring elements seem ultimately to dissolve into a higher unity "tous les contraires / . . . deviendront frères."[16] The conflictual tropes—the antitheses, the oxymorons—are meant as a figural imitation of nature's "universal antithesis," of the "ubiquity of antinomy": *totus in antithesi*.[17] Ultimately, the rhetoric of harmonious contrast and opposition is seen as an imitation of God's own creative devices.

Yet the truth of Hugo's texts is not in such mimetic harmony. In novel after novel, his rhetoric seems to obey imperatives deeper than those of his overt themes. The system of antitheses, the dense network of oxymorons that call for transcendence, the metaphorical structures with their built-in principles of conversion, a linguistic playfulness that undercuts the language of ideologies, the polysemic character of his nature imagery, the elaborate figures of effacement involving the writing process itself—all these devices and features suggest that the structures underlying Hugo's explicit themes are shifting forces, that his texts have a way of spinning out *other* meanings.

Such a view obviously runs counter to received ideas concerning

Hugo's unironic, utopian faith in *le peuple*, in progress, in providential history. But a literalist reading of Hugo clearly fails to take into account elements of parody and fantasy, as well as the deeper subversions implicit in his art. There is hardly an image, a motif, a theme in his work, that is not polyvalent. The destructive creativity of the ocean; the civilizing and corrupting force of Paris, absent and unreal city (both Babylon and New Jerusalem); the historical ambiguities of Napoleon; the discrediting and revitalizing of the epic; the displacement of the heroic quest, which requires the demise of the hero—at whatever level one seriously examines Hugo's novels, they reveal themselves as problematic. The conversion of worldly defeats into spiritual victories and the disappearance of conventional "characters" in favor of a poetic voice link Hugo's texts to traditional tragic values, yet also make them surprisingly modern.[18]

Tensions and complexities come into greater relief as soon as one studies more closely the social and political motifs in his work. Indignation in the face of pauperism, fortified by a brand of humanitarian idealism, seemingly led him to espouse the cause of *le peuple*. It is impossible to read his pungent speech "La Misère" (1849), or the haunting account of his visit to the subterranean slums known as the "caves" of Lille (1851), without being struck by his compassion, as well as by his understanding of the radical implications of the social question. Hugo himself, speaking of Mirabeau, stressed the priority of *questions sociales* in radical thinking.[19] Yet the preoccupation with physical degradation seemed to intensify in his mind the inviolability of selfhood, the priority of the individual over collective "social" issues.

The term and the notion of *le peuple* are specifically fraught with contradictory values. In his speech on "La Misère" to the Assemblée Législative, Hugo maintained that the proletariat has the double instinct of truth and justice. The Goyaesque vision of poverty in the "caves" of Lille also inspired one of the pieces of *Les Châtiments* but did not in this case project, as it had in the political speech, a prophetic view of popular unrest and revolutionary fervor.[20] It is indeed precisely *Les Châtiments* which most vehemently denounces the submissive, spineless masses whose political consciousness seems totally asleep. The entire volume, far from proclaiming the revolutionary mission of *le peuple*, is an indictment of their prostitution to the dictatorship of Louis Bonaparte.[21] Nor is this a passing anger. Hugo mistrusts the masses. The populace is a blind force; a mistaken people is not worth one righteous individual.[22] Such latent hostility, clashing with utopian faith in the working classes, helps us better understand in what sense Gwynplaine sees himself as a "master of crowds" and as a spokesman for the *silent* people.[23]

Even more complex, as noted throughout this study, are Hugo's ambiguous attitudes toward history. Anachronism, in every sense of the word, provides tension and drama. Hugo's remarkable evolution from the political right to the left is in a sense no evolution at all. Latent revolutionary tendencies are alive in him well before he fully grasps them, just as a nostalgia for conservative positions continues to clash with his professed socialist utopianism. These political anachronisms no doubt have emotional but also intellectual and cultural roots associated with the vocation of literature. Books are at the same time viewed as sacred repositories and as a challenge to the past. Their revolutionary potential, as the future continues to be conceived in terms of the past, remains fundamentally self-destructive. Spiritual paternity has both progressive and regressive features.

These dialectical tensions between past and future cast light on the historical nature of Hugo's imagination. They condition the recurrent interest in the historical novel, as well as the need to subvert its premises and conventions. In a sense, all of Hugo's narratives are historically oriented. Not only dates but gaps and discontinuities play a major role in his fiction. But the historical novel and its variants are most often an opportunity to probe and challenge the very possibility of historical meaning. The tollgate of calamities that is history does not, Hugo fears, automatically open onto progress. In the deepest sense, Hugo's relentless preoccupation with history corresponds to a strong antihistorical bias.

History is the brutal fait accompli. The key word *siècle*, which measures large periods of time but also denounces the worldly spirit, refers not only to epic dimensions but to the sequential nightmare, the *mur des siècles* of "La Vision d'où est sorti ce livre," the somber opening poem of *La Légende des siècles*.[24] There is ultimately for Hugo a sense in which the text is not about history: it is history that is seen as an enigmatic text—"texte obscur écrit dans une langue mystérieuse"[25]—constantly in need of translation and interpretation. Viewed in this hermeneutic and visionary perspective, history—as Sheila Gaudon excellently put it—becomes a metaphor for the Last Judgment.[26] The prophetic no less than the mythic mode dehistoricizes history.

Hugo's deep-seated distrust of the linearity of history illustrates Mircea Eliade's claim, in our own day, that all of modern Western culture feels anguish about its progress-oriented notion of history and longs for the "paradise of archetypes and repetition," for the *axis mundi* that would offer resistance to historical time.[27] In Hugo's visionary narratives, the linearity of plot and of melioristic themes is repeatedly countered by a symbolism of spiraling descent and cyclical structures.

Vision remains of the essence, but cannot be accounted for in simple thematic terms. It is easy, of course, to list the Hugolian themes that lend themselves to visionary treatment. Transformations and transmutations of all sorts, sea changes, erasures of boundaries, monsters of the flesh and of the psyche, voyages into the night—these are among the most obvious. Behind the dream-spectacle hides a sense of guilt which is never far removed from the obsession with capital punishment and from the horrors of parricide and fratricide. Laughter itself, so hauntingly present in Hugo's fiction, is most often a signal of antagonism and hatred. The freedom of laughter may signify the laughter of freedom. It may imply the unavoidable vengeance of the oppressed. The buffoon becomes the prophet of revolution. In the meantime however, his is the laughter of cruelty: the grimace. And behind the grimace can be read a deeper anxiety: the latent fear of a dehumanizing fall from grace, which, in its extreme form, seems to indict all of creation.

But more enigmatic even than these identifiable themes are the metaphorical structures that project them. Figures of verticality, in particular, affect both the social and mythopoetic vision in Hugo's narratives—though in different and at times contradictory ways. *Abyss* remains an ambivalent term, connoting the misery and revolutionary potential of the city's "underworld," as well as the poet's private descent into the elating but dangerous world of reverie and contemplation. In this personal, revelatory exploration, the axis of verticality points to suffering and possible madness. Hence the importance of carceral images (spaceless jails, unwalled prisons of the mind) and of the inverted Tower of Babel, symbol of dizzying perspectives.[28]

The inverted or reflected tower, which functions as a fearsome *mise en abyme* beginning in *Han d'Islande,* is associated with the fever of "optical illusions."[29] *In Notre-Dame de Paris,* Frollo has a hallucination in which a steeple reflected in the Seine appears to be a Tower of Babel; this occurs in a chapter entitled "Fièvre." Such fever doubtless suggests fear of the eye's desire, the inability to separate the aggression of the *voyeur* from the insight of the *voyant.* Despite bucolic pieces such as "Oui, je suis le rêveur . . ." in which the nature poet, an indiscreet witness to the trysts of spring, is seen as "l'oeil du bon dieu,"[30] the ocular motif is essentially one of anxiety. Precisely to the extent that the poet's eye tends to be all-invasive, Hugo seems to experience with increasing intensity the fear of vision, the terror of his own dreams. His daughter Adèle recorded in her diary that in his exile years, he could not go to bed without a kind of dread, that he complained of waking up with a "sacred horror" of his nightly visitations.[31] But even more than his nightmares, his penchant for prolonged reverie and the allurements of his creative imagination filled him with apprehension and awe. In *Promontorium somnii*—a striking text on the relation of genius to dreams—Hugo transforms a lunar summit, glimpsed years earlier through a telescope at the Observatoire, into the symbolic mental topography of visionary extravagance, of *fureur sacrée,* of poetic madness. Inverting the old adage, Hugo writes: "Quos vult AUGERE Juppiter dementat."[32]

Hugo's expressed belief that *dementia* is the affliction and distinction of genius is not a mere literary echo of the ancient saying that genius and madness went together.[33] Hugo appears genuinely convinced that the creative impulse, in one way or another, has to do with chaos. The fear is often repressed, or tamed by a playful fantasy. The paroxysm of creation is at times charmingly stylized, as in the eroticized fantasy play *La Forêt mouillée*, where the poet has a sparrow glorify nature's mutinous conduct ("L'ordre, c'est le délire"). For the "seer" in the enchanted, rain-drenched forest, the rites of spring are an "immense tumulte."[34] But not everywhere are tumult and disorder presented in such reassuring tones. *La Forêt mouillée* and "Oui, je suis le rêveur . . ." are contemporaneous with the tragic "Ce que dit la Bouche d'Ombre." They are the self-reassuring by-products of an obsessive vision that relates violence to all creation and all creativity.

There is indeed much to suggest that the dynamics of violence and the nocturnal chaos of creativity reflect Hugo's deep-seated unease with artistic vision and with the writing process itself. His novels are perhaps, in that sense, more revealing than his poetry; they refer less directly, but more disturbingly, to the "vertiginous spiral" of the creative self.[35] No one believed more intensely than Hugo in the destiny and function of genius. His verse repeatedly projects the figural presence of the poet. Certain poems of *Les Contemplations* propose an expansion of the poet's figura of such magnitude that it ultimately appears dispossessed of personality, emptied of the biographical self. This effacement is of course quite the opposite of a disappearance. What is involved is a figural presence which, by means of symbolic associations (Lucifer, Adam, Prometheus, Orpheus), becomes an allegory of the poetic process.[36]

In the novels, however, the figural presence of the poet and the poetic process itself tend to be treated with parody and irony. It is remarkable indeed that, while Hugo's poetry is rich in idealized artist-types (some of them inspired by historical figures: Dürer, Virgil, Palestrina, Dante), his narratives seem to present only caricatures of the writer: Gringoire, the ineffectual philosopher-dramatist in *Notre-Dame de Paris*; Ursus, the mountebank-ventriloquist in *L'Homme qui rit*; Gernardus Geestemunde, sinister spiritual leader of a gang of bandits, whose ultimate scriptural message to posterity is the confession of a crime.

The "spiritual chaos" that Geestemunde bears within him is only one among many indications, in the novels, of the symbolic link between poetic vision and a fascination with evil. To be sure, the literalized metaphor of the poet-abyss, the image of the *noir génie*, appears in his poetry too. "O strophe du poète . . . ," in book 5 of *Les Contemplations*, evokes in striking images the relation of violence between the poet and his poetry, the rape and infernal marriage that condemns both to live in the underworld of the poet's soul and that metamorphoses the victim-muse ("Prisonnière au plus noir de son âme profonde") into a sinister Proserpina.[37] But it is Hugo's fictional world that, in subtle and complex ways, suggests the bond linking poetic reverie, the art of writing, and the forces of evil. Deciphering the occult, penetrating into the unnameable dark, is the function of the visionary artist; but it is also a fateful transgression. The enigmatic commerce with evil is perceived as constitutive of the literary act.

Ego Hugo is thus not merely a self-centered, vainglorious motto. It corresponds to Hugo's intuition of the tragic intimacy with darkness, with the "désolation du Mal mystérieux." It also corresponds to his latent identification of all principles of authorship and authority that bring the author of a literary text into an evil complicity (or is it a complicity in evil?) with God himself, defined as "collaborateur ténébreux."[38] The author of the literary creation and the author of the greater Text thus meet in a common theology of darkness. In his last three novels—*Les Travailleurs de la mer*, *L'Homme qui rit*, and *Quatrevingt-Treize*—Hugo seems to stress particularly the relation among authority, textuality, and malevolent forces.

This identification of author as God and of God as author is, needless to say, very different from Baudelaire's affirmation that the artist is answerable only to himself, that he perpetuates only himself, that he is his own king, his own priest, his own God. It is also totally unlike Flaubert's repeated assertion that the author in his text should be like God in his universe, present everywhere and visible nowhere. It is true that Hugo had written in the preface to *Cromwell*: "Like God, the true poet is present everywhere at once in his work."[39] (One might even wonder whether Flaubert, perhaps unconsciously, did not recall Hugo's statement.) But for Hugo, the metaphor came close to an act of faith: the world was the space of inscription. Such a notion of the world as book clearly brought transcendence and immanence into an unconventional relationship. In the philosophical companion-piece to *Les Misérables*, it is in the same passage in which he states that "authority implies the author" that he also refers to the "auteur suprême."[40] It would hardly be exaggerated to say that Hugo's conception of creation was "lettristic."[41]

Like Dante in the *Convivio*, Hugo might have been tempted himself to play with symbolic etymology: Dante had proposed that the word *autor*—not to be confused with *auctor*—was derived from the Latin verb *avieo*, meaning to bind. Hugo would surely have found congenial the notion of the author as a binder of vowels, entrusted with the secret mastery of language. According to this tradition, the letter of the text is a scriptural transcription of the world's *sacrality*.[42] It is clear, in any case, that Hugo remained convinced of the deep correlation between the authority of the text and the authority of the Word. The two authorities ultimately tended to blend in his mind. The effacement of lines of demarcation between inner and outer reality abolished all distance and separation. The principle of authority ended up by merging with the principle of identity. This transgressive assimilation is perhaps best illustrated in "Le Satyre," as the infinite enlargement of the Orphic faun not only elevates him to the stature of Universal Pan but allows him to *absorb* infinity: "L'espace immense entra dans cette forme noire."[43] Once again, the darkness of the poet's shape— "forme noire"—casts a tragic shadow on the poetic function.

The peculiar power of Hugo's narratives stems in large part from their ability to conceal and reveal the sense that writing itself is a tragic act. If there is survival through the written word (and even that survival, as we have seen, is an expression of guilt), it is also true that the process of writing, as thematized in Hugo's novels, remains forever incomplete, caught in the progressions and regressions of becoming; for text feeds on text, and must desire its own undoing. Like the treacherous snow in *Les Travailleurs de la mer*, which obliterates the letters of Gilliatt's name, the written page is unstable. Words, moreover, have too sharp a contour to account for the flux of ideas. Though the master rhetorician prides himself on his power over words, he must deplore the limitations of language: "Expression has frontiers," Hugo comments in *L'Homme qui rit*. No matter how one perseveres in one's struggle with words, language cannot adequately account for diffuse states of being, for the inner depth, the "sombre immensité intérieure" of man.[44]

There is another sense in which, for Hugo, the act of writing has tragic undertones. Much as he was drawn to humanitarian hope in progress, the obsessive image of the Tower of Babel is a steady reminder that utopia is beyond reach. Its alternately upsurging and inverted structure undermines eschatological schemes. The writer's tools are again directly involved. The symbolic skyscraper, thrusting upward and downward into the unknown, is built on language and with language but is also liable to be destroyed by it. For Hugo, the vertical construct is a never-to-be-achieved project from whose height (or depth) he can contemplate his own sacred awe. For the image of the tower and even more so the image of the promontory mirrored and inverted in the sea (genius is defined as "un promontoire dans l'infini")[45] are heights and depths from which the visionary artist, perceiving the shadow, can survey with fear what he most desires, and dream of what he most fears. The promontory, in Hugo's imagination, is associated with Saint John at Patmos unveiling the apocalypse, but also with Moses in his terrifying encounter with God, and finally with the notion of transgression itself. There is no genius without sacred terror. The great artist, we are told, shudders at his own depth: "Il a l'horreur de sa profondeur."[46]

This almost religious awe, instilled in the visionary artist by his creative self, is especially disturbing because the mystery of selfhood (the "théologie du moi," as Anne Ubersfeld aptly called it)[47] is inextricably bound up, in Hugo's mind, with the even more puzzling mystery of supreme Selfhood. The "moi de l'infini," as the supreme author is defined in Les Misérables, is deeply involved with the forces of darkness. Like his tragic "collaborator" Germain Pilon, like all the visionary and creative figures in his work, he seems to lean to the darker side of his own creation.

Among Hugo's drafts, under the heading "Infinity in Art," there is an astonishing sentence. It was written after he completed Les Misérables, when he was at work on William Shakespeare, and it provides a disquieting answer to Job's age-old question about the mystery of God and the mystery of evil. Hugo writes: "Evil, in nature as well as in destiny, is a dark beginning of God continuing beyond us into the invisible."[48] This sentence, which seemingly roots God's reality in the reality of evil, echoes and illumines many other statements about the noir génie's fascination with the "sob" of creation and the deep mourning that afflicts all of nature.[49]

The sentence remained buried in Hugo's notes. Though its formulation is striking, it says hardly anything that his poetry and above all his great visionary novels did not suggest in enigmatic and even more disturbing ways. However, because of its explicit formulation, the sentence reveals with particular clarity the inadequacy of a naïve reading of Hugo as the reassuring bard of progress, of light, of redemptive love, and of Satan's ultimate salvation.

Notes

Selected Bibliography

Credits for Illustrations

Index

Notes

1. Approaches

1. Victor Hugo, "Quentin Durward ou l'Ecossais à la cour de Louis XI," in Hugo, *Oeuvres Complètes*, ed. Jean Massin (Paris: Club Français du Livre, 1967), II, 431–438. See also Hugo's notes for a projected preface to *La Légende des siècles*, ibid., X, 671–672; *William Shakespeare*, ibid., XII, 204; and the "Annexes" to *L'Homme qui rit*, ibid., XIV, 390. References throughout, including the volume and page citations in the text, are to this chronological edition of Hugo's works: *Oeuvres Complètes*, ed. Jean Massin, 18 vols. (Paris: Le Club Français du Livre, 1967–1970) [hereafter referred to as *O.C.*].

2. Lamartine's letter, dated 1 July 1831, is reprinted in *O.C.*, IV, 1035. Algernon Charles Swinburne, "Victor Marie Hugo," in Swinburne, *The Complete Works* (London: Heinemann, 1926), XIII, 4, 5, 21; also idem, *A Study of Victor Hugo* (London: Chatto and Windus, 1886), p. vi. Walter Pater, "Postscript," in *Appreciations"* (London: Macmillan, 1910), pp. 241–261. See Nathalie Babel Brown, *Hugo and Dostoevsky* (Ann Arbor: Ardis, 1978), pp. 11, 14–15. Brown quotes at length from Dostoevsky's interesting presentation of the four installments of a Russian translation of *Notre-Dame de Paris*, which appeared in *Vremya* (September–December 1862) at the time Dostoevsky was still under the spell of the recently published *Les Misérables*. See also Joseph Frank, *Dostoevsky: The Seeds of Revolt, 1821–1849* (Princeton: Princeton University Press, 1976), pp. 108, 110, 121. Frank speaks of the young Dostoevsky's worship of Victor Hugo, whom he considered a "prophetic mouthpiece of God," providing the "moral foundations of the modern

world." Leo Tolstoy, *What is Art,* in Tolstoy, *The Complete Works* (Boston: Dana Estes, 1904), XXII, 299–300.

3. Gustave Flaubert, *Correspondance,* ed. Jean Bruneau (Paris: Pléiade, 1973, 1980), I, 195; II, 164, 385. Idem, *Correspondance* (Paris: Conard, 1926–1933), IV, 333. Charles Baudelaire, "Victor Hugo," in Baudelaire, *Oeuvres Complètes* (Paris: Pléiade, 1961), pp. 701–713. Baudelaire in this article calls Hugo a "génie sans frontières." Arthur Rimbaud, letter of May 1871 to Paul Demeny, in Rimbaud, *Oeuvres* (Paris: Garnier, 1960), pp. 344–350.

4. Jean-Paul Sartre, *L'Idiot de la famille* (Paris: Gallimard, 1971, 1972), I, 841; III, 162–163, 203, 283.

5. Idem, *Situations II* (Paris: Gallimard, 1948), pp. 12–13, 246–250. Hugo, *O.C.,* XII, 314. Hugo's powerful self-identification with the institution of literature is of course symptomatic of larger sociocultural issues. Jeffrey Mehlman appropriately speaks of Hugo's role in the French nineteenth century as "metonym of Literature itself," as "Literature incarnate." Mehlman, *Revolution and Repetition: Marx/Hugo/Balzac* (Berkeley: University of California Press, 1977), pp. 44–46. Hugo's aphorism appears in book 3 of *William Shakespeare, O.C.,* XII, 314.

6. André Gide, *Anthologie de la poésie française* (Paris: Pléiade, 1949), p. xxxii. Jean Cocteau, "Le Mystère laïc," in Cocteau, *Oeuvres Complètes* (Lausanne: Marguerat, 1946), X, 21. Some of these observations appeared earlier in *The Times Literary Supplement* (London), August 7, 1981.

7. See in particular Mikhail Bakhtin, *Epopée et roman* (Paris: Recherches Internationales, 1973). This work has appeared in English as "Epic and Novel," trans. Caryl Emerson and Michael Holquist, in Holquist, ed., *The Dialogic Imagination of M. M. Bakhtin* (Austin: University of Texas Press, 1981), pp. 3–40. See also Bakhtin, *Rabelais and His World* (Cambridge, Mass.: MIT Press, 1968).

8. See Hugo's oration at Balzac's funeral, 21 August 1850, *O.C.,* VII, 316–318. On Hugo's novels as romances or *romans poèmes,* see Richard B. Grant, *The Perilous Quest* (Durham: Duke University Press, 1968), esp. ch. 1; and Henri Meschonnic, "Vers le roman poème," in *O.C.,* III, i-xx. On the nineteenth-century notion of epic, see Léon Cellier, *L'Epopée romantique* (Paris: Presses Universitaires de France, 1954); and Herbert J. Hunt, *The Epic in Nineteenth Century France* (London: Oxford University Press, 1941).

9. Jean Gaudon, "Digressions hugoliennes," in *O.C.*, XIV, i–xvii.

10. See "But de cette publication" (preface), ibid., V, 38.

11. *Les Feuilles d'automne*, ibid., IV, 373, 458.

12. "Le Tas de Pierres," ibid., XIV, 1214; "Guerre aux Démolisseurs," ibid., IV, 509.

13. On the specific year 1830 (the time of *Notre-Dame de Paris*) as a time of transition and "emptiness," see Claude Duchet and Guy Rosa, "Sur une Edition et Deux Romans de Victor Hugo," *Revue d'Histoire Littéraire de la France* 79 (September–October 1979): 824–834. In his Introduction to *Notre-Dame de Paris* (Paris: Pléiade, 1975, Jacques Seebacher stressed the notion of "temps creux" (p. 1045). On viewing the revolution-to-be as a matter of the past, see Claude Duchet, "The Object-Event of the Ram's Charge: An Ideological Reading of an Image," *Yale French Studies* 59 (1980): 172. Duchet speaks intelligently of the need to conciliate "the order of historical values with those of desire."

14. *O.C.*, V, 25.

15. *O.C.*, X, 593. John Porter Houston makes the interesting point that Hugo's visionary writings are "paradoxically unsusceptible of complete visualization." Houston, *The Demonic Imagination: Style and Theme in French Romantic Poetry* (Baton Rouge: Louisiana State University Press, 1969), p. 153. On the crucial distinction between *regarder* and *voir*, see Jean Gaudon, *Le Temps de la contemplation* (Paris: Flammarion, 1969), passim, but esp. the chapter entitled "Contempler." The line from "Le Satyre" is: "Il peignit l'arbre vu du côté des racines" (*O.C.*, X, 593.

16. *O.C.*, X, 672.

17. Such Saint-Simonian notions of the writer's mission were well summed up, in 1830, by Hugo's friend Sainte-Beuve in "Espoir et voeu du mouvement littéraire et poétique après la révolution de 1830"—an article that first appeared in *Le Globe*, 11 October 1830, and that was reprinted in Sainte-Beuve, *Premiers Lundis* (Paris: Pléiade, 1949).

18. *O.C.*, IX, 255, 256–257.

19. Ibid., XIV, 1221.

20. Stendhal, *Courrier anglais* (Paris: Le Divan, 1935), II, 55–62. Many of the names invented by Hugo are clearly meant as a joke: Cumbysulsum, Orugix, Musdoemon, Symgrantax, Oglypiglap, and so on.

21. *O.C.*, II, 93–95.

22. Ibid., II, 387, 138–139.

23. Ibid., II, 216, 234.

24. On the royal slave in French literature, see the excellently documented study by Léon-François Hoffmann, *Le Nègre romantique* (Paris: Payot, 1973), esp. pp. 59, 61–62, 81–82. See also Julien J. Lafontant, "A Tribute to Victor Hugo's *Bug-Jargal*," *Rocky Mountain Review* 32, no. 4 (1978): 195–210.

25. For a discussion of the figure of the negro in terms of archetypal erotic animalization, see Roger Toumson's Présentation of an edition of *Bug-Jargal* recently published in Haiti, in which the title of Hugo's novel is given on the title page as *Bug Jargal, ou la révolution haïtienne* (Fort-de-France: Désormeaux, 1979).

26. In view of the fact that the insurrection interrupts and delays the wedding night, one may be tempted to agree with Georges Piroué that images of ravishment correspond to a secret wish to have his bride deflowered by his "noir frère herculéen." Piroué, Présentation of *Bug-Jargal*, in *O.C.*, I, vi.

27. Ibid., II, 694.

2. The Condemned Man

1. For a survey of texts that, in the 1820s, discussed the death penalty, see Gustave Charlier, "Comment fut écrit 'Le Dernier Jour d'un condamné,' " *Revue d'Histoire Littéraire de la France* 22 (1915): 321–360. Charlier also refers to a number of prison memoirs that might have served as sources for Hugo's novel.

2. *Mémoires de Vidocq* (Paris: Amis du Club de Livre, 1959), p. 82.

3. On Hugo's inquiries into prisons and prison conditions, see P. Savey-Casard, *Le Crime et la peine dans l'oeuvre de Victor Hugo* (Paris: Presses Universitaires de France, 1956).

4. For some excellent remarks on the tyranny of the present indicative, see Jean Massin's Présentation of the novel in Hugo, *Oeuvres Complètes*, ed. Jean Massin, 18 vols. (Paris: Le Club Français du Livre, 1967–1970), III, 614ff [hereafter referred to as *O.C.*].

5. In the introduction to his tale *Krotkaia* (1876), Dostoevsky imgines a hypothetical stenographer who would link realism to fantasy, and gives as his model Hugo's "masterpiece" *Le Dernier Jour d'un condamné*. Dostoevsky, *Journal d'un Ecrivain* (Paris: Pléiade, 1972), p. 751. Flaubert expressed his admiration to Louise Colet in a letter of

9 December 1852, in which he praises the total absence of didacticism in Hugo's novel. Its impact, according to Flaubert, is directly related to the absence of authorial commentary. Flaubert, *Correspondance* (Paris: Pléiade, 1970), II, 204.

6. *O.C.*, III, 664.

7. In *Actes et Paroles, II*, ibid., XII, 866.

8. *Claude Gueux* (1834) is a fictionalized account (about twenty pages long in most editions) of a real case that Hugo had read about in *La Gazette des Tribunaux*. It tells how a poor and uneducated worker, without a job, is driven to steal in order to support the woman he lives with and his daughter; how, condemned to five years of prison for this petty crime, he is cruelly persecuted by the inspector of the prison workshop (an early incarnation of Javert) and forcibly separated from his best friend and prison companion; how, after much patient suffering, much deliberation, and repeated warnings, he decides to kill the sadistic overseer. Claude Gueux, whose last name means "beggar" or "tramp," is of course condemned to death and duly executed. Hugo clearly conceived the text as a tract denouncing social injustice. It takes a hard look at prison, at capital punishment, and, in the didactic conclusion, calls for a determined effort to fight illiteracy and to educate the people. The following sentence sums up Hugo's larger design, as well as the seminal virtue of *Claude Gueux* in terms of Hugo's later work: "We have given the history of Claude Gueux's life in some detail because we believe that every paragraph of this story could serve as chapter headings in a work that would provide a solution to the great problem of the people in the nineteenth century" (*O.C.*, V, 250). When one considers that almost thirty years would elapse before the publication of *Les Misérables*, one is struck by the persistence of Hugo's central preoccupations.

9. The detail has its realistic justification: the right hand of parricides was cut off prior to execution. It is nonetheless revealing that in this nightmare group of undifferentiated criminals, the parricide should be singled out.

10. *O.C.*, III, 669. The importance of *Le Dernier Jour d'un condamné* has not escaped psychoanalytically oriented critics. See Charles Baudoin, *Psychanalyse de Victor Hugo* (Geneva: Mont Blanc, 1943; rpt. Armand Colin, 1972); and Charles Mauron, "Les Personnages de Victor Hugo," in *O.C.*, II, i–xli. See in particular the latter's development on the relation of the spider to the notion of *anankē*.

11. *O.C.*, X, 268. The association between the guillotine and a

repressed sense of family guilt is strongly confirmed by a curious detail pointed out by Yves Gohin: the thirteen-year-old Victor, confined with his brother in a boarding school and under the tyrannical surveillance of a hated aunt, hears of the condemnation and execution of a man who had killed his aunt and had afterward also killed his brother, who had suspected him of the crime. The name of that murderer was Dautun— a name that appears, under a huge spider web, on one of the walls of the Bicêtre prison in *Le Dernier Jour d'un condamné*. Gohin, "Les Réalités du crime et de la justice pour Victor Hugo avant 1829," *O.C.*, III, vii.

12. Cesare Beccaria, *Dei Delitti e delle pene* (Florence: Felice Le Monnier, 1950), chs. 1 and 9.

13. Michel Foucault, *Surveiller et punir: Naissance de la prison* (Paris: Gallimard, 1975), esp. pp. 28, 92, 117, 120, 132, 148, 169, 174, 210, 219, 304–305. Foucault indeed refers to *Le Dernier Jour d'un condamné* and to *Claude Gueux* (see pp. 261–269).

14. "Ecrit en 1846," in *Les Contemplations*, *O.C.*, IX, 256; *William Shakespeare*, ibid., XII, 274.

15. Richard Grant is right, of course, in observing that a substantial number of poems in *Les Orientales* refer in some manner to the Greek war of independence, and that the "historical inspiration" cannot be ignored. Richard B. Grant, "Sequence and Theme in Victor Hugo's *Les Orientales*," *PMLA* 94 (October 1979): 895.

16. In 1807 Madame Hugo and her three sons—Abel, Eugène, and Victor—joined their father, who was then a field officer in Napoleon's army in Italy (he was later to become a general) and had recently led a successful expeditionary force against the guerrilla-bandit Fra Diavolo. The rows of hanged men on trees and the deep impression made by this sight on young Victor are described in *Victor Hugo raconté par un témoin de sa vie*, the biographical narrative written by Victor Hugo's wife, largely with information provided by him, and so to speak under his supervision (*O.C.*, I, 850).

17. See Michael Riffaterre, "La Poésie métaphysique de Victor Hugo: Style, symbole et thèmes de *Dieu*," *Romanic Review* 51 (December 1960): 268–276. See also Victor Brombert, "Victor Hugo: The Spaceless Prison," in Brombert, *The Romantic Prison* (Princeton: Princeton University Press, 1978), pp. 88–119; this paragraph and the following use and develop in a different perspective some ideas presented in my earlier work.

18. Dostoevsky may well have remembered this episode when he wrote the scene of the prisoners' bath in *Notes from the House of the Dead*.

19. See Joseph de Maistre, *Les Soirées de Saint-Pétersbourg*, Neuvième Entretien (Paris: Garnier, 1815). Also Pierre Halbwachs, "Le Poète de l'histoire," in *O.C.*, VII, xiii.

20. *O.C.*, III, 661. The double meaning of the word *révolution* is in fact part of a larger project of articulating the personal drama on the drama of history. In the introductory pages to *Littérature et philosophie mêlées* (1834), Hugo writes: "Pourquoi, en effet, ne pas confronter plus souvent qu'on ne le fait les révolutions de l'individu avec les révolutions de la société?" (ibid., V, 25).

3. The Living Stones of Notre-Dame

1. See Richard B. Grant, *The Perilous Quest: Image, Myth, and Prophecy in the Narratives of Victor Hugo* (Durham: Duke University Press, 1968), pp. 46–72, a very persuasive analysis of the importance of the spider image.

2. Charles Baudelaire, "La Beauté" (Paris: Pléiade, 1961), p. 20. The image, in the poem, refers to the metaphor of a sphinx-like statue of beauty. But the image is applicable throughout to Baudelaire's city poetry.

3. On the prison images in *Notre-Dame de Paris*, see Victor Brombert, *The Romantic Prison* (Princeton: Princeton University Press, 1978), p. 103.

4. "Feuilles paginées," in Victor Hugo, *Oeuvres Complètes*, ed. Jean Massin, 18 vols. (Paris: Le Club Français du Livre, 1967–1970), IV, 961–962 [hereafter referred to as *O.C.*].

5. In the 1832 notice added to the novel, Hugo refers to Paris as "la cité de la presse, de la parole, de la pensée" (*O.C.*, IV, 23). See also the twenty-sixth letter of *Le Rhin* (ibid., VI, 406–407), where the physical growth of the capital (its climbing stones) and the "saint travail de la civilisation, de la paix et de la pensée" are clearly linked with revolutionary change.

6. Ibid., IV, 108. Two texts by Hugo cast light on this aspect of the novel: the earlier "Sur la destruction des monuments en France" (1825), ibid., II, 569–572; and the almost contemporaneous article "Guerre aux démolisseurs!" (1832), ibid., IV, 499–509.

7. Pierre-Simon Ballanche, *Oeuvres* (Paris: Bureau de l'encyclopédie de connaissances utiles, 1833; rev. ed. Geneva: Slatkine, 1967), II, 333. Hugo's assertion is to be found in his essay on Walter Scott's *Quentin Durward*, *O.C.*, II, 437.

8. G. W. F. Hegel, *Ästhetik*, 2 vols. (Frankfurt: Europäische Verlagsanstalt, n.d.), pt. 2, sect. 2, ch. 3c. See in particular II, 452.

9. The complete sentence reintroduces the stone motif: "Moi, je suis quelque chose d'affreux, ni homme, ni animal, un je ne sais quoi plus dur, plus foulé aux pieds et plus difforme qu'un caillou!" (*O.C.*, IV, 259).

10. 1 Peter 2: 2–5. For ingenious remarks about the political implications of this reference to the First Epistle of Peter, see Jacques Seebacher, Introduction to Victor Hugo, *Notre-Dame de Paris* (Paris: Pléiade, 1975), p. 1071.

11. See Anne Ubersfeld's fine chapter, "D'une Théorie du grotesque," in Ubersfeld, *Le Roi et le Bouffon* (Paris: Corti, 1974), pp. 461–474.

12. *O.C.*, IV, 95. The lines in question are: "pendent opera interrupta minaeque / murorum ingentes aequataque machina caelo" (*Aeneid*, IV, 88–89). It is interesting to note that Virgil's text conjures up Babel-like constructs: huge threatening walls and scaffoldings that reach up to heaven. W. Wolfgang Holdheim, in a very interesting discussion of Hugo's attempt to fuse dramatic and epic elements, makes some relevant comments concerning architectural metaphors. Holdheim, *Die Suche nach dem Epos: Der Geschichtsroman bei Hugo, Tolstoi und Flaubert* (Heidelberg: Carl Winter Universitätsverlag, 1978), esp. pp. 30, 38–39, 49, 69, 85.

13. The point was elaborated, many years later, in *William Shakespeare:* "La civilisation a des phrases. Ces phrases sont les siècles. Elle ne dit pas ici ce qu'elle dit là. Mais ces phrases mystérieuses s'enchaînent (*O.C.*, XII, 320).

14. Paul Zumthor put it very well: "Le temps mythique est désormais 89; mais sa relative proximité l'empêche de projeter jusqu'à nous une véritable perspective chronologique: son ombre nous déborde, et s'allonge dans un inconnu au-delà de nous." Zumthor, "Le Moyen Age de Victor Hugo," ibid., IV, xxx.

15. "La lettre ne doit jamais se pétrifier quand les choses sont progressives. Si la lettre résiste, il faut la briser." Hugo, *Journal des idées et des opinions d'un révolutionnaire de 1830*, ibid., V, 109.

16. Ibid., IV, 144. It is interesting to note that language, in its transformational nature, was from the outset seen by Hugo as the opposite of petrification, as the sign of man's *progressive* movement: "Une langue ne se fixe pas. L'esprit humain est toujours en marche, ou, si l'on veut, en mouvement." Hugo, Preface to *Cromwell*, ibid., III, 76.

17. Hugo had a keen sense of the importance of proper names. This onomastic preoccupation characterizes all his texts, and is made explicit in "Post-Scriptum de ma vie": "A name must be a figure. The poet who does not know this knows nothing" (ibid., VI, 1121). Quoted by Michel Grimaud, "De Victor Hugo à Homère-Hogu: L'Onomastique des *Misérables*," *L'Esprit Créateur* 16 (Fall 1976): 220–230.

18. See the preface to *Cromwell*, *O.C.*, III, 53.

19. *Victor Hugo raconté par un témoin de sa vie*, ibid., IV, 1192.

20. Ibid., IV, 250. In the theoretically oriented chapter "Ceci tuera cela," Hugo in fact refers to the less hieratic styles, such as the Gothic, as tending to be "detached from religion" (ibid., IV, 140).

21. *Les Feuilles d'automne*, no. 37, ibid., IV, 445–454.

22. The relevant pages by Sainte-Beuve and Montalembert have been reproduced by Jean Massin in *O.C.*, IV, 1234, 1243, 1294. The title of a suggestive essay by Jacques Seebacher, dealing with a wide range of questions, characteristically stresses emptiness. Seebacher, "Le Système du vide dans *Notre-Dame de Paris*," *Littérature* 5 (February 1972): 95–106. And it is revealing that Hugo himself, referring to his fictional output in the opening poem of *Les Feuilles d'automne*, speaks of his "roman ironique et railleur" (*O.C.*, IV, 374). He could, of course, have had in mind *Han d'Islande*.

23. *O.C.*, IV, 254. Richard B. Grant quite appropriately speaks of the "demonic quality of the church." Grant, *The Perilous Quest*, p. 69.

24. *Les Contemplations*, *O.C.*, IX, 354.

25. For a detailed account of this drama of friendship and family, see Raphaël Molho, "Critique, Amour et Poésie: Sainte-Beuve et 'Les' Hugo," ibid., IV, i–xxvi.

26. On the importance of the coronation of Charles X in Reims, see Jacques Seebacher's astute observations in his introduction to *Notre-Dame de Paris* (Paris: Pléiade, 1975), pp. 1048–76.

27. *Journal des idées et des opinions d'un révolutionnaire de 1830*, *O.C.*, V, 108.

28. See in particular C. A. Sainte-Beuve, "Espoir et voeu du

mouvement littéraire et poétique après la révolution de 1830," *Le Globe*, 11 October 1830, reproduced in Sainte-Beuve, *Premiers Lundis*, in *Oeuvres* (Paris: Pléiade, 1949); and Pierre Leroux, "Aux Artistes," *Revue Encyclopédique*, November–December 1831.

29. "Littérature et philosophie mêlées," *O.C.*, V, 38.

30. For instance, in 1823, "it would be an almost criminal mistake for the writer to think himself above the general interest and the country's needs." Hugo, "Quentin Durward, ou l'Ecossais à la cour de Louis XI," ibid., II, 432.

31. "Le bruit sourd que font les révolutions, encore enfouies dans la sape" (ibid., IV, 367).

32. "Réponse à un acte d'accusation," *Les Contemplations*, ibid., IX, 75. Adèle Hugo recalls as follows Hugo's political mood in the 1830s: "M. Victor Hugo, qui venait de faire son insurrection et ses barricades au théâtre, comprit que tous les progrès se tiennent et qu'à moins d'être inconséquent il devait accepter en politique ce qu'il voulait en littérature." *Victor Hugo raconté par un témoin de sa vie*, ibid., IV, 1190.

33. On the specific figure of the battering ram in the revolutionary tradition, see Claude Duchet's enlightening pages on Malraux's use of the motif in his article "The Object-Event of the Ram's Charge: An Ideological Reading of an Image," *Yale French Studies* 59 (1980): 155–174.

34. "Rêverie d'un passant à propos d'un roi," *Les Feuilles d'automne*, *O.C.*, IV, 380–381.

35. From the 1872 notebook; quoted by Jean Massin, ibid., IV, 105.

36. Ibid., VI, 406.

37. "Bièvre," in *Les Feuilles d'automne*, ibid., IV, 439. In *Notre-Dame de Paris*, Hugo refers to the "marée montante du pavé de Paris" (ibid., IV, 92).

38. See in particular the first part of Mikhail Bakhtin's *Rabelais and His World* (Cambridge, Mass.: MIT Press, 1968). See also his interesting essay "Epic and Novel," in *The Dialogic Imagination of M. M. Bakhtin*, ed. Michael Holquist (Austin: University of Texas Press, 1981), pp. 3–40.

39. Bakhtin, *Rabelais and His World*, p. 128. The references to laughter in *Notre-Dame de Paris* are, respectively, in *O.C.*, IV, 168, 77, 74, 325, 171, 331, 250, 339.

40. IX, 294. On the grotesque as an affirmation of the sublime, see Ubersfeld, "D'Une Théorie du grotesque," in *Le Roi et le Bouffon*, pp. 461–474.

41. See in particular a letter to Louise Colet, dated 15 July 1853, in Flaubert, *Correspondance*, ed. Jean Bruneau (Paris: Pléiade, 1980), II, 385.

42. *O.C.*, IV, 76, 163. Some of the other painters mentioned are Teniers, Salvator Rosa, Rembrandt (several times), and Masaccio. On Hugo's likely mental associations of certain painters with his description of the Cour des Miracles, see Claude Gély, *Victor Hugo, poète de l'intimité* (Paris: Nizet, 1969), pp. 257ff.

43. See in particular the beginning of "Les Cariatides" in the poem "La Révolution," *O.C.*, X, 226–232.

44. Ubersfeld argues this point very cogently in *Le Roi et le Bouffon*, p. 86.

45. *William Shakespeare*, *O.C.*, XII, 205, 271, 273. See in particular the beginning of the section entitled "Les Esprits et les masses."

46. Ibid., IV, 287, 34. *Victor Hugo raconté par un témoin de sa vie*, ibid., IV, 1194. The connection between this act of "violence populaire" and the novel was obviously made by the Hugos themselves, since Adèle claimed that the novel appeared the day of the sack, 13 February 1831. In fact, *Notre-Dame de Paris* appeared in March.

47. *Journal des idées et des opinions d'un révolutionnaire de 1830*, ibid., V, 114.

48. *Feuilles paginées, II*, ibid., IV, 963.

49. Sainte-Beuve, at about the same time, in his private notes, maliciously refers to Hugo as "le cyclope."

50. *Les Feuilles d'automne*, *O.C.*, IV, 440.

51. Preface to *Cromwell*, ibid., III, 71–74.

52. See also *Les Feuilles d'automne:* "Et les passants ne sont, le soir, sur les quais sombres, / Qu'un flux et qu'un reflux de lumières et d'ombres." In the manuscript the first line here quoted mentions Rembrandt specifically: "Et j'ai cru voir souvent Rembrandt sur les quais sombres" (ibid., IV, 444).

53. The text is explicit: "la rivière, en reflétant le ciel, prolongeait l'abîme au-dessous de lui" (ibid., IV, 252–253).

54. Jean-Bertrand Barrère, in his excellent study of Hugo's fantasy, shrewdly observed that the "views from above" serve at the same time to simplify and to intensify the "enchevêtrement des lignes." Barrère,

La Fantaisie de Victor Hugo (Paris: Klincksieck, 1973), I, 147.

55. *Les Misérables*, *O.C.*, XI, 531.

56. Ibid., XII, 465, 226; XIV, 85.

57. Hugo's remarks about Dante in *William Shakespeare* are worth quoting, especially since they involve an architectural image: "Dante tord toute l'ombre et toute la clarté dans une spirale monstrueuse. Cela descend, puis cela monte. Architecture inouïe" (ibid., XII, 183).

58. Ibid., XIV, 1254.

59. Ibid., XIV, 336.

60. Ballanche, *Oeuvres*, VI, iii.

61. *O.C.*, II, 437.

62. "Que l'histoire soit à refaire, cela est évident. Elle a été presque toujours écrite jusqu'à présent au point de vue misérable du fait; il est temps de l'écrire au point de vue du principe." Hugo, *William Shakespeare*, ibid., XII, 315.

63. This is basically the conviction of Jacques Seebacher, who, in the Pléiade edition of *Notre-Dame de Paris*, speaks of the "dégradation du roman historique" (p. 1068). In a more recent study, Stirling Haig shrewdly stresses the importance of Gringoire, an often neglected and often maligned character, as a marker of authorial presence and of a nineteenth-century point of view. Haig, "From Cathedral to Book, from Stone to Press: Hugo's Portrait of the Artist in *Notre-Dame de Paris*," *Stanford French Review* 3 (Winter 1979): 343–350. In his private notes, Hugo entertained himself with the fiction of being the great-grandson of Pierre Gringoire (*O.C.*, IV, 961). On dislocation, fragmentation, and disfiguration in the novel, see Suzanne Nash, "Writing a Building: Hugo's *Notre-Dame de Paris*," *French Forum* 8 (May 1983): 122–133.

64. The article from *Le Journal des Débats*, 24 July 1832, has been reprinted in *O.C.*, IV, 1237–44. Sainte-Beuve defines Hugo's novel as follows: "un peu fantastique toujours, anguleux, hautain, *vertical* pour ainsi dire, pittoresque sur tous les bords, et à la fois sagace, railleur, désabusé."

65. "La rêverie est un regard qui a cette propriété de tant regarder l'ombre qu'il en fait sortir la clarté." Hugo, *William Shakespeare*, ibid., XII, 226. On Hugo's *concupiscentia oculorum* and on the symbolism of blindness in his work, see Jean Gaudon's admirable *Le Temps de la contemplation* (Paris: Flammarion, 1969).

66. *O.C.*, XII, 356.

67. Ibid., IX, 271.

68. Ibid., XIV, 334.

4. Les Misérables

1. An entry in Hugo's notebook for 1860 reads as follows: "Peut-être Waterloo / commencer par là (19 oct)—grand récit épique mêlé au roman." Victor Hugo, *Oeuvres Complètes*, ed. Jean Massin, 18 vols. (Paris: Le Club Français du Livre, 1967–1970), XII, 1502 [hereafter referred to as *O.C.*]. Jean Gaudon drew my attention to this most interesting entry. See his excellent "Digressions hugoliennes," in *O.C.*, XIV, xiv.

2. For a systematic and intelligent analysis of confrontations and conjunctions in *Les Misérables*, see André Brochu, *Hugo. Amour/Crime/Révolution. Essai sur "Les Misérables"* (Montréal: Les Presses de l'Université de Montréal, 1974). This study, extremely rich in insights, is one of the best pieces of criticism on *Les Misérables*.

3. André Brochu speaks of an "habile contrepoint" in the thematic articulation of fall and ascent implicit in the contrast established between Napoleon and Valjean (ibid., p. 80).

4. *The Perilous Quest* (Durham: Duke University Press, 1968) is the well-chosen title of Richard B. Grant's study of image, myth, and prophecy in Victor Hugo's narratives. Grant speaks indeed of the "apolitical world of Jean Valjean" (p. 165).

5. See Bernard Leuilliot, "Présentation de Jean Valjean," in *Hommage à Victor Hugo* (Strasbourg: Bulletin de la Faculté des Lettres de Strasbourg, 1962), p. 53.

6. In his discussion of this theme of regressivity, Jean Gaudon concludes amusingly that the "false nephews" never live up to the uncles (Introduction to *La Légende des Siècles* (Paris: Garnier, 1974), p. xxxvi.

7. O.C., VI, 719–721. See Claude Gély, *Les Misérables de Hugo* (Paris: Hachette, 1975), p. 5.

8. *O.C.*, XII, 1180.

9. Ibid., XI, 292.

10. See the interesting discussion of the problem in Brochu, *Hugo. Amour/Crime/Révolution*, pp. 178ff.

11. Brochu has an excellent development on this affective transfer. Ibid., pp. 212ff.

12. See the relevant passages of Lamartine's *Cours Familier de*

Littérature ("Considérations sur un chef-d'oeuvre ou le danger du génie"), quoted in *O.C.*, XII, 1608, 1616.

13. Mikhail Bakhtin, *Rabelais and His World* (Cambridge, Mass.: MIT Press, 1968), p. 62.

14. Ibid., p. 88. It is odd that although Bakhtin recognized Hugo's insights into Rabelais and into the relationship of laughter to the "struggle between life and death," he criticized him for his alleged failure to understand the "regenerating and renewing power of the lower stratum" (ibid., p. 126). Such a judgment fails to take into account poems such as "La Révolution" and "Le Satyre," as well as Hugo's central meditation on the nature of genius in *William Shakespeare* and in his novel *L'Homme qui rit*.

15. Quoted in *Les Misérables*, ed. Marius-François Guyard (Paris: Classiques Garnier, 1957), I, 412.

16. *O.C.*, XII, 176.

17. Jean Massin, in a footnote, broadens the Cambronne-Ezekiel parallel: "pour Victor Hugo, Ezéchiel est le Cambronne de la poésie" (ibid., XII, 176). The note refers to the Cambronne chapter in *Les Misérables*.

18. Ibid., XI, 282, 443. The word *gueule*, with its connotation of loudness (*gueuler*) and vulgarity (*fort en gueule*) adds to the sentence's savor.

19. Ibid., XI, 531. Social philosophers, striving for human happiness, are later compared to miners working against the hard rock of selfish interests (ibid., XI, 607).

20. See Raphaël Molho's excellent remarks on this "inverted" religion in "Esquisse d'une théologie des *Misérables*," *Romantisme* 9 (1975): 105–108.

21. Henri Meschonnic, "Vers le roman poème: les romans de Hugo avant *Les Misérables*," *O.C.*, III, ii.

22. See Victor Brombert, "Victor Hugo: The Spaceless Prison," in Brombert, *The Romantic Prison* (Princeton: Princeton University Press, 1978), esp. pp. 114–119.

23. Pierre Albouy, "La Préface philosophique des *Misérables*," in Albouy, *Mythographies* (Paris: Corti, 1976), pp. 121–137. First published in *Hommage à Victor Hugo*, pp. 103–116.

24. Thus Grant refers to the "apolitical world of Jean Valjean" (*The Perilous Quest*, p. 165), and Georges Gusdorf remarks very rightly that even though Valjean appears on the barricades, he remains a stranger

to the revolutionary ideology. Gusdorf, "Quel horizon on voit du haut de la barricade," in *Hommage à Victor Hugo*, pp. 175–196.

25. Several critics have pointed out the parallel. See in particular Paul Zumthor, *Victor Hugo, poète de Satan* (Paris: Laffont, 1946), pp. 319ff; and, more recently, Jean Gaudon, "Je ne sais quel jour de soupirail . . . ," *O.C.*, XI, xlix–lx.

26. Bernard Leuilliot suggests that the early version of the name, Vlajean (*Voilà Jean!*), indicates Hugo's desire to associate the figure of Jean Valjean with that of the "visionary genius" of Patmos. In support, he quotes Hugo's conviction, stated in his private notes, that a name "must be a figure." Leuilliot, "Présentation de Jean Valjean," in *Hommage à Victor Hugo*, pp. 51–67.

27. In *Les Travailleurs de la mer*, Hugo writes of the "opiniâtreté insubmersible du moi" (*O.C.*, XII, 707).

28. Lamennais, *Les Evangiles* (Paris: Pagnerre-Perrotin, 1846), p. 308; and idem, *De la Société première et de ses lois* (Paris, 1848), p. 9. Both passages are quoted and excellently discussed in Paul Bénichou, *Le Temps des prophètes: doctrines de l'âge romantique* (Paris: Gallimard, 1977), pp. 166, 170.

29. See Pierre Albouy's discussion of the question of "survival" in "La Préface philosophique des *Misérables*," in *Mythographies*, pp. 129–130.

30. In "Philosophie. Commencement d'un livre," Hugo establishes a clear parallel between supreme authority and the author as authority ("l'autorité implique l'auteur"—*O.C.*, XII, 61).

31. Georges Piroué, *Victor Hugo romancier, ou les dessus de l'inconnu* (Paris: Denoël, 1964), p. 222. See the entire discussion of Hugo's authorial intrusions and of Hugo's respect for the mysterious link between being and action, the visible and the invisible, the sign and the unsignified (pp. 220–222). I owe to Piroué the notion of the "inviolabilité" of the characters and of the essential privacy of their soul.

32. How else is one to explain the obstetrical image of stanza 43, in which the *mages* are seen as bringing forth God "par l'esprit et le scalpel"? Jacques Seebacher appropriately speaks of a "progressive fusion of nature, man, and God, thanks to the poet-prophets." Seebacher, "Sens et Structure des Mages," *Revue des Sciences Humaines* 3 (July–September 1963): 347–370.

33. For some relevant examples, see Edmond Estève, "Le 'théâtre

monacal' sous la Révolution," in idem, *Etudes de Littérature Préromantique* (Paris: Champion, 1923), pp. 88–137.

34. For a more extensive discussion of this theme of the abolished prison, see the chapter on Victor Hugo in Victor Brombert, *The Romantic Prison* (Princeton: Princeton University Press, 1978), esp. pp. 114–119.

35. *O.C.*, XI, 389. The visionary element is stated from the outset in the digression: "C'est que le couvent . . . est un des appareils d'optique appliqués par l'homme sur l'infini."

36. On the parallel with Balzac's novel, as well as echoes of Diderot and Greuze, see Jacques Seebacher, "La Mort de Jean Valjean," in *Hommage à Victor Hugo*, pp. 69–83, esp. the beginning of the article.

37. Pierre Barbéris, "A propos de 'Lux': la vraie force des choses (sur l'idéologie des 'Châtiments')," *Littérature* 1 (February 1971): 92–105. Barbéris specifically reproaches Hugo for his unwillingness to see the modern industrial hell and for his escape into humanistic individualism.

38. "Discours de réception à l'Académie Française," *O.C.*, VI, 160. The same speech characteristically refers to Hugo's love for the "people" and to his contempt for "populaces."

39. Jacques Seebacher, in an interesting discussion of Valjean's death ("La Mort de Jean Valjean," pp. 69–83), suggests that this "drowning in infinity" is a form of suicide.

5. The Toilers of the Sea

1. The title "Abîme" had already been used by Hugo for one of the philosophical poems of *La Légende des siècles*. Victor Hugo, *Oeuvres Complètes*, ed. Jean Massin, 18 vols. (Paris: Le Club Français du Livre, 1967–1970), IX, 649–653 [hereafter referred to as *O.C.*].

2. Ibid., XII, 159, 242. *William Shakespeare* is Hugo's most celebratory text. He had agreed to write a preface for his son's translations of the complete works of the English poet. But this preface grew so exceedingly in size and scope and became such a vast encomium of genius that Hugo decided to publish it separately, in 1864, the year of the three hundredth anniversary of Shakespeare's birth.

3. Clearly the "work" in question is a collaborative effort. In that same text, Hugo refers to the "mystérieux travail de la mer et du vent" (ibid., XII, 535).

4. Charles Baudoin relates the image of footprints in the snow not to death but to a "birth complex" and to Hugo's early experience of sexual taboos. Baudoin, *Psychanalyse de Victor Hugo* (Paris: Armand Colin, 1972), p. 72.

5. Jean-Bertrand Barrère, *La Fantaisie de Victor Hugo* (Paris: Klincksieck, 1972), II, 354.

6. Jean Gaudon, *Le Temps de la contemplation* (Paris: Flammarion, 1969), p. 400.

7. In a letter of 6 December 1862, Hugo congratulated Flaubert for having powerfully and poetically resuscitated a vanished world (*O.C.*, XII, 1207).

8. "Océan," in *La Légende des siècles*, ibid., IX, 675–685.

9. In his notes Hugo writes: "Il s'était trouvé à Paris en 1789. Il était enthousiaste de la révolution.—Il est probable qu'il avait pris un peu la Bastille" (ibid., XII, 573).

10. Pierre Albouy, *La Création mythologique chez Victor Hugo* (Paris: Corti, 1963), p. 348.

11. Jean-Luc Mercié, in his Présentation of the novel, makes a number of very interesting comments about the ambiguities of progress. He views the revolver in particular as a symbol of "progrès à l'envers," a kind of "perfection in evil" (*O.C.*, XII, 511.

12. Hugo comments on this "epic" fiction—"le drame qu'on ne peut pas jouer"—in his notes for *L'Homme qui rit* (ibid., XIV, 388). More than fifty years earlier, he had pointed in that direction in the article on Walter Scott published in *La Muse française* (ibid., II, 431–438).

13. Joseph Campbell, *The Hero with the Thousand Faces* (New York: Pantheon, 1949), p. 10. Quoted in Richard B. Grant, *The Perilous Quest* (Durham: Duke University Press, 1968), p. 182. See also ibid., pp. 189, 197.

14. Roger Caillois, *La Pieuvre: essai sur la logique de l'imaginaire* (Paris: La Table Ronde, 1973), esp. pp. 13, 17, 31, 75–84, 201, 208, 218. It seems that *pieuvre*, until 1866 a dialect word used on the Channel Islands, became thanks to Hugo the accepted term, replacing the word *poulpe*, which was henceforth used only to designate the animal as seafood. According to Caillois, the word *pieuvre* was included in the dictionary of the Académie Française as late as 1878, and the example given was taken precisely from Hugo. On the phonetic value of the word *pieuvre* and the semantic displacements of the image, see Annamaria

Laserra, "Il polipo e la piovra," *Micromégas* 23–24 (January–August 1982): 49–76.

15. "La mer apparaît comme un guet-apens; un clairon invisible sonne on ne sait quelle guerre" (*O.C.*, XII, 602).

16. I am paraphrasing here Hugo's evocation of the ocean, which had originally been destined to appear at the beginning of *L'Homme qui rit* and which is now included as an appendix in Jean Massin's chronological edition of the complete works. The sentence builds up to the word *chaos:* "L'océan trouble toutes les lignes, désagrège toutes les symétries, complique tous les niveaux de révolte et de dislocation, et remplace les nuances, les cadences, les gammes paisibles, les musiques discrètes par une harmonie à lui qui se compose de chaos" (ibid., XIV, 401).

17. The poem "La Conscience" in *La Légende des siècles* is the point of departure of Charles Baudoin's *Psychanalyse de Victor Hugo*. Baudoin relates the eye, and the "*complexe spectaculaire*" in general, to fratricidal guilt.

18. Barrère, who drew attention to the precedence of the drawn image over the written word in Hugo's works, concludes that Hugo's fictional imagination works best when he can first experiment by sketching and drawing (*La Fantaisie de Victor Hugo*, I, 210, 343). See also Jean-Luc Mercié, "*Les Travailleurs de la mer*, ou les avatars du roman parisien," *O.C.*, XII, 506; Mercié likewise comments on the generative virtue of the drawings.

19. "La Pente de la revêrie," in *Les Feuilles d'automne*, *O.C.*, IV, 426–429.

20. "Le 'crime' de la mer" is Pierre Albouy's striking formulation in *La Création mythologique chez Victor Hugo*, p. 345.

21. The image of the mask is, in this poem also, associated with cosmic evil: "Et tout, même le mal, est la création, / Car le dedans du masque est encore la figure" (*O.C.*, IX, 374, 376).

22. Roger Caillois makes the point that the *pieuvre*, as an incarnation of the principle of evil, leads Hugo to a "méditation presque théologique" (*La Pieuvre*, p. 75).

23. The blasphemous nature of the sentence ("Quand Dieu veut, il excelle dans l'exécrable") has obviously troubled some translators and editors. It has, for instance, been omitted in the translation by W. Moy Thomas, published by J. M. Dent and E. P. Dutton (Everyman's Library), n.d.

24. *"Actes et paroles, I,"* *O.C.*, VII, 90–97.

25. In a contemporaneous text, Hugo writes: "Tout ce globe est un phénomène de permanence et de transformation." Hugo, "Philosophie. Commencement d'un livre, ibid., XII, 16.

26. Once again, "Philosophie. Commencement d'un livre" is a revealing text. Speculation on the close tie between *achèvements* and *ébauches* culminates in the terse conclusion: "toute mort naît" (ibid., XII, 35).

27. *William Shakespeare*, ibid., XII, 159, 173–183.

28. Hugo is even more specific: "l'oeuvre des génies est du surhumain sortant de l'homme" (ibid., XII, 171).

29. The association of writer with God is quite striking in the progression of the sentences around the word *procédé:* "on voit venir Dieu. Saisissement suprême! on surprend presque son procédé. Un peu plus il semble qu'on créerait soi-même" (ibid., XII, 810).

30. Gaudon, *Le Temps de la contemplation*, p. 202.

31. "La Révolution," *O.C.*, X, 231–232.

6. *L'Homme qui rit*

1. Victor Hugo, *Oeuvres Complètes*, ed. Jean Massin, 18 vols. (Paris: Le Club Français du Livre, 1967–1970), XIV, 390 [hereafter referred to as *O.C.*].

2. Ibid., XIV, 388. Various other statements in his project stress this *psychomachia:* the novel is seen as part of a series of "affirmations de l'Ame"; the aim of art is "l'affirmation de l'âme humaine." Hugo, at one point, even had in mind this one-sentence preface: "J'ai senti le besoin d'affirmer l'âme" (ibid., XIV, 387–388).

3. Léon Cellier rightly sees in Ballanche's universalizing statement one of the keys to the romantic notion of a new epic concerned with the destiny of mankind. Cellier, *L'Epopée romantique* (Paris: Presses Universitaires de France, 1954), p. 72.

4. "Sur Mirabeau," *O.C.*, V, 192–221. *William Shakespeare*, ibid., XII, 307.

5. "Le genre humain est au cachot" (ibid., XIV, 350). *Cachot* is one of Pascal's favorite expressions for describing the human condition. See Victor Brombert, "Pascal's Dungeon," in Brombert, *The Romantic Prison* (Princeton: Princeton University Press, 1978), pp. 18–29.

6. The association of the gibbet and the Cross is not new. At the

time he was writing *Le Dernier Jour d'un condamné*, Hugo jotted down the following: "Attachez Dieu au gibet, vous avez la croix"—a sentence he repeated word for word in the closing statement of his preface to *Lucrèce Borgia* (1833). *O.C.*, III, 1201; IV, 656.

7. In the contemporaneous comic fantasy in verse *Mangeront-ils?* (1867), Hugo has the king say about the outlaw: "Dans son gibet, je reconnais mon trône" (ibid., XIII, 520).

8. Ibid., IV, 490.

9. Hugo, in this same chapter, speaks of the degrading parody of parody: the politically organized laughter has a purpose ("Ce rire a une mission"): to devitalize the lower classes (*le peuple*), to reduce them once again to the level of *populace* (ibid., XI, 940–942).

10. See Mikhail Bakhtin, *Rabelais and His World* (Cambridge, Mass.: MIT Press, 1968), passim; see also his essay "Epic and the Novel" in *The Dialogic Imagination of M. M. Bakhtin*, ed. Michael Holquist (Austin: University of Texas Press, 1981).

11. In *William Shakespeare*, Hugo makes a point of evoking the "cours d'hôtelleries," where Elizabethan plays were often performed (*O.C.*, XII, 161).

12. Hugo refers to Shakespeare's "vaste rire divin" (ibid., XII, 233).

13. Ibid., IV, 557.

14. "Rêverie d'un passant à propos d'un roi," in *Les Feuilles d'automne*, ibid., IV, 381.

15. Ibid., X, 217–247.

16. Ibid., XII, 945.

17. See, on this laughter of revolution, the valuable comments of Jean Massin and Pierre Albouy in their Présentations of the poem "La Révolution" (ibid., X, 199–216) and of *L'Homme qui rit* (ibid., XIV, 5–26).

18. Ibid., X, 1175.

19. Ibid., XVII, no. 19.

20. Ibid., VI, 433–434.

21. Ibid., XI, 707.

22. Ibid., XI, 442.

23. Ibid., VIII, 631, 643, 647.

24. Ibid., XIV, 365.

25. Ibid., XIV, 394–395.

26. Ibid., XIV, 354.

27. Ibid., XV, 677–678.

28. Ibid., XIII, 497, 545, 520. The interdependence is clearly stated by the king: "Il faut . . . que je le possède, étant son possédé!"

29. Charles Baudelaire, "L'Héautontimorouménos," *Oeuvres Complètes* (Paris: Pléiade, 1961), p. 74; idem, "De l'Essence du rire," ibid., pp. 977, 980.

30. "A André Chenier," in *Les Contemplations, O.C.*, IX, 70.

31. Ibid., XII, 216.

32. Ibid., XII, 457–458.

33. Ibid., XII, 216.

34. Ibid., IX, 357.

35. Ibid., XIV, 44. On Gwynplaine's ultimate smile as an initiatory sign, see the valuable comments in Léon Cellier, "Chaos vaincu: Victor Hugo et le roman initiatique," in *Hommage à Victor Hugo* (Strasbourg: Bulletin de la Faculté des Lettres de Strasbourg, 1962), pp. 213–223. Reprinted in Cellier, *Parcours initiatiques* (Neuchâtel: Baconnière, 1977), pp. 164–175.

36. This symbolism of mutilation has been discussed most interestingly in René Girard, "Monstres et demi-dieux dans l'oeuvre de Hugo," *Symposium* 19 (Spring 1965): 50–57.

37. *O.C.*, XIV, 389.

38. Ibid., X, 591.

39. See the notes for his famous speech "La Misère," ibid., VII, 216.

40. Ibid., XIV, 388.

41. Georges Piroué, *Victor Hugo romancier, ou les dessus de l'inconnu* (Paris: Denoël, 1964), pp. 68, 102.

42. The passage in question carries the title "Extrait du livre des songes" and is followed by the subtitle "Ecrit en langue mixte" (*O.C.*, XII, 1533.

43. Ibid., XIV, 390.

44. *William Shakespeare*, ibid., XII, 265.

45. Lucien Dällenbach, *Le Recit spéculaire* (Paris: Seuil, 1977), pp. 16, 41, 49.

46. When the *gouffre en haut* is revealed to the hierarchy-conscious Javert, his authoritarian mind cannot cope with this dizzying perspective, which situates God as much *below* as *above*. Les Misérables, *O.C.*, XI, 915.

47. Ibid., XIV, 401.

48. For a more thorough discussion of the initiatory nature of the interlude, see Cellier's already mentioned inspired essay "Chaos vaincu." Cellier describes the interlude as an "Eleusis populaire."

49. See "A Celle qui est restée en France" and "Magnitudo parvi," in *Les Contemplations*, *O.C.*, IX, 396, 209. For a masterful discussion of the poetics of occultation in the work of Hugo, see Jean Gaudon, *Le Temps de la contemplation* (Paris: Flammarion, 1969).

50. The title of Richard B. Grant's book, *The Perilous Quest*, although relevant to all of Hugo's fiction, is particularly apt in the case of *L'Homme qui rit*. Grant rightly stresses the relation of myth to prophecy.

51. *O.C.*, X, 280.

52. Ibid., XIV, 162, 274. Henri Meschonnic very perceptively noted that the imagery of anguish in *L'Homme qui rit* tends to be Biblical in inspiration. Meschonnic, "Le Poème Hugo," in *O.C.*, XIV, xlviii–xlix.

53. Ibid., IV, 427.

54. Ibid., IV, 429.

55. Ibid., XII, 203, 693. To measure the extent to which the banal image of the abyss is, in Hugo's mind, linked to the hell of poetic creation, one might profitably refer to the short poem "O strophe du poète," in *Les Contemplations*, ibid., IX, 289.

56. Ibid., X, 1175, 1189.

57. Ibid., XI, 533.

7. The Violence of History

1. "La Révolution" and "Le Verso de la page," as well as their sequel "La Pitié suprême," were all written within a very short span of time (1857–1858). For further background, see the ingenious and patient scholarship of the late Pierre Albouy, who suceeded in reconstructing the original poem. Albouy, "Une Oeuvre de Victor Hugo reconstituée," *Revue d'Histoire Littéraire de la France* 60 (July–September 1960): 388–423.

2. For intelligent discussions of these questions, see Jean Gaudon's introduction to *La Légende des siècles* (Paris: Garnier, 1974); and Pierre Albouy's "Présentation" of "Le Verso de la page" in Victor Hugo, *Oeuvres Complètes*, ed. Jean Massin, 18 vols. (Paris: Le Club Français du Livre, 1967–1970), X, 251–258 [hereafter referred to as *O.C.*].

3. For some fine insights into the tensions between historic and "pastoral" elements in *Quatrevingt-Treize*, see Sandy Petrey, *History in the Text: "Quatrevingt-Treize" and the French Revolution*, Purdue University Monographs in Romance Languages (Amsterdam: John Benjamins, 1980). One may, however, wish to question Petrey's assertion that the presentation of historical situations in the novel "continually undermines its impulse toward transhistorical truth" (p. 97).

4. It is revealing that the young Stalin, while a seminarist in Tiflis, was punished by lengthy confinement in a cell for reading *Quatrevingt-Treize*. One can only speculate on how intrigued he might have been by the figure of the fanatical and ruthless ex-priest. See the interesting documentation on young Djugashvili's readings of Hugo and on his punishment by the monks, in Robert C. Tucker, *Stalin as Revolutionary*, 1879–1929 (New York: Norton, 1973), pp. 86, 130–132.

5. One might establish a parallel with the last line of the poem "La Rose de l'Infante": "Tout sur terre appartient aux princes, hors le vent" (*O.C.*, X, 608).

6. See Jean Gaudon's excellent discussion of Hugo's antitheses and of the "déroute de la logique" which allows him to abolish all apparent contraditions. Gaudon, *Le Temps de la contemplation* (Paris: Flammarion, 1969), pp. 391–403.

7. On this theme of *double appartenance*, see Guy Rosa's important Présentation of the novel in *O.C.*, XV. 229–260. On the inner contradiction of the novel, see Rosa, " 'Quatrevingt-Treize' ou la critique du roman historique," *Revue d'Histoire Littéraire de la France* 75 (March–June 1975), 329–343.

8. For a general discussion of the prison image as symbol and metaphor of the human condition, see Victor Brombert, *The Romantic Prison* (Princeton: Princeton University Press, 1978); for a detailed discussion of Hugo's use of the image, see ch. 6, "Victor Hugo: The Spaceless Prison."

9. Saint Augustine, *The Confessions*, bk. IV, chs. 10–11.

10. Georg Lukács, *Le Roman historique* (Paris: Payot, 1972), pp. 83–84, 291; Pierre Barbéris, "A propos de 'Lux': la vraie force des choses (sur l'idéologie des 'Châtiments')," *Littérature* 1 (February 1971): 92–105.

11. P. J. Proudhon, "Ce que la révolution doit à la littérature," in *Mélanges*, in *Oeuvres Complètes* (Brussels: Lacroix, Verboeckhoven, 1868), XVII, 37–38; idem, *De la Justice dans la révolution et l'église*

(Paris: Marcel Rivière, 1935), IV, 233, 316; Karl Marx, *The Eighteenth Brumaire of Louis Bonaparte* (New York: International Publishers, 1963), pp. 7–8.

12. See Jean Massin's Présentation of "La Révolution," in *O.C.*, X, 199–216. Massin suggests a link between this revelation and Hugo's acceptance of the necessity of the Terror in his poem "Nox" (pp. 200–201).

13. Jean Gaudon makes a very convincing case for the importance of this double temptation in his introduction to *La Légende des siècles* (Paris: Classiques Garnier, 1974), pp. xix, xxi.

8. Epilogue

1. Quoted in Bernard Leuilliot, "Présentation de Jean Valjean," in *Hommage à Victor Hugo* (Strasbourg: Bulletin de la Faculté des Lettres de Strasbourg, 1962), p. 59. Quoted earlier in Jean Delalande, *Victor Hugo à Hauteville House* (Paris: Albin Michel, 1947), pp. 26–27; and in Jean-Bertrand Barrère, *Victor Hugo à l'oeuvre* (Paris: Klincksieck, 1965), p. 13. See Charles Hugo, "Chez Victor Hugo, par un passant," in Victor Hugo, *Oeuvres Complètes*, ed. Jean Massin, 18 vols. (Paris: Le Club Français du Livre, 1967–1970), XII, 1573–1588 [hereafter referred to as *O.C.*].

2. "Le Tas de Pierres," ibid., XV-XVI, 390, 378.

3. Ibid., VI, 535.

4. "Feuilles paginées" (1827–1830), ibid., III, 1195. Hugo's formula is: "Se totaliser dans un livre complet."

5. In this chapter, the institution of literature is quite specifically described as "la seconde tour de Babel du genre humain" (ibid., IV, 144).

6. See the planned dedication for *L'Homme qui rit*, ibid., XIV, 387.

7. See *William Shakespeare*, ibid., XII, 187.

8. Ibid., XIV, 387.

9. "De Maistre est féroce avec foi . . . Ce sombre livre est au sommet de la théocratie" (ibid., XII, 429–430).

10. It may be worth recalling that Michelet proclaimed the "inconciliable opposition du Christianisme avec le Droit et la Révolution."

Preface to 1868 edition of Jules Michelet, *Histoire de la Révolution Française* (Paris: Pléiade, 1952), I, 15.

11. "Torment of the mind after the work has been completed! / Astonishment of the eagle-spirit seeing its brood! / Misgivings of the dreamer about what he has dreamed" (*O.C.*, X, 261.

12. "Did this prophet share his own secret? / This vast soul driven to great risks, / Did he have the total revelation of his thought?" (ibid., X, 230–231).

13. "Fraught with vague fears, I lived in intimacy / With this dark world that stirred within me" (ibid., VIII, 889).

14. *William Shakespeare*, ibid., XII, 252.

15. Ibid., III, 50.

16. Ibid., X, 246; also X, 287.

17. Hugo uses this expression in discussing what he calls Shakespeare's "réflexion double." But it is clear, in the context, that it is his own art he has in mind (ibid., XII, 237).

18. Michel Butor, obviously interested in this early case of the disappearance of the fictional personage, noted that only the poet-narrator remained "véritablement actif." Butor, "Victor Hugo romancier," in idem, *Répertoire II* (Paris: Editions de Minuit, 1964), pp. 215–242.

19. "La Misère" and "Les Caves de Lille," *O.C.* VII, 207–213; 371–383. "Sur Mirabeau," ibid., V, 217. Interestingly, Hannah Arendt saw the "social question" as being predominant in the tradition of the French Revolution. Arendt, *On Revolution* (New York: Viking, 1981, p. 55.

20. See in particular the end of the speech—which in fact was not delivered (*O.C.*, VII, 382–383). As for the poem in *Les Châtiments*, partly inspired by the Lille visit ("Joyeuse Vie," ibid., VIII, 643–646), it stresses the hopelessness of these victims in the human hell of modern cities.

21. For a lucid and thorough study of this aspect of *Les Châtiments*, and of Hugo's anger against *le peuple* after the plebiscite in support of the reestablishment of the Empire, see Sheila Gaudon, "Prophétisme et utopie: le problème du destinataire dans *Les Châtiments*," *Saggi e Ricerche di Letteratura Francese* 16 (1977): 403–426.

22. In "Le Verso de la page," Hugo dramatizes the conflict between the individual and the collective consciousness: "Le songeur et la foule ont des rencontres rudes"; and again: "Tout un peuple égaré ne pèse pas un juste" (*O.C.*, X, 271, 274.

23. *L'Homme qui rit*, ibid., XIV, 202, 364.

24. Ibid., X, 817.

25. Ibid., XI, 606.

26. Gaudon, "Prophétisme et utopie," p. 420.

27. Mircea Eliade, *The Myth of the Eternal Return* (Princeton: Princeton University Press, 1954). See in particular chapter 4, "The Terror of History," pp. 141–162.

28. Michel Butor's suggestive title for one of his essays on Hugo is "Babel en creux" (Butor, *Répertoire II*). On the association of Babel and Piranesi, see Jean Gaudon's analysis of the image of "Babel renversée" in Hugo's unfinished poem *Dieu*. Gaudon, *Le Temps de la contemplation* (Paris: Flammarion, 1969), pp. 311–312.

29. *O.C.*, II, 216.

30. Ibid., IX, 110.

31. Ibid., IX, 1495.

32. Ibid., XII, 464 ("God makes mad those he wants to elevate").

33. In discussing the *exceptional* yet *unfree* nature of genius, Kierkegaard gives a sentence attributed to Seneca: "Nullum unquam exstitit magnum ingenium sine aliqua dementia" ("No great genius has ever existed without being possessed of some madness"). Sören Kierkegaard, *Journals and Papers* (Bloomington: Indiana University Press, 1970), II, 85. The correct sentence, in Seneca's *De Tranquillitate animi* (XVII, 10)—a sentence that Seneca in fact attributes to Aristotle—is somewhat different, though it says substantially the same thing: "Nullum magnum ingenium sine mixtura dementiae fuit."

34. *O.C.*, IX, 16, 13.

35. *Promontorium somnii*, ibid., XII, 465.

36. This allegorization of the poetic process has been excellently studied in Suzanne Nash, *Les Contemplations of Victor Hugo: An Allegory of the Creative Process* (Princeton: Princeton University Press, 1976).

37. *O.C.*, IX, 289.

38. Ibid., X, 231–232.

39. Baudelaire, "Exposition universelle de 1855" in idem, *Oeuvres Complètes* (Paris: Pléiade, 1961), p. 959. Preface to *Cromwell*, *O.C.*, III, 72.

40. "Philosophie. Commencement d'un livre," *O.C.*, XII, 61.

41. Some of Hugo's notions about the world as book seem to bring him close to the Kabbalistic tradition. See Shira Wolosky, "Derrida, Jabès, Levinas: Sign-Theory as Ethical Discourse," *Prooftexts* 2 (1982):

283–302. Wolosky's statement that the "lettristic" conception of creation implies "a particular conception of the relation between creation and its Creator" (p. 293) is highly relevant to Hugo. On the world as a "space of inscription," see Jacques Derrida, *De la Grammatologie* (Paris: Les Editions de Minuit, 1967), pp. 65–66, which is quoted and commented on by Wolosky.

42. On this "scriptural transcription," which is essentially of a theological nature, see Roger Dragonetti, "La Littérature et la lettre," *Lingua e stile* 4, no. 2 (1969): 205–222. The passage in question from Dante's *Convivio* is IV, vi, 3–6. In Italian and in French, the proposed etymology is even more suggestive, since *lego* (*je lie*) sounds like the first person singular of the verb "to read" (*je lis*).

43. "Immense space entered into this black shape" (*O.C.*, X, 600).

44. Ibid., XIV, 232.

45. *William Shakespeare*, ibid., XII, 250.

46. Ibid., XII, 242.

47. Anne Ubersfeld, *Le Roi et le Bouffon* (Paris: Corti, 1974), p. 474.

48. "Le mal est, soit dans la nature, soit dans la destinée, un commencement obscur de Dieu qui se continue au delà de nous dans l'invisible" (*O.C.*, XII, 356).

49. Ibid., XII, 806; X, 231–232.

Selected Bibliography

The following bibliography is limited to studies that are directly relevant to my analyses and that have been cited or alluded to in my text. Everyone working on Hugo will of course also want to consult the works of Hugo specialists such as Paul Berret, Raymond Escholier, Claudius Grillet, Henri Guillemin, Edmond Huguet, René Journet, André Maurois, Albert Py, Guy Robert, Jacques Roos, Géraud Venzac, and Auguste Viatte. Good general bibliographies can be found in Jean Gaudon, *Le Temps de la contemplation*, and in Anne Ubersfeld, *Le Roi et le Bouffon*.

Albouy, Pierre. "Une Oeuvre de Victor Hugo reconstituée." *Revue d'Histoire Littéraire de la France* 60 (July–September 1960): 388–423).

———— "La 'Préface Philosophique' des 'Misérables.' " In *Hommage à Victor Hugo*, pp. 103–116. Strasbourg: Bulletin de la Faculté des Lettres de Strasbourg, 1962. Reprinted in Albouy, *Mythographies*, pp. 121–137. Paris: José Corti, 1976.

———— *La Création mythologique chez Victor Hugo*. Paris: José Corti, 1963.

———— "Hugo, ou le *je* éclaté." In *Mythographies*, pp. 66–81. Paris: José Corti, 1976.

———— Présentation of "Le Verso de la page." In Victor Hugo, *Oeuvres Complètes*, X, 251–258. Paris: Le Club Français du Livre, 1969.

———— Présentation of *L'Homme qui rit*. In Victor Hugo, *Oeuvres Complètes*, XIV, 5–26. Paris: Le Club Français du Livre, 1970.

———— *Mythographies*. Paris: José Corti, 1976.

Alighieri, Dante. *Il Convivio*. Ed. Maria Simonelli. Bologna: R. Patron, 1966.

Arendt, Hannah. *On Revolution*. New York: Viking Compass, 1981.

Augustine, Saint. *Confessions*. New York: Sheed and Ward, 1942.

Babel Brown, Natalie. *Hugo and Dostoevsky*. Ann Arbor: Ardis, 1978.

Bakhtin, Mikhail. *Epopée et roman*. In *Recherches Internationales*, no. 76 (1973). Rpt. as "Epic and Novel." In *The Dialogic Imagination of M. M. Bakhtin*, pp. 3–40. Trans. Caryl Emerson and Michael Holquist, ed. Michael Holquist. Austin: University of Texas Press, 1981.

———— *Rabelais and His World*. Cambridge, Mass.: MIT Press, 1968.

Ballanche, Pierre-Simon. *Oeuvres*. Paris: Bureau de l'Encyclopédie des Connaissances Utiles, 1833. Rev. ed., 2 vols., Geneva: Slatkine, 1967.

Barbéris, Pierre. "A Propos de Lux: La Vraie Force des choses (sur l'idéologie des 'Châtiments')." *Littérature* 1 (February 1971): 92–105.

Barrère, Jean-Bertrand. *La Fantaisie de Victor Hugo*. 3 vols. Paris: José Corti, 1949, 1950, 1960. Rev. ed. Paris: Klincksieck, 1972–1973.

———— *Hugo, l'homme et l'oeuvre*. Boivin, Connaissance des Lettres, n.d. [1952].

———— *Victor Hugo à l'oeuvre*. Paris: Klincksieck, 1965.

Baudelaire, Charles. *Oeuvres Complètes*. Paris: Pléiade, 1961, 1963.

Baudoin, Charles. *Psychanalyse de Victor Hugo*. Geneva: Editions du Mont-Blanc, 1943. Rpt. Paris: Armand Colin, 1972.

Beccaria, Cesare. *Dei Delitti e delle pene*. Florence: Felice Le Monnier, 1950.

Béguin, Albert. *L'Ame romantique et le rêve*. Paris: José Corti, 1939.

Bénichou, Paul. *Le Temps des prophètes*. Paris: Gallimard, 1977.

Brochu, *Hugo. Amour/Crime/Révolution. Essai sur "Les Misérables."* Montreal: Presses de l'Université de Montréal, 1974.

Brombert, Victor. *The Romantic Prison: The French Tradition*. Princeton: Princeton University Press, 1978.

Butor, Michel. *Répertoire II*. Paris: Editions de Minuit, 1964.

Caillois, Roger. *La Pieuvre: Essai sur la logique de l'imaginaire*. Paris: La Table Ronde, 1973.

Campbell, Joseph. *The Hero with the Thousand Faces*. New York: Pantheon, 1949.

Cellier, Léon. *L'Epopée romantique*. Paris: Presses Universitaires de France, 1954.

———— "Chaos Vaincu: Victor Hugo et le roman initiatique." In *Hommage à Victor Hugo*, pp. 213–223. Strasbourg: Bulletin de la Faculté des Lettres de Strasbourg, 1962. Rpt. in *Parcours initiatiques*, pp. 164–175. Neuchâtel: A la Baconnière, 1977.

Charlier, Gustave. "Comment fut écrit 'Le Dernier Jour d'un Condamné.' " *Revue d'Histoire Littéraire de la France* 22 (1915): 321–360.

Cocteau, Jean. "Le Mystère laïc." In Cocteau, *Oeuvres Complétes*, X, 21. Lausanne: Marguerat, 1946.

Dällenbach, Lucien. *Le Récit spéculaire: Essai sur la mise en abyme.* Paris: Editions du Seuil, 1977.

Delalande, Jean. *Victor Hugo à Hauteville House.* Paris: Albin Michel, 1947.

De Maistre, Joseph. *Du Pape.* Ed. Jacques Lovie and Joannès Chetail. Geneva: Droz, 1966.

——— *Les Soirées de Saint-Pétersbourg.* Paris: Garnier, 1815.

Derrida, Jacques. *De la Grammatologie.* Paris: Editions de Minuit, 1967.

Dostoevsky, Fyodor. Introduction to *Krotkaia (Douce).* In *Journal d'un Ecrivain.* Paris: Pléiade, 1972. Orig. pub. 1876.

Dragonetti, Roger. "La Littérature et la lettre." *Lingua e Stile* 4 (1969): 205–222.

Duchet, Claude. "The Object-Event of the Ram's Charge: An Ideological Reading of an Image." *Yale French Studies* 59 (1980): 155–174.

——— and Guy Rosa. "Sur une édition et deux romans de Victor Hugo." *Revue d'Histoire Littéraire de la France* 79 (September–October 1979): 824–834.

Eliade, Mircea. *The Myth of the Eternal Return.* Trans. W. R. Trask. New York: Pantheon, 1954. Rpt. Princeton: Princeton University Press, 1971.

Estève, Edmond. "Le 'Théâtre monacal' sous la Révolution." In *Etudes de Littérature préromantique.* Paris: Champion, 1923.

Flaubert, Gustave. *Correspondance.* Vols. 1 and 2. Paris: Pléiade, 1973, 1980.

——— *Correspondance.* 9 vols. Paris: Conard, 1926–1933.

Foucault, Michel. *Surveiller et punir: Naissance de la prison.* Paris: Gallimard, 1975.

Frank, Joseph. *Dostoevsky: The Seeds of Revolt, 1821–1849.* Princeton: Princeton University Press, 1976.

Gaudon, Jean. *Le Temps de la contemplation.* Paris: Flammarion, 1969.

——— "Je ne sais quel jour de soupirail . . ." In *Hommage à Victor*

Hugo, pp. 149–160. Strasbourg: Bulletin de la Faculté des Lettres de Strasbourg, Rpt. in Victor Hugo, *Oeuvres Complètes*, XI, xlix–lx. Paris: Le Club Français du Livre, 1969.

—— "Digressions hugoliennes." In Victor Hugo, *Oeuvres Complètes*, XIV, i–xvii, Paris: Le Club Français du Livre, 1970.

—— "Vers une rhétorique de la démesure: 'William Shakespeare.' " *Romantisme* 3 (1972): 78–85.

—— Introduction to Victor Hugo, *La Légende des Siècles*, pp. i–lii. Paris: Garnier, 1974.

Gaudon, Sheila. "Prophétisme et Utopie: Le Problème du destinataire dans *Les Châtiments*." *Saggi e Ricerche di Letteratura Francese* 16 (1977): 403–426.

Gély, Claude. *Victor Hugo poète de l'intimité*. Paris: Nizet, 1969.

—— *Les Misérables de Hugo*. Paris: Hachette, 1975.

Gide, André. Préface to *Anthologie de la poésie française*. Paris: Pléiade, 1949.

Girard, René. "Monstres et demi-dieux dans l'oeuvre de Hugo." *Symposium* 19 (Spring 1965): 50–57.

Glauser, Alfred. *La Poétique de Hugo*. Paris: Nizet, 1978.

Gohin, Yves. "Les Réalités du crime et de la justice pour Victor Hugo avant 1829." In Victor Hugo, *Oeuvres Complètes*, III, i–xxvi. Paris: Le Club Français du Livre, 1967.

Grant, Richard B. *The Perilous Quest: Image, Myth, and Prophecy in the Narratives of Victor Hugo*. Durham: Duke University Press, 1968.

—— "Sequence and Theme in Victor Hugo's *Les Orientales*." *PMLA* 94 (October 1979): 894–908.

Grimaud, Michel. "De Victor Hugo à Homère-Hogu: L'Onomastique des *Misérables*." *L'Esprit Créateur* 16 (Fall 1976): 220–230.

Gusdorf, Georges. "Quel horizon on voit du haut de la barricade." In *Hommage à Victor Hugo*. Strasbourg: Bulletin de la Faculté des Lettres de Strasbourg, 1962.

Guyard, Marius-François. Introduction to Victor Hugo, *Les Misérables*. Paris: Garnier, 1957.

Haig, Stirling. "From Cathedral to Book, from Stone to Press: Hugo's Portrait of the Artist in *Notre-Dame de Paris*." *Stanford French Review* 3 (Winter 1979): 343–350.

Halbwachs, Pierre. "Le Poète de l'histoire." In Victor Hugo, *Oeuvres Complètes*, VII, i–xxxiii. Paris: Le Club Français du Livre, 1968.

Hegel, Georg Wilhelm Friedrich. *Ästhetik*. 2 vols. Frankfurt: Europäische Verlagsanstalt, n.d.

Holdheim, W. Wolfgang. *Die Suche nach dem Epos: Der Geschichtsroman bei Hugo, Tolstoi und Flaubert*. Heidelberg: Carl Winter Universitätsverlag, 1978.

Hoffmann, Léon-François. *Le Nègre Romantique*. Paris: Payot, 1973.

Hofmannsthal, Hugo von. *Victor Hugo*. Leipzig: Schuster und Loeffler, n.d.

Houston, John Porter. *The Demonic Imagination: Style and Theme in French Romantic Poetry*. Baton Rouge: Louisiana State University Press, 1969.

―――― *Victor Hugo*. Boston: Twayne, 1974.

Hugo, Victor. *Oeuvres Complètes*. Ed. Jean Massin. 18 vols. Paris: Le Club Français du Livre, 1967–1970.

―――― *Les Misérables*. Ed. Marius-François Guyard. 2 vols. Paris: Garnier, 1957.

―――― *Quatrevingt-Treize*. Ed. Jean Boudout. Paris: Garnier, 1957.

―――― *Dieu: L'Océan d'en haut*. Critical edition by René Journet and Guy Robert. Paris: Nizet, 1960.

―――― *Dieu: Le Seuil du gouffre*. Critical edition by René Journet and Guy Robert. Paris: Nizet, 1961.

―――― *L'Ane*. Ed. Pierre Albouy. Paris: Flammarion, 1966.

―――― *La Légende des siècles*. Introd. by Jean Gaudon. Ed. André Dumas. Paris: Garnier, 1974.

―――― *Notre-Dame de Paris* and *Les Travailleurs de la mer*. Ed. Jacques Seebacher and Yves Gohin. Paris: Pléiade, 1975.

Hunt, Herbert James. *The Epic in Nineteenth-Century France*. Oxford: Blackwell, 1941.

Kierkegaard, Sören. *Journals and Papers*. 2 vols. Bloomington: Indiana University Press, 1967, 1970.

Lafontant, Julien J. "A Tribute to Victor Hugo's *Bug-Jargal*." *Rocky Mountain Review* 32, no. 4 (1978): 195–210.

Lamartine, Alphonse de. "Considérations sur un Chef d'Oeuvre ou le Danger du Génie." In *Cours Familier de Littérature*. Paris: Privately printed, 1856–1858.

Lamennais, Hughes Félicité Robert de. *Les Evangiles*. Paris: Pagnerre-Perrotin, 1846.

―――― *De la Société première et de ses lois*. Paris: Garnier, 1848.

Laserra, Annamaria. "Il polipo e la piovra." *Micromégas* 23–24 (January–August 1982): 49–76.

Leroux, Pierre. "Du Style symbolique." *Le Globe*, 8 April 1829. Rpt. in Leroux, *Oeuvres*, I, 328–338. Paris: Société Typographique, 1850–51.

———— "Aux Artistes." *Revue Encyclopédique*, November–December 1831.

Leuilliot, Bernard. "Présentation de Jean Valjean." In *Hommage à Victor Hugo*. Strasbourg: Bulletin de la Faculté des Lettres de Strasbourg, 1962.

Lukács, Georg. *The Historical Novel*. London: Merlin Press, 1962.

———— *Theory of the Novel*. Cambridge, Mass.: MIT Press, 1971.

Massin, Jean. Présentation of *Le Dernier Jour d'un condamné*. In Victor Hugo, *Oeuvres Complètes*, III, 607–637. Paris: Le Club Français du Livre, 1967.

———— Présentation of "La Révolution." In Victor Hugo, *Oeuvres Complètes*, X, 199–216. Paris: Le Club Français du Livre, 1969.

Marx, Karl. *The Eighteenth Brumaire of Louis Bonaparte*. New York: International Publishers, 1963.

Mauron, Charles. "Les Personnages de Victor Hugo: Etude psychocritique." In Victor Hugo, *Oeuvres Complètes*, II, i–xlii. Paris: Le Club Français du Livre, 1967.

Mehlman, Jeffrey. *Revolution and Repetition: Marx/Hugo/Balzac*. Berkeley: University of California Press, 1977.

Mercié, Jean-Luc. "*Les Travailleurs de la mer* ou les avatars du roman parisien." In Victor Hugo, *Oeuvres Complètes*, XII, 485–512. Paris: Le Club Français du Livre, 1969.

Meschonnic, Henri. "Vers le roman poème: Les Romans de Hugo avant *Les Misérables*." In Victor Hugo, *Oeuvres Complètes*, III, i–xx. Paris: Le Club Français du Livre, 1967.

———— "Le Poème Hugo." In Victor Hugo, *Oeuvres Complètes*, XIV, xix–lxvi. Paris: Le Club Français du Livre, 1970.

———— *Ecrire Hugo*. Paris: Gallimard, 1977.

Molho, Raphaël. "Critique, Amour et Poésie: Sainte-Beuve et 'Les' Hugo." In Victor Hugo, *Oeuvres Complètes*, IV, i–xxvi. Paris: Le Club Français du Livre, 1967.

———— "Esquisse d'une théologie des 'Misérables.' " *Romantisme* 9 (1975): 105–108.

Nash, Suzanne. *"Les Contemplations" of Victor Hugo: An Allegory of the Creative Process*. Princeton: Princeton University Press, 1976.

———— "Transfiguring Disfiguration in *L'Homme qui rit:* A Study of Hugo's Use of the Grotesque." In *Pretext—Text—Context*. Ed. Robert L. Mitchell. Columbus: Ohio State University Press, 1980.

———— "Writing a Building: Hugo's *Notre-Dame de Paris*." *French Forum* 8 (May 1983): 122–133.

Pater, Walter. *Appreciations*. London: Macmillan, 1910.

Péguy, Charles. *Clio: Dialogue de l'Histoire et de l'âme païenne*. Paris: Pléiade, 1957.

Petrey, Sandy. *History in the Text: "Quatrevingt-Treize" and the French Revolution*. Purdue University Monographs in Romance Languages. Amsterdam: John Benjamins, 1980.

Peyre, Henri. *Hugo*. Paris: Presses Universitaires de France, 1972.

———— *Qu'est-ce que le Symbolisme?* Paris: Presses Universitaires de France, 1974.

Piroué, Georges. *Victor Hugo romancier ou les dessus de l'inconnu*. Paris: Denoël, 1964.

———— "Les Deux *Bug-Jargal*." In Victor Hugo, *Oeuvres Complètes*, I, i–viii. Paris: Le Club Français du Livre, 1967.

Poulet, Georges. *Essais sur le temps humain, II: La Distance intérieure*. Paris: Plon, 1952.

Proudhon, Pierre Joseph. *De la Justice dans la Révolution et l'Eglise*. Paris: Marcel Rivière, 1935.

———— *Qu'est-ce que la propriété?* In Proudhon, *Oeuvres Complètes*, Marpon et Flammarion, 1866.

———— "Ce que la Révolution doit à la littérature." In *Mélanges*, in Proudhon, *Oeuvres Complètes*, vol. 17. Brussels: A Lacroix–Verboekhoven, 1868.

Ricatte, Robert. "*Les Misérables:* Hugo et ses personnages." In Victor Hugo, *Oeuvres Complètes*, XI, i–xxiv. Paris: Le Club Français du Livre, 1969.

Richard, Jean-Pierre. "Petite lecture de Javert."*Revue des Sciences Humaines*, no. 156 (1974): 597–611.

———— *Microlectures*. Paris: Editions du Seuil, 1979.

Riffaterre, Michael. "La Poésie métaphysique de Victor Hugo: Style, symboles et thèmes de *Dieu*." *Romanic Review* 51 (December 1960): 268–276.

———— *Essais de stylistique structurale*. Paris: Flammarion, 1971.

—————— *La Production du texte*. Paris: Editions du Seuil, 1979.

Rimbaud, Arthur. "Lettre à P. Demeny." In Rimbaud, *Oeuvres*. Paris: Garnier, 1960.

Rosa, Guy. Présentation of *Quatrevingt-Treize*. In Victor Hugo, *Oeuvres Complètes*, XV, 229–260. Paris: Le Club Français du Livre, 1970.

—————— "*Quatrevingt-Treize* ou la critique du roman historique." *Revue d'Histoire Littéraire de la France* 75 (March–June 1975): 329–343.

Rosa, Guy, and Claude Duchet. "Sur une édition et deux romans de Victor Hugo." *Revue d'Histoire Littéraire de la France* 79 (September–October 1979): 824–834.

Sainte-Beuve, Charles Augustin. "Espoir et voeu du mouvement littéraire et poétique après la révolution de 1830." In Sainte-Beuve, *Premiers Lundis*. Paris: Pléiade, 1949.

—————— "Les Feuilles d'automne." *Revue des Deux Mondes*, 15 December 1831). Rpt. in Victor Hugo, *Oeuvres Complètes*, IV, 1231–37. Paris: Le Club Français du Livre, 1967.

—————— "Les Romans de Victor Hugo." *Journal des Débats*, 24 July 1832. Rpt. in Victor Hugo, *Oeuvres Complètes*, IV, 1237–44. Paris: Le Club Français du Livre, 1967.

Sartre, Jean Paul. *Situations II*. Paris: Gallimard, 1948.

—————— *Les Mots*. Paris: Gallimard, 1964.

—————— *L'Idiot de la famille*. 3 vols. Paris: Gallimard, 1971–1972.

Savey-Casard, Paul. *Le Crime et la peine dans l'oeuvre de Victor Hugo*. Paris: Presses Universitaires de France, 1956.

Seebacher, Jacques. "La mort de Jean Valjean." In *Hommage à Victor Hugo*, pp. 69–83. Strasbourg: Bulletin de la Faculté des Lettres de Strasbourg, 1962.

—————— "Sens et structure des *Mages*." *Revue des Sciences Humaines* 3 (July–September 1963): 347–370.

—————— "Esthétique et Politique chez Victor Hugo: 'L'Utilité du Beau.' " *Cahiers de l'Association Internationale des Etudes Françaises*, no. 19 (March 1967): 233–246.

—————— "Le Système du vide dans 'Notre-Dame de Paris.' " *Littérature* 5 (February 1972): 95–106.

—————— Introduction to *Notre-Dame de Paris*, pp. 1045–76. Paris: Pléiade, 1975.

—————— "Gringoire, ou le déplacement du roman historique vers l'histoire." *Revue d'Histoire Littéraire de la France* 75 (March–June 1975): 308–320.

——— "La Polémique chez Victor Hugo." *Cahiers de l'Association Internationale des Etudes Françaises*, no. 31 (May 1979): 207–222.

Seneca. *De Tranquillitate animi*. Milan: Signorelli, 1953.

Stendhal. *Courrier anglais*. 5 vols. Paris: Le Divan, 1935.

Swinburne, Algernon Charles. *A study of Victor Hugo*. London: Chatto and Windus, 1886.

——— "Victor Marie Hugo." In Swinburne, *The Complete Works*, vol. 13. London: William Heinemann, 1926.

Tolstoy, Leo. *What is Art?* In Tolstoy, *The Complete Works*. Boston: Dana Estes, 1904.

Toumson, Roger. Présentation of *Bug-Jargal*. Fort de France, Haiti: Editions Désormeaux, 1979.

Tucker, Robert. *Stalin as Revolutionary, 1879–1929*. New York: Norton, 1973.

Ubersfeld, Anne. *Le Roi et le Bouffon: Etude sur le théâtre de Hugo de 1830 à 1839*. Paris: José Corti: 1974.

Vidocq, François-Eugène. *Mémoires*. Paris: Les Amis du Club du Livre, 1959.

Zumthor, Paul. *Victor Hugo, poète de Satan*. Paris: Laffont, 1946.

——— "Le Moyen Age de Victor Hugo." In Victor Hugo, *Oeuvres Complètes*, IV, i–xxxi. Paris: Le Club Français du Livre, 1967.

Wolosky, Shira. "Derrida, Jabès, Levinas: Sign-Theory as Ethical Discourse." *Prooftexts* 2 (1982): 283–302.

Credits for Illustrations

1. Bibliothèque Nationale, MSS, n.a.fr. 24.807, f. 3.
2. Maison Victor Hugo, 279; Collection Bulloz, 77115.
3. Bibliothèque Nationale, MSS, n.a.fr. 13.356, f. 1.
4. Maison Victor Hugo, 317; Collection Bulloz, 80918.
5. Maison Victor Hugo, 38; Collection Bulloz, 77069.
6. Maison Victor Hugo, 118; Collection Bulloz, 46102.
7. Maison Victor Hugo, 240; Collection Bulloz, 46210.
8. Maison Victor Hugo, 238; Collection Bulloz, 46208.
9. Bibliothèque Nationale, MSS, n.a.fr. 13.459, f. 16.
10. Maison Victor Hugo, 242; Collection Bulloz, 77623.
11. Bibliothèque Nationale, MSS, n.a.fr. 24.745, f. 57.
12. Bibliothèque Nationale, MSS, n.a.fr. 24.745, f. 232.
13. Bibliothèque Nationale, MSS, n.a.fr. 24.745, f. 382.
14. Bibliothèque Nationale, MSS, n.a.fr. 24.745, f. 159.
15. Bibliothèque Nationale, n.a.fr. 24.745, f. 123.
16. Bibliothèque Nationale, MSS, n.a.fr. 24.745, f. 85.
17. Bibliothèque Nationale, MSS, n.a.fr. 24.745, f. 222.
18. Bibliothèque Nationale, MSS, n.a.fr. 24.745, f. 2.
19. Bibliothèque Nationale, MSS, n.a.fr. 13.370, f. 86.
20. Maison Victor Hugo, 272; Collection Bulloz, 46224.
21. Maison Victor Hugo, 255; Collection Bulloz, 46220.
22. Maison Victor Hugo, 256; Collection Bulloz, 77107.
23. Maison Victor Hugo, 257; Collection Bulloz, 77108.
24. Maison Victor Hugo, 199; Collection Bulloz, 77098.
25. Maison Victor Hugo, 127; Collection Bulloz, 46112.
26. Maison Victor Hugo, 205; Collection Bulloz, 46124.
27. Maison Victor Hugo, 211; Collection Bulloz, 46211.

Frontispiece: Maison Victor Hugo, not catalogued; Collection Bulloz, 81339.

Index